Futile Pleasures

for Chris Holmes

CONTENTS

When I was young, I gave my mind
And plied myself to fruitless poetry,
Which, though it profit the professor naught,
Yet is it passing pleasing to the world.

—HIERONIMO in Thomas Kyd's *The Spanish Tragedy*

Futilitarianism: An Introduction

"From now to the end of consciousness," wrote Susan Sontag, "we are stuck with the task of defending art."[1] This assertion particularly rings true now, especially if we broaden Sontag's "art" to include the liberal arts. In recent years, the apparent escalation of the crisis in higher education has placed contemporary humanists on the defensive. Year after year, publishers, conference panels, and blogs continue to churn out, at an astonishing rate, apologetic justifications for the value of the humanities in general and literature and literary studies in particular.[2] In the ongoing wake of the global financial meltdown of 2007–8 and the subsequent Great Recession—an economic downturn from which colleges and universities, and especially the humanities, have proven to be far from exempt—it makes perfect sense that, in seemingly unprecedented ways, so many scholars working in the humanities would feel compelled to rush valiantly, like knights in shining armor, to the discipline's defense. I say "seemingly unprecedented," though, because these defenses can often appear familiar to those trained in the study of earlier historical periods. However determined by the particularities of the current situation, the defenses of literature that mark our specific historical moment are themselves marked by previous historical moments, from which the humanities' most gallant champions draw the energy that fuels their arguments.

Hence, Gregory Jusdanis, in his 2010 book *Fiction Agonistes: In Defense of Literature*, channels the spirit of a real knight, the Renaissance courtier and poet Sir Philip Sidney, in his rousing defense of the value of literature and the arts. Commenting that "we" humanists "once believed that culture made us into better human beings, that we could find solutions to our problems in literature, or that art provided us with solace for the imperfections and injustices of life," Jusdanis attempts to revitalize such arguments for our current moment, which has fallen away, he claims, from these beliefs.[3] In this effort, he draws on a humanist tradition best represented by Sidney's *Defence of Poesy*; that tradition, according to Jusdanis, argued that "poetry was both pleasurable and pedagogically useful," a position that "stands in contract [*sic*] to modern philosophy, which presents the aesthetic experience as self-enclosed, affording satisfaction with little instrumental value," with the result that these days "few people touch on the issue of literature's social function."[4] However inadvertently, the typo here implies that the "contrast" Jusdanis attempts to draw cannot be entirely sustained. The aesthetic philosophy he poses in contradistinction to early humanist defenses of literature has long been critiqued by generations of historicist and materialist critics invested in establishing the (social, political, ethical) efficacy of literature. Indeed, modern humanists instead seem bound, as if by contract, to repeat the humanist ideals that Jusdanis laments we have cast aside.

Such rehearsals of humanist commonplaces are not confined to the academy; popular journalistic accounts often succumb to the same compulsion. After the *New York Times* columnist Frank Bruni published an op-ed piece singing the praises of the liberal arts education he received from a particularly memorable Shakespeare professor with whom he studied in college,[5] he received an e-mail from Joel Benenson, a prominent pollster and political consultant, personally "attest[ing] to the value of Shakespeare." It turns out that Benenson, who was working as a chief advisor for Hillary Clinton's campaign for the 2016 Democratic presidential nomination, had majored in theater at Queens College; it was through his study of Shakespeare that he gained an "understanding of the rhythm and nuance of language," as he explained to Bruni, who promptly advertised this good press in a follow-up column. "If Hillary Clinton goes the distance," Bruni remarked, "she may have Shakespeare to thank."[6] At a moment when the number of English majors nationwide is steadily declining, when the humanities-educated President Barack Obama devotes funding for education almost exclusively to developing STEM (science, technology, engineering, and mathematics) programs, and when even academic publishers have started seeing literary studies as unmarketable and unpublishable—when, in sum, a B.A. in English seems to be, as the opening number to the musical *Avenue Q* would have it, a "useless degree"—it is hardly surprising that Bruni would welcome and broadcast the testimony for the value of literary study handed to him by such a major political player.

As Bruni's invocation of Shakespeare and Jusdanis's of Sidney suggest, current debates over the worth and significance of the humanities invite us to return to the literature of the English Renaissance, though not, I would suggest, in the straightforwardly nostalgic way that defenses such as theirs seem to encourage us to undertake. In offering the unassailable value of Renaissance literature as something of a useful solution to, or savior from, the contemporary crisis in and of the humanities, both academic and journalistic accounts overlook the degree to which that crisis is itself an extension of debates that rifted the Renaissance, in ways that prevent either the period's literature or its defenses of literature from constituting a simple panacea for the problems that currently plague us. As tempting as it is to celebrate the Renaissance as a paradise lost, a cultural moment when literature enjoyed enormous prestige before the fall into the deplorable current state of affairs, this study begins with the observation that early modern writers were no less anxious and ambivalent about the value of literature than their contemporary counterparts, however much they tried to mask that ambivalence with the commonplaces so routinely rehearsed today.

Precisely because it squares so well with our own assumptions about the meaning and virtue of our work, the Renaissance humanist idea that the pleasure of literature can be sublimated as socially and ethically useful or productive—that its potential negativity, in other words, can be dialectically recuperated or redeemed as a positive good—has served as the primary standard by which the value of literary writing has been measured. Because the intellectual and ideological roots of the American academy, like the United States itself, can be traced back in part to the Protestant or Puritan work ethic forged in the context of early modern English culture, it is no wonder that contemporary Anglo-American critics operate according to an ends-oriented understanding of the humanities.[7] While such claims may assuage our moral anxieties about the value of literature, especially in the face of the growing corporatization of the academy, our adherence to an instrumental view of aesthetics calls out for reexamination because it diminishes what may be, in the final analysis, literature's most useful or valuable quality: its distinctive ability to confound the very use of utility as a metric for determining value. If automatically defending the utility of the literary always ends up being, ironically enough, an exercise in futility, then it may be more helpful to critique the rhetorical and institutional forces that activate such defense mechanisms, and the charges to which they respond, in the first place. In reexamining the struggles that early modern writers had with these issues, we may be in a better position to reevaluate the current (read: perpetual) crisis in the liberal arts and so to imagine alternatives to the redemptive logic that marks present as well as past justifications for the value of literature.

In sixteenth- and seventeenth-century England, as Jusdanis notes, poets such as Sidney insistently justified the profit and value of their work on the basis of the notion—borrowed from antiquity, and in particular from Horace—that the purpose of poetry is to please and instruct, that it must be both delightful and useful.[8] However, many of the same writers soon came to realize that this notion might be nothing more than wishful thinking, that the relationship between poetic pleasure and poetic utility might be far more complex, even antagonistic, than they had hoped. Concerns over what happens when the delighting and the teaching functions of poetry come into conflict with each other, or when the delighting overtakes the teaching, or when the delighting teaches us how to be bad, were expressed most explicitly by religious authorities intent on curbing what they saw as the deleterious effects of poetry and the theater. Calvinist killjoys were not, however, the only voices that articulated alarm about the potential dangers of poetic delight. Embedded, though not always explicit, in the era's literature itself are similar worries about the volatility of poetic pleasure.

This book examines those worries by attending to the rhetoric of pleasure and the pleasure of rhetoric in early modern literature, with the aim of theorizing what I call literature's "futilitarian" impulse. With this term I intend more generally to parody—and, in doing so, to defamiliarize—the injunction to utility that so often marks attempts to redeem the value of literature. More specifically, "futilitarian" designates the troublesome quality of literature explored in the following chapters—namely, the prospect that poetic pleasure may be pointless at best, poisonous at worst, and profitless either way, that literature, in other words, might need to count itself among what Palamon, in William Shakespeare and John Fletcher's *The Two Noble Kinsmen*, calls "all those pleasures/That woo the wills of men to vanity" (2.2.100–1).[9] If we take the word "vanity" not only in its common sense of narcissistic self-love, with all the connotations of queer antisociality such narcissism implies, but also in its root sense of futility and meaninglessness (from the Latin *vanus*: empty, void, idle), we can begin to see why literature's potential for vanity is the source of such concern. Because it troubles the values of utility, productivity, profitability, and didacticism that were promoted, at least nominally, by the cultures of Renaissance humanism, early modern writers often entertain the possibility of futile pleasure but never fully embrace it, some going so far as to reject it.

One of the primary goals of this study is to trace the various ways in which these dynamics get played out in the work of some representative, more or less canonical, English Renaissance writers. Following a wide-ranging first chapter that establishes and develops the cultural, critical, and theoretical frameworks within which my analyses are set, the rest of the book analyzes Shakespeare's *Richard II* (Chapter 2), Roger Ascham's *The Scholemaster* and Thomas Nashe's *The Unfortunate Traveller* (Chapter 3), book 6 of Edmund Spenser's *The Faerie Queene* (Chapter 4), and finally John Milton's *Paradise Lost* (Chapter 5). All of these writers struggle in their own ways against poetry's futilitarian drive. Some seem to be more successful than others in combating that impulse, at least at the level of narrative, as the examples of Shakespeare and Milton will suggest. Others, like Spenser, become melancholically resigned to the inertia and dissatisfaction they experienced when poetry proved to be less profitable than they had hoped. Of all these writers, only Nashe attempts to revel—unapologetically, no less—in the prodigality and vanity of poetic pleasure, but only at the extreme cost of facing the disillusionment, emptiness, and literal unprofitability that the word "vanity," in its most deeply negative registers of meaning, implies. What this variegated landscape of textual pleasures and vanities reveals, we will see, is a literary culture unable to commit either to rigid standards of poetic utility or to an aestheticist project of pure futility, and incapable of reconciling those two choices as well.[10]

Although the chapters ahead attend, where appropriate, to some of the historically specific and materially situated forces that impacted the ambivalence with which these writers approached the pleasures and virtues of their work, my aims and procedures in this book are more theoretical than historical. Rather than restricting my attention to the particular cultural sources or causes of that ambivalence, I am more interested in tracing its rhetorical, logical, and narrative effects on both early modern literature and the critical assumptions we bring to that literature in the first place. In this way, my approach differs from some of the most influential recent frameworks that early modern scholars have brought to debates over the value of literature and to the question of pleasure. On the one hand, critics working from sociohistorical and economic viewpoints have helpfully illuminated the material forms of profit and value that literature was supposed to secure.[11] On the other hand, scholars interested in the humors, passions, and senses have elucidated how early modern writers and readers would have understood the experience of reading, and particularly the effects of aesthetic pleasure on the reading body.[12]

While I have gained much from reading these previous studies, this book nevertheless endeavors to pursue a less literalized approach to both the "profit" and the "pleasure" of literature. Given that early modern writers do not always use these terms in their literal or material senses, I read these notions instead as tropes or figures that condense and displace certain fantasies—about rhetoric, style, eroticism, foreignness, ethics, spiritual redemption, and so forth—that circulated in the literary culture of early modern England. Indeed, from the perspective of this book, the literalizing tendencies in historicist and materialist criticism are symptomatic of the larger intellectual and cultural logics this book questions. By grounding the vicissitudes of literature in strictly empirical and materialist contexts, critics working in these modes often recapitulate conventional humanist views about the efficacy of literature, defensively guarding their own work both from the suspect idle pleasures of reading and from literature's potential *un*reliability as a source of profitable cultural value and meaning.[13]

Throughout this book I thus demonstrate the surprising ways in which contemporary critics, in an effort to cling to a redemptive humanist vision of literature as an edifying and civilizing force, have replayed the same structures of ambivalence I seek to uncover in early modern literature. As a result, with few exceptions, critics have mostly reinforced the demand for utility; in the process, they have failed to recognize not only the potential pleasure in futility with which early modern writers struggled but also the ways in which we might harness that pleasure in our own critical writing. Accordingly, this book performs the play with pleasure and futility that it discusses; it attempts to enact, in its own methodology and style, a futilitarian perspective that deliberately indulges in, rather than defends against, the potential futility of literariness. At the same time, though, this book strives not merely to play but, more important, to do so without ever losing sight of the potential dangers and costs of such indulgence. Consequently, readers who expect to find a theory, let alone a practice, of purely pointless pleasure here are bound to be disappointed. My overarching aim is to question, not abandon, the demand for utility; by the logic of my argument, the act of abandoning utility altogether is an impossible, perhaps even an unimaginable, enterprise. If this book offers a half-hearted defense of pleasure, this is because Renaissance writers, as my readings show, remain ambivalent about the feasibility of enacting the pleasures of futility. My objective here is thus to recapture, explore, and play with the ambivalence, contingency, and irony that mark both early modern and modern debates about literary value.

In drawing such links between Renaissance literary culture and the contemporary critical scene, this book joins a growing body of scholarship that bridges the gap between the two periods. In the past fifteen years, critics working under the banners of presentism and queer theory have argued against an entrenched tradition in early modern studies that insists on the historical alterity of the Renaissance.[14] Working with more nuanced notions of history and temporality—haunting, repetition and recursion, sedimentation and palimpsestic traces—presentist scholarship has investigated the ongoing relevance of Renaissance literature to contemporary political, religious, sexual, racial, and ecological concerns. Surprisingly, however, presentist work in early modern studies has yet to address explicitly the contemporary crisis in the humanities. This book redresses that gap by arguing that this supposed crisis recapitulates many of the tensions inherent in the conceptions of poetic value that were forged in early modern England.[15] I am motivated in this endeavor not by an antipathy toward history but, rather, by a sense that the conflicts inherent in Renaissance understandings of literature have a much longer history and more persistent logic than those who insist on historical difference may realize.

Because *Futile Pleasures* aims to examine forms of poetic pleasure—of literary play, errancy, and vanity—that have been occluded by the historicist and materialist scholarship that has reigned in early modern studies since the 1980s, I have also found it necessary to revive modes of reading, particularly deconstructive approaches, that were more active in the years prior to historicism's rise to prominence. It is clear that the historical and cultural turn in early modern studies, and in the humanities more broadly, during the last several decades has constituted a massive reaction and backlash against the speculative play, ostentatious rhetorical games, and formalist abstractions of poststructuralist theory and the linguistic turn.[16] For the most part, as Jonathan Goldberg notes, poststructuralist frameworks failed to take hold in early modern studies.[17] And yet, for a brief moment, there was a small handful of books that attempted to draw parallels, rather than sharp divisions, between early modern and postmodern conceptions of linguistic and narrative play.[18] Scholars quickly recoiled from those parallels and soon began promoting history as a post-theoretical means of salvation for a field tainted by the apparently unhistorical heresies of deconstruction.[19]

Against this backlash, one of the polemical aims of this book is to reengage with and expand the pleasures and insights of poststructuralism, especially as they have been reformulated and reactivated by critics working in and around queer theory. Yet I should stress from the outset that this book does not treat deconstructive and queer theories as crystal-clear lenses exterior to and independent of the early modern literature it analyzes. Instead, I view these frameworks as symptomatic reconfigurations of the ambivalences that early modern writers themselves struggled with. For one thing, the privileged styles of such criticism (play, digression, deferral, contradiction, surprise, coincidence, and a general resistance to ends) reiterate the forms of rhetorical and narrative pleasure I seek to trace in Renaissance literature. For another, such approaches have often been rejected in terms uncannily akin to those that Renaissance writers use to devalue poetic pleasure. As I will show, especially in Chapter 2, the xenophobia and homophobia of the terms with which so many Anglo-American critics have dismissed deconstruction—as vain, self-indulgent, effeminate, queer, French—often echo the rhetorical tactics that early modern English writers used to stereotype unproductive, excessive, and futile pleasures. As one of the most recent objects of a longstanding hedonophobia that reaches back (at the very least) to the Renaissance, deconstruction, in all its queerness, can provide us with the analytical leverage to recapture (not to say recuperate) the futilitarian pleasures of early modern literature.

More specifically, I draw from deconstructive and queer criticism a methodological commitment to close reading—or, better yet, to slow reading—however *démodé* a practice it may seem to be in an intellectual era marked by archive fervor, thematic criticism, countless materialisms, distant "reading," and quantitative approaches to literature. In the relevant secondary literature on early modern poetic theory and practice, scholars often merely cite and paraphrase the key passages, pronouncements, and texts, with the effect of reinforcing the already-known-in-advance platitudes about poetic value that have circulated for centuries. A slow rereading of the primary texts, with careful attention to their form and style, reveals the surprising ways in which these platitudes fail to hold up in the face of such close analysis. If the effect (or purpose) of paraphrase is "to blur, confound, and hide discontinuities and disruptions in the homogeneity of its own discourse," in the words of Paul de Man, then a resistance to paraphrase, a more patient and careful reading of the actual language a text uses, can help bring out such "discontinuities and disruptions," highlighting forms of irony that put pressure on the commonplaces we routinely elicit from the texts we quickly turn to, and merely glance at, in order to flatter our sensibilities.[20]

Beyond whatever particular content or results it might yield, close reading is also an important practice here because it not only registers but also *enacts* the kinds of queer—idle, unproductive, futile—pleasures that this book seeks to theorize. "To close read," Elizabeth Freeman writes, "is to linger, to dally, to take pleasure in tarrying, and to hold out that these activities can allow us to look both hard and askance at the norm."[21] Surely those pleasures constitute one of the primary reasons why the humanities are always under attack—and, consequently, on the defensive—in the first place. I suspect most of my readers have been, at one point or another, recipients of the charge that such close, lingering attention to the letter of the text and to seemingly insignificant details is excessive, useless, or beside the point. As Barbara Johnson describes it, slow reading "does not carry with it a justification through practical or political usefulness."[22] Because ours is a culture that values speed—fast food, fast cars, high-speed Internet, quick and easy answers, decisions, actions, and results—the kind of slow reading preached, if not always practiced, in literary studies can only be seen as counterproductive. It seems to me, though, that attempting to sacrifice the pleasures of slow reading at the altar of utility will hardly win us any allies anyway. Writing in 1881, in the wake of the Industrial Revolution, Friedrich Nietzsche argued that philology—that "venerable art which demands of its votaries . . . to go aside, to take time, to become still, to become slow"—is "more necessary than ever today," which he clarifies as "an age of 'work,' that is to say, of hurry, of indecent and perspiring haste, which wants to 'get everything done' at once."[23] If we must justify the utility of our work, then we should justify it, as did Nietzsche, on the grounds that it seems to fly in the face of the need for speed, for immediate utility, and, indeed, for justification altogether.

From our contemporary vantage point—increasingly corporatized, digitized, and globalized as it is—the culture of hurry that made Nietzsche worry has only intensified, bolstering the demand that any literal or figurative investment in the arts and liberal arts must be redeemed. With the notion of "redemption," I refer not necessarily to the strictly economic sense of the term but to the more ethical or spiritual senses covered by early modern writers' understanding of the word. This broader, less material notion of redemption links the Renaissance with contemporary discussions of the value of literature. Two and a half decades ago, Leo Bersani launched a massive critique of what he identified as the modern era's "culture of redemption," which operates, as he explains, according to the "crucial assumption" that "art repairs inherently damaged or valueless experience."[24] Hardly confined to the modern era, this reparative assumption can be seen as being rooted in the various theological and philosophical debates that formed the context in which, and for which, the authors I examine in this book wrote. But it also determines the various theoretical debates that formed the context in which, and for which, this book itself was written.

Since Bersani's book was published, the force of his antiredemptive stance—especially as that argument was taken up and pushed further by Lee Edelman in *No Future: Queer Theory and the Death Drive*—has been one of the primary engines driving an important conversation in queer theory.[25] In recent years, critics have proposed a number of alternatives—reparativity, optimism, hope, utopia, idealism—to what they see as an undue emphasis on the various forms of negativity theorized by Bersani, Edelman, and others.[26] To the extent that *Futile Pleasures* engages with and contributes to this theoretical debate, it does so through an implicit argument that we've been here before. Not only does the early modern period serve, to varying degrees, as a reference point for a number of these critics (Shakespeare for Edelman, Gottfried Wilhelm Leibniz for Michael Snediker, Baruch Spinoza for Sara Ahmed, Sir Thomas More for José Esteban Muñoz), but the period's Protestant, and more broadly idealist, poetics can also be detected in the rhetorical texture of the redemptive stance that Bersani and Edelman critique—the hope that art can deliver us, over time, from negativity, contingency, and futility. Muñoz's *Cruising Utopia*, for example, opens with a beautiful lyrical vision that, absent the word "queerness," reads as though it could have been written by Sir Philip Sidney or George Herbert or any number of other early modern writers invested in building a bridge to the world to come:

> Queerness . . . allows us to see and feel beyond the quagmire of the present. The here and now is a prison house. . . . Some will say that all we have are the pleasures of this moment, but we must never settle for that minimal transport; we must dream and enact new and better pleasures, other ways of being in the world, and ultimately new worlds. . . . Often we glimpse the worlds proposed and promised by queerness in the realm of the aesthetic. The aesthetic, especially the queer aesthetic, frequently contains blueprints and schemata of a forward-dawning futurity.[27]

The futurity and optimism debate in queer theory might best be read, then, as nested within the following series of philosophical and theological frameworks, each of which inhabits, like a piece of a temporal *matryoshka* doll, a *longue durée* more vast than the previous one(s) in the series: the legacy of poststructuralism since the mid-twentieth century; the legacy of Hegelian idealism since the early nineteenth century; the legacy of Protestantism since the sixteenth century; the legacy of Christian spiritualism more generally since the middle of the first century; and the legacy of Western metaphysics since at least Plato. Within this schema of nested frames, the early modern period serves as an important epistemic layer. Protestant culture's distrust of sensuous forms, its reformulation of salvational doctrine, its cultivation of a work ethic that valorized productivity and thereby, as Max Weber famously argued, fostered the development of capitalism: these shifts still reverberate today. It is important to note that they help inform Anglo-American culture's redemptive view of aesthetic and literary utility as well as the distrust that goes along with that view—a supreme distrust toward pleasure, toward contingency, and toward the fusion of pleasure and contingency that goes by the name of "vanity."

Early modern literature manifests that distrust in a number of telling ways, two of which in particular will claim our primary attention in the readings to follow. The first is a *rhetorical* tendency of projecting the vanity of pleasure onto a range of dissolute and disreputable queer figures: women, sodomites, prostitutes, Catholics, atheists, aristocrats, foreigners (especially the French and the Italians), and even, to my great surprise, a small menagerie of nonhuman species (bees, caterpillars, ostriches, cormorants). The second is a *narrative* tendency of teleologically subordinating pleasure to virtue under the guise or alibi of reconciling them (to invoke the title and story of Ben Jonson's masque *Pleasure Reconcil'd to Virtue*). Simply put, these are disciplinary tactics, and my argument for the unpredictable contingencies of pleasure in early modern literature may seem to be directed, in a counterdisciplinary fashion, against these tactics' repressive force. Such an understanding of my efforts here would not be wholly inaccurate. Following the lead of much recent work in queer theory, especially in the field of early modern studies, I have indeed endeavored to practice what James Bromley characterizes as "a non-teleological reading practice," one that attends to errant stylistic and narrative energies that seem to resist, or even cause the complete failure of, forms of reconciliation, recuperation, and redemption.[28]

At the same time, though, and as I have already begun to suggest, early modern literature prevents us from offering a positive, celebratory account of pleasure as liberating, transgressive, or even therapeutic. In *The Unrepentant Renaissance*, Richard Strier rightly pushes against a tradition of scholarship, exemplified in more recent decades by New Historicism and the "new humoralism," that overemphasizes the repressive and regulatory tenor of Renaissance views of pleasure and the passions.[29] The benefits of Strier's argument are enormous, but one should be cautious about erring too far in the opposite direction—that is, toward a purely hedonistic, epicurean Renaissance. Where early modern literature is concerned, an indulgence in pleasure comes more often than not, we will see, with a high price: an unremitting drive toward the futility of fatality, toward *nothing*.

In Shakespeare's *Antony and Cleopatra*, the self-indulgent Antony recognizes this cost even as early as act 1: "The present pleasure, / By revolution low'ring, does become / The opposite of itself" (1.2.113–15). As if uncannily anticipating modern psychoanalytic, poststructuralist, and queer-theoretical accounts of an attractive and senseless drive that "pushes pleasure beyond itself, to the point of becoming the enemy of pleasure, that which lies 'beyond the pleasure principle,'"[30] Antony knows that the irresistibility of pleasure is matched only by his inability to resist the narrative teleology that will lead from pleasure to his downfall. Where pleasure cannot be reformed or recuperated, it must be extinguished. Indeed, it must be extinguished even where it *is* reformed and recuperated—extinguished, that is, through the very acts of reformation and recuperation. This, in the end, is the narrative that early modern literature tells repeatedly about pleasure's vanity in order to grapple with the unpredictable contingency of its own vain pleasures. It is also the narrative that we have adopted and endlessly rehearsed in order to grapple with the futilitarian pleasures, queer vanity, and indefensible play in which we humanists, like our early modern counterparts, continue to indulge, against both our better judgments and the judgments levied against us.

The overarching organization of this book is meant to mirror the narrative structure so often employed in Renaissance literature's treatments of pleasure, a structure that allows for the exploration of errant, futilitarian pleasures before the teleological demand for utility submits or sublimates those pleasures to purposeful ends. Chapter 1 provides the necessary exposition, outlining the social standards of utility and profitability against which practicing writers in the Renaissance pitched their literary performances. Chapter 2 focuses this general discussion on a particular text, Shakespeare's *Richard II*, which plays out its ambivalence toward its own pleasures by staging the submission of pleasure to utility. Following these introductory investigations, Chapters 3 and 4 will lead us to wander through the *selva oscura* of chivalric romance. In these two chapters, I demonstrate how writers like Nashe and Spenser, and even the supremely didactic Ascham, appear to abandon their intentions of utility, surrendering to the formal pleasures of their drifting, desultory texts. The demand for utility recurs with something of a vengeance in the final chapter, which examines Milton's *Paradise Lost*, a text that, like *Richard II*, abjects the disreputable pleasures in which it traffics. Finally, the book's coda offers a forward-glancing epilogue, elaborating what I hope to be this book's potential implications, if not its utility and value.

As tempting as it is to schematize the chapters of this book according to such a narrative, it is also necessary to stress that this pattern cannot do justice to the ironies, complexities, and ambivalences that mark the particular texts studied in each chapter. In fact, the four principal case studies of the book can also be seen as forming a chiasmus that performs this ambivalence. While Chapters 2 and 5, on Shakespeare and Milton, respectively, both foreground the largely successful neutralization of pleasure, they also attempt to pry open moments of contingency in which the *possibility* of adopting and enacting that pleasure gets imagined, however briefly. By a symmetrical inversion, while Chapters 3 and 4 address romance—the one mode of Renaissance writing where errant, aimless pleasure can be practiced and performed to a greater degree than in any other genre, thus providing a necessary counterpoint to the manuscript's insistent attention to the impossibility of abandoning oneself to such pleasures—they also stress the high prices paid by writers working in this disreputable mode. Each case, then, is taken to exemplify not one or the other pole of the utility/futility opposition, and much less that opposition's dialectical reconciliation or synthesis, but rather the more unstable and ambivalent tension that constitutes the opposition in the first place.

In the coda I will have more to say about how that tension, and the apparent double bind it creates, has affected the form and style of this book no less than the form and style of the texts this book examines. For now, as a preview of the chapters ahead, it may be helpful to signal the metonymic and errant forms that my own arguments take. Seemingly heterogeneous ideas, topics, texts, and contexts are frequently yoked together (whether by violence, I leave others to judge) on the basis of echoes, coincidences, and other counterintuitive, nonessential associations, and often this book argues its points less by way of direct, propositional statements than through implication, indirection, and patterns of imagery. I trust that this mode is at least partially justified by the book's critique of the logics of utility and teleology and its attempted countervalorization of the pleasures of contingency and error.

Precedent for this critique, and for the critical styles that accompany it, can be found in the work of deconstructive and queer theorists who have similarly employed "forms [that] are intelligible but do not emerge out of teleological necessity," as Carolyn Dinshaw describes her methodology of queer history.[31] Yet models for my stylistic choices can also, more importantly, be found in the work of the early modern writers I analyze, and indeed each chapter attempts to imitate, in a self-reflexive manner, the futilitarian play with errancy, delay, amplification, dilation, circumlocution, irresolution, and even (in the case of *Paradise Lost*) chaos in which these writers indulge in their efforts to circumvent, postpone, or flout the teleological demand for useful, redemptive ends.

As my insistent qualifying language here suggests, though, it would be false (and more than a little foolish) to claim for this project a pure madness without method. However much the following chapters attempt, in the spirit of Renaissance writers and their poststructuralist counterparts, to loosen the inextirpable *cordons sanitaires* that rigidly separate criticism from the literature it investigates, I have also been repeatedly reminded, and so repeatedly tried to remind myself, that a scholarly monograph is not, alas, in the end, a poem or a romance. Given that this book, like the texts it treats, is no more invested in abandoning itself to absolute futility than in submitting wholeheartedly to the demands of utility—indeed, given that this project makes a claim about the impossibility of the former and the inescapability of the latter—it seems only reasonable to admit the teleological necessity of utilitarian ends on our work. From the viewpoint of this study, however, such an admission is acceptable only as long as the pleasurably dilatory journey that leads us to those ends can create some leeway for viewing their power with skepticism.

CHAPTER 1

Pleasure without Profit

Simply, a day comes when we feel a certain need to *loosen* the theory a bit, to shift the discourse, the idiolect which repeats itself, becomes consistent, and to give it the shock of a question. Pleasure is this question.

—ROLAND BARTHES, *The Pleasure of the Text*

Early in the Legend of Temperance, the second book of the 1590 edition of Edmund Spenser's *The Faerie Queene*, Guyon, the Knight of Temperance, and his spiritual guide, the Palmer, stumble upon a fountain next to which a woman, Amavia, lies bleeding to death while her baby boy, later given the name Ruddymane, splashes around playfully in a gruesome mixture of the fountain's water and his mother's blood. Amavia tells Guyon that she stabbed herself because her husband, Mortdant, had fallen victim to the wiles of Acrasia, the Circean enchantress who presides over the Bower of Bliss, the legend's supreme emblem of intemperate pleasure and the setting for its climactic events. After Amavia dies, Guyon and the Palmer bring Ruddymane to a castle occupied by three sisters; with Medina, the temperate middle sister, they ultimately entrust the baby. At the end of canto 2, Medina asks Guyon to tell his story, which he then proceeds to do, recounting the events that set him on his quest and led him to find Ruddymane. When he interrupts the story, claiming that it is "too hideous to be told," Medina gently encourages him to continue:

Tell on, fayre Sir, said she, that dolefull tale,
From which sad ruth does seeme you to restraine,
That we may pitty such vnhappie bale,
And learne from pleasures poyson to abstaine:
Ill by ensample good doth often gayne.[1]

Medina articulates a lucid encapsulation of the idea, pervasive throughout the literature of early modern humanism, that the ultimate end or purpose of poetry is to offer profitable precepts for moral edification. Spenser himself seems to adhere to this view when he states, in the letter to his friend Sir Walter Raleigh printed with the 1590 *Faerie Queene*, that he composed the poem with the aim of "fashion[ing] a gentleman or noble person in vertuous and gentle discipline" (714).

If, however, we were to pause more carefully on the form of Medina's statements, we might notice a slight snag in meaning that a hasty reading would lead us to miss. The syntactic ambiguity of the line "And learne from pleasures poyson to abstaine" makes it unclear whether "pleasures poyson" is what we're supposed to learn from or abstain from. The problem here is redoubled by the fact that if Medina's moral—that is, that morals can be "gayne[d]" from stories such as Guyon's and from poems such as *The Faerie Queene*—is unclear, then that is likely because Spenser himself scrambles the line simply for the sake of poetic pleasure. If he had written the line as "And learn to abstaine from pleasures poyson," he might have articulated the moral more clearly, but he appears to sacrifice that clarity of instruction from the first in order to generate and sustain the vain poetic delight in the stanza's chain of B rhymes ("restraine," "abstaine," "gayne"), thereby leaving a stain of ambiguity on Medina's otherwise plain moral vein.

One could, of course, easily resolve the vagueness of Medina's phrase by claiming that the obvious answer to the question—are we supposed to learn or abstain from pleasure's poison?—is "both": her point seems to be that we should learn from pleasure's negative example the positive moral of how to abstain from pleasure. Medina's comment would thus chime well with one of the primary arguments that John Milton, a poet deeply inspired by Spenser, later makes in *Areopagitica*: namely, that we must be exposed *to* the negativity of evil in order to gain practice in distinguishing good *from* evil. Milton himself probably has comments like Medina's in mind when he pays tribute to his beloved Spenser as not only a "sage and serious poet" but also "a better teacher than Scotus or Aquinas."[2] Such claims form the basis of Stanley Fish's career-long argument that Milton invokes and enacts the vanity of error as a dialectical means of instructing his readers to goodness.[3] As Fish has always stressed, however, this dialectical process is easier said than done given that Milton's readers, like Spenser's, are fallen creatures, as are Milton and Spenser themselves. To return to Medina's line, then: if pleasure is what we are supposed to learn from *and* abstain from, then we are left with a potential conflict between the virtuous ends of poetry and the pleasurable means used to reach those ends.

However slight it may appear to be, the barely perceptible ambiguity and irony contained in Medina's little phrase is hardly anomalous in the broader context of the literary culture of sixteenth- and seventeenth-century England. Again and again in early modern literature, writers run up against the limits of the mandate that literature be useful and profitable. And in all of these cases, "pleasure" functions as a key figure for those limits. Another brief example, this time from Shakespeare, can supply an even more acute glimpse of the hesitation and ambivalence that pleasure instantiates, the way in which it loosens otherwise taut, straightforward rehearsals of humanist commonplaces about poetry's value. Toward the beginning of *The Taming of the Shrew*, when Lucentio arrives in Padua to study moral philosophy, his servant Tranio attempts to convince him to supplement his austere education in ethics with the pleasures of poetry and music: "No profit grows where is no pleasure ta'en./In brief, sir, study what you most affect" (1.1.39–40). This simple nugget of wisdom—one we might wish to pronounce and publicize in order to recruit undeclared undergraduates to the English major—proves to be, like Medina's comment, less unambiguous than it appears at first glance. Although Tranio's comment explicitly forecloses the possibility of a profit without pleasure, the form of his statement implicitly leaves open the possibility of a pleasure without profit: even if pleasure is necessary for the production of profit, as Shakespeare, Spenser, and their contemporaries reiterated to the point of banality, there is still no assurance that profit will grow where pleasure *is* taken.

The degree to which that lack of assurance poses problems for early modern writers, and for the mainstream views of literature that circulated in early modern humanism, cannot be overstated, even if it has been largely overlooked by a field committed to the task of establishing literature's social and cultural efficacy. Not that such a task is erroneous or inaccurate per se; indeed, it all too dutifully recapitulates the avowed commitments of early modern writers themselves. Over the course of the sixteenth and seventeenth centuries, various religious, socioeconomic, political, philosophical, and scientific revolutions all collided with the effect of recalibrating and strengthening standards of poetic utility, profit, and value inherited from antiquity and the Middle Ages. In the context of the period's heated debates over poetry's virtue, or lack thereof, these standards become the primary point of accord between poetry's attackers and defenders, constituting the very ground of the field on which they do battle. Regardless of whether they agreed *with* those standards, practicing poets had to agree *to* them. Unlike the French and English decadents of the nineteenth century and their modernist heirs, early modern writers cannot adopt aestheticism, the doctrine of art for art's sake, as a purpose or program.

This does not necessarily mean, however, that poetic futility was simply unthinkable in the early modern period (nor does it mean that poetic futility has been simply thinkable in the modern period). To the contrary, futility quite often functions as a primary concern in early modern writing.[4] The issue is that those worries cannot be expressed explicitly or faced directly, given the pervasiveness of what Jeff Dolven recognizes as "the cultural imperative that [poets] use poetry to teach virtue."[5] As the initial examples from Spenser and Shakespeare help us to see, concerns over poetic futility come into relief implicitly or indirectly, at an oblique angle to dominant strands of early modern literary theory. In order to explore how poetic pleasure exceeds or confounds the good intentions made on its behalf, we must first defy the recourse to intention that still marks literary and cultural criticism. Instead of continuing to privilege what these writers *say* about what poetry does, we should redirect our attention to what early modern poetry actually does or does not, can or cannot, do. In using early modern writers' explicitly stated intentions as standards by which to examine their poetry, we have rendered ourselves incapable of accounting for the more unsettling and unprofitable role that pleasure plays in articulating, or disarticulating, the value of poetry. The aim of this chapter is to offer a preliminary investigation of what those intentions were, why pleasure throws a wrench into the system of values they reinforce, and how these dynamics persist in the context of contemporary theoretical debates.

Reading Pleasure

Among the various heroic legends that the Renaissance inherited from antiquity, the allegory of the choice of Hercules, or Hercules at the crossroads, proved especially compelling to early modern poets and painters. As told by Xenophon in the *Memorabilia*, one of his Socratic dialogues, the story concerns the moment when the young Hercules, about to pass from childhood to adolescence, stumbles upon two women at a fork in a road.

The first of the two women, representing Pleasure or Vice, attempts to sweet-talk Hercules down the path of sensual delights and decadent ease; the second, representing Duty or Virtue, convinces Hercules that the route she offers, though less attractive and more laborious than the one Pleasure urges him to take, will culminate in more lasting and honorable rewards.[6] While the allegory became a favorite among Continental artists, from Albrecht Dürer in Germany to Paolo Veronese and Annibale Carracci in Italy, in Renaissance England it had its greatest impact on the work of the country's writers—explicitly in a masque like *Pleasure Reconcil'd to Virtue*, where Ben Jonson stages the harmonious rapprochement between the two figures, and implicitly in a play like *Antony and Cleopatra*, in which Shakespeare dramatizes the tragic consequences of choosing the wrong path.

One possible explanation for Renaissance writers' attraction to this allegory has to do with its relevance to their ambivalent conceptions about their own vocations *as* writers. Generally speaking, much of Renaissance literature can be read as an attempt to answer the paradigmatic question posed in the October eclogue of Spenser's *The Shepheardes Calender*: "O pierlesse Poesye, where is then thy place?"[7] Yet any attempt to answer that question in a positive way—to establish that "poesy" has not only a place in civil society but also a vaunted and valuable one—often tends to be shadowed by the fear that poetic pleasure is potentially, and maybe even fundamentally, irreconcilable with virtuous duty. In this light, it would be difficult for writers of the period not to identify on some level with the emblematic image of Hercules at the crossroads, unable to have it both ways.

The fear of Renaissance writers that their work might be profitless pervades not only the fictional texts they wrote, but also the period's more explicit theoretical pronouncements on poetry, often manifesting as a hesitation or embarrassment about the very practice of imaginative writing. As Richard Helgerson shows, both amateur aristocratic poets (such as Sir Philip Sidney) and professional writers (of the Elizabethan stage, for instance) rarely thought highly of their own work.[8] Against the assumptions of both the professional and the amateur, Helgerson poses the third category of "the laureate," of which Spenser, Jonson, and Milton are his prime examples. Among his poetic contemporaries, Spenser, for example, "alone presented himself as a poet, as a man who considered writing a duty rather than a distraction."[9] We might notice, however, how both views—those shared by the professional and the amateur, on the one hand, and those professed by the laureate, on the other—use duty as the standard by which to measure the utility of poetry. Clearly that standard functions as a defense against the possibility of poetry's vanity. Yet as we will see, the fragility of those defenses begins to come into focus when one reads more carefully the strange place that pleasure occupies in this system of values.

When Renaissance writers codified their conceptions of the practice of poetry, they fused Aristotelian poetics with Horatian ethics in order to make their texts safe for consumption by civil society. As a result, they demanded that poetry be both *dulce* and *utile*: sweet and useful, pleasurable and profitable, delightful and instructive. Poets, according to Horace, "aim either to do good or to give pleasure—or, thirdly, to say things which are both pleasing and serviceable for life."[10] But what was, for Horace, a construction that permitted, at least rhetorically, three options for the poet—*either* to please *or* to instruct *or* to please and instruct—was not so flexible for English humanists such as Sidney, who recast Horace's preference for the third option as a prescription, as the only option.[11] In a sentence printed on the title pages of books authored by everyone from Robert Greene to King James I, Horace asserts: "He who combines the sweet and the useful wins every vote" (*Omne tulit punctum qui miscuit utile dulci*). For these writers, though, it is obvious that the sole purpose of poetry was not merely to please *and* to instruct—a simple mixture of the two, as the Horace motto suggests—but to please *in order to* instruct. According to the demands of humanism, the pleasure of poetry must always be oriented toward instruction in moral virtue, civic productivity, and spiritual atonement. The pleasure of the text is nothing more, therefore, than a means to an end, a means justified only by the value of that end. Poetic pleasure is just a spoonful of sugar to make the moral medicine go down.[12]

Considering the Renaissance conception of poetic pleasure as a means to an end, it comes as no surprise to find that the era's writers tend to locate pleasure as much in the style, structure, and form of a text as in its thematic content or readerly reception.[13] For example, the period's fiery debates about the genre of romance, which I discuss at greater length in Chapters 3 and 4, center on the dangerous pleasures performed by large-scale formal elements such as narrative variety and digression, the errancy and *entrelacement* that defined romance in contradistinction to the more reputable (because more teleological) form of epic. As Victoria Kahn explains, "In a well known verbal and structural pun, the erring of the multiple plot [of romance] represented a form of moral error; the aesthetic pleasure that readers took in the variety of characters and subplots was a form of moral weakness."[14] Yet discussions of poetic pleasure tended to center on smaller-scale formal features as well, as writers located the delights of poetry in the effects of language on the ear and on the mind—its rhythm, its melody, its harmony, and its incessant play with the sounds, shapes, and senses of words.

While poetic theorists such as George Puttenham insisted on the beneficial aspects of such play when it is committed "to some purpose and not in vain,"[15] there is a corresponding preoccupation with the ease by which poetic and rhetorical devices can become vices if they are enjoyed in vain and *not* to some purpose—enjoyed, that is, to an immoderate degree or for their own sake. In his detailed catalogue of various rhetorical figures, for instance, Puttenham provides two different entries for the typical poetic technique of alliteration. On the one hand, he calls it *paroemion*, or the "Figure of Like Letter," claiming that it is "much used by our common rhymers, and doth well if it be not too much used."[16] On the other hand, when it *is* used too much, it becomes the vice he later identifies as *tautologia*, or the "Figure of Self-Saying," in which the poet "takes *too much delight* to fill his verse with words beginning all with a letter."[17]

In the context of a Protestant dispensation that insisted quite strictly on the Pauline distinction between the letter that killeth and the spirit that giveth life, it is no mere coincidence that the features of poetry most often associated, then as well as now, with excessive, self-indulgent, and pointless pleasure—puns, alliteration, rhyme, anagrams, and other plays of the signifier—are precisely those elements that bring to the foreground what Jacques Lacan designates as "*l'instance*" (variously translated as "the agency," "the instance," or "the insistence") of the letter.[18] When spirit, meaning, and sense become subordinated to the shapes and sounds of the letter, broadly conceived, we catch a glimpse, however momentary, of that "pure materiality" or "ribbon of infra-language" that Roland Barthes associates with the pleasure of the text.[19] This is not to say that the insistence of the letter offers the *only* source of literary pleasure. Nor is it to say that spiritualizing engagements with literature cannot be a source of pleasure. Rather, the letter localizes those distinctly poetic and literary pleasures that can only be viewed as vain and profitless from the perspective of a utility-based system of meaning. "Literariness," as Geoffrey Hartman puts it, "'illuminates' rather than writes over or evangelizes the letter."[20] The scare quotes that Hartman places around the verb "illuminates" suggest that what literariness paradoxically illuminates, or makes readable, in the letter is the darkness or shade, the real unreadability, that the letter itself throws over the spiritualizing demand for meaning and profit.[21] However problematic it may always turn out to be, that shade constitutes the distinct stuff out of which poetic pleasure, and therefore poetry as such, is made.

Pleasure, then, like the letter in relation to the spirit (and often *as* the letter in relation to the spirit), must be merely supplementary to, left in the end as nothing more than a mere by-product of, the more valuable ends toward which it should be directed. But it is also, again like the letter, a *necessary* supplement: for early modern writers, pleasure, not utility, distinguishes poetry from other forms of writing and learning. Sidney claims in his *Defence of Poesy*, for example, that "of all sciences . . . is our poet the monarch," because the poet not only "show[s] the way" to learning, virtuous action, and salvation, but also provides "so sweet a prospect into the way, as will entice any man to enter into it. Nay, he doth, as if your journey should lie through a fair vineyard, at the first give you a cluster of grapes, that full of that taste, you may long to pass further."[22] The preparatory stage of enticement is crucial, or else poetry would be as dull as moral philosophy or historiography. Pleasure, Sidney suggests, defines poetry *as poetry*. In making this point, Sidney has recourse to a familiar metaphor: by way of pleasure, he states, poets "doth intend the winning of the mind from wickedness to virtue: even as the child is often brought to take most wholesome things by hiding them in such other as have a pleasant taste."[23]

Given how central pleasure is to the definition of poetry, why must it be redirected toward, so as to serve, more useful and reputable ends? We can gain some sense of an answer to this question by broadening our perspective beyond defensive apologists for poetry such as Sidney and considering instead Renaissance writers who maligned its reputation. Take, for example, Stephen Gosson's 1579 diatribe against poets and playwrights, *The School of Abuse*, to which Sidney's *Defence* is generally thought to be a reply. In the course of his attack, Gosson strikingly twists the traditional figure of poetry as a honey-coated cup of medicine in a manner that anticipates Medina's curious phrasing in Spenser's Legend of Temperance: "Where hony and gall are mixed, it will be hard to seuer the one from the other. The deceitfull Phisition giueth sweete Syrropes to make his poyson goe downe the smoother."[24] Taking this (in)version of the figure alongside its more commonplace manifestation, we can see that poetry works as a drug, a *pharmakon*, in the double sense of poison *and* remedy that Jacques Derrida traces in his close reading of Plato's *Phaedrus*.[25] Within the textured logic of this trope, pleasure thus acts as the misleading varnish that prevents us from knowing in advance whether or not poetry offers useful, reparative benefits.

If pleasure defines and distinguishes poetry, and if pleasure prevents us from knowing with certainty whether or not poetry is useful, then poetry can be defined as a mode of writing that lacks a guarantee of its own utility. The relationship between pleasure and utility is therefore more contradictory, or at least more convoluted, than a conventional ends-oriented understanding of Renaissance poetic theory may lead us to believe. Indeed, the complexity is inscribed within the very logic by which Renaissance writers theorize poetry and establish its value. None of this, though, should be taken to mean that textual pleasure is simply useless. The point is not that literature cannot produce useful effects, but that it always *can* not; its futility, like its utility, is a contingent possibility. As a way of reconsidering the ends-oriented logic by which contemporary humanists, no less than our early modern counterparts, routinely and stridently measure literature, we must reckon with poetry's potential for futility.

The Queerness of Futility

"Pleasure," says Lord Henry Wotton in Oscar Wilde's classic futilitarian novel, *The Picture of Dorian Gray*, "is the only thing worth having a theory about."[26] The blunt aristocratic confidence with which Lord Henry proclaims this principle is belied by the sheer difficulty involved in constructing any theory of pleasure. Indeed, for many modern thinkers, pleasure has often proven to be slippery. It was certainly so for Karl Marx; in the *Grundrisse*, he locates it at the limits of historical analysis: "The difficulty lies not in understanding that the Greek arts and epic are bound up with certain forms of social development. The difficulty is that they still afford us artistic pleasure and that in a certain respect they count as a norm and as an unattainable model."[27] Nearly a century and a half later, Stephen Greenblatt cites Marx's comment in the course of his own attempt to come to terms with the possible contradiction between the historicity and transhistoricity of pleasure. At the end of his brief discussion, Greenblatt asserts that "neither the work of art nor the person experiencing the work of art nor the historical situation in which the work is produced or received fully *possesses* the pleasure that is art's principle reason for being and its ticket to survival."[28] Pleasure, in this portrait, may be "*art's* principle reason for being," but it is an excessive remainder, something that cannot be possessed or mastered. Does this mean that pleasure has no positive or stable raison d'être of its own?

The contours of this question help to account for the intricacies involved in many attempts, perhaps even any attempts, to cordon off pleasure from other related terms. Think of that entire strain of French thought, from Lacan's seminar on *The Ethics of Psychoanalysis* to Barthes's *The Pleasure of the Text* and beyond, that attempts to divorce pleasure from simplistic or stable forms of gratification and satisfaction, resulting in a split between *plaisir* (pleasure) and *jouissance* (bliss). Any line that can be drawn between these two categories, however, is difficult to maintain, according to Barthes.

Before he even demarcates the distinction, he collapses it: "Terminologically," he writes in a parenthetical comment, "there is always a vacillation . . . The distinction will not be the source of absolute classifications, the paradigm will falter, the meaning will be precarious, revocable, reversible, the discourse incomplete."[29] In his essay "Pleasure: A Political Issue," Fredric Jameson attempts to reread these French theories of *jouissance* in conjunction with the terms of certain strands of Anglo-American philosophy; while the essay begins by addressing the issue of pleasure, it ends by discussing the concept of the sublime.[30] It would appear, then, that any attempt to confront pleasure head-on leads writers into other intersecting but not completely compatible categories of analysis.

This kind of diversion effect has a profound impact on the way any such endeavor takes shape. In his introduction to *The Use of Pleasure*, the second volume of *The History of Sexuality*, Michel Foucault admits that his reconceptualization of pleasure led to a "long detour" between the publication of the first and second volumes of the project, so much so that he had to acknowledge "the likelihood of delaying and upsetting the publication schedule that [he] had projected." In a gesture at once defensive and defiant, he then goes on to dedicate his text "to those for whom to work hard, to begin and begin again, to attempt and be mistaken, to go back and rework everything from top to bottom, and still find reason to hesitate from one step to the next . . . to those, in short, for whom to work in the midst of uncertainty and apprehension is tantamount to failure," and to whom he bluntly says, "all I can say is that clearly we are not from the same planet."[31] Such examples of detour, delay, hesitation, difficulty, and failure accrue, seemingly exponentially, the more one delves into modern commentaries on pleasure. They lead to the simple preliminary premise that pleasure eludes and deludes us.

Any contemporary understanding of pleasure—even if it is focused on early modern culture—must inevitably come to grips with this vast field of modern thought in which pleasure, however designated or defined, has both aided and complicated attempts to articulate fruitful conjunctions among the aesthetic, erotic, economic, ethical, political, and religious spheres. Some of the names that immediately come to mind, in addition to those just invoked, include Immanuel Kant, G. W. F. Hegel, John Stuart Mill, Jeremy Bentham, Friedrich Nietzsche, Sigmund Freud, Max Weber, Theodor Adorno and Max Horkheimer, Herbert Marcuse, Pierre Bourdieu, Gilles Deleuze and Félix Guattari, Guy Hocquenghem, Laura Mulvey, Gayle Rubin, and Terry Eagleton, among many others. In the course of writing this book I have had occasion to draw on many of these thinkers, especially Lacan and above all Barthes, but I think it is also worthwhile to suspend any desire to seek in these philosophers and theorists an ultimate explanatory framework. Such suspension is necessary, I hasten to add, not because these modern thinkers offer ideas that are anachronistic to a consideration of early modern literature and culture but, rather, because they are, quite simply (though not without consequence), the usual cast of characters on which one tends to rely for any serious intellectual investigation of pleasure.

Because pleasure, as this list makes clear, has most often been discussed from the points of view of Marxism, psychoanalysis, or a combination of the two (especially where they intersect in the form of various strands of feminist thought), theorists have tended to view pleasure as a symptom, or even as a source, of class- or gender-based privilege and repression, resulting in an "impulse to demystify pleasure," according to Tim Dean. "Our habits of thinking," Dean elaborates, "exhibit a marked propensity for making pleasure disappear or allowing it to manifest only someplace else."[32] Barthes has these habits of thinking in mind when he more pointedly and acerbically writes, "No sooner has a word been said, somewhere, about the pleasure of the text, than two policemen are ready to jump on you: the political policeman and the psychoanalytical policeman: futility and/or guilt, pleasure is either idle or vain, a class notion or an illusion."[33] The approaches critiqued by both Dean and Barthes reinforce, in their suspicion toward pleasure, an opposition between repression and liberation that both early modern literature and poststructuralist theory invite us to question. Beyond holding open the general possibility that pleasure never signifies nor ramifies in any binary (much less singular) way, one of the implicit aims of this book is to suggest how uneasily the question of literary pleasure fits into conventional Marxist or psychoanalytic paradigms and pieties.

Overall, then, this project emphatically does not subscribe to—indeed, it wants to put tremendous amounts of pressure on—what Joseph Litvak aptly describes as "the self-congratulatory illusion that the aesthetic and the erotic turn magically into the ethical and the political."[34] For the early modern writers I examine, it is the relative inability to predict or control, precisely and efficaciously, the political and ethical (as well as the psychological and physical) effects of pleasure that makes it such an intense site of concern—a rich, albeit unstable, nexus where various worries about aesthetic value come into contact, conflict, and crisis. How that form of value relates to other—particularly, though not exclusively, economic—forms of value is not a question I am all that interested in answering in any explicit and determined way, at least at this moment and within the necessarily discrete parameters of this project. I am more interested in tracing how aesthetic and erotic, textual and sexual, pleasures come to figure each other in ways that cannot be reduced to psychological, socioeconomic, or political explanations.

When such reductions do take place, especially under the sign of Marxism, they often draw on and reciprocally reinforce a deeply ingrained bias against what our culture's dominant homophobia continues to view as the "elitist or aristocratic tendencies of gay male aestheticism," in the words of David Halperin.[35] Witness, for instance, how Jameson characterizes what he identifies in Barthes's *The Pleasure of the Text* as "Barthesian hedonism and Barthes' own complacent, stubborn commitment to the *instant*, whether of reading or writing, his self-indulgence (here, self-indulgently, transformed into a very *theory* of self-indulgence), his blissful renunciation of the 'high seriousness' of the Anglo-American critic's sense of the moral vocation of criticism itself."[36] It is difficult not to notice how the rhetoric Jameson uses here ("hedonism," "complacen[cy]," "instant" gratification, "self-indulgence") rehearses many of the standard stereotypes on which the machinery of homophobia relies. Earlier in the essay—which was first published in the early days of the AIDS crisis—Jameson includes a strange, out-of-the-blue reference to "gay promiscuity," which he connects in passing to one of the archetypes of "bourgeois individualism": the adventurer.[37] Given what we know about Jameson's Marxist project and its attempt to demystify the ideology of "bourgeois individualism," this association can scarcely be seen as a compliment to gay men.

Implicit in Jameson's homophobically inflected hedonophobia is a longstanding genealogical narrative that sees poststructuralist theorists such as Barthes as inheritors of a modern(ist) avant-garde elitism. That elitism can be traced back to a Kantian aesthetics of disinterest that takes on a particularly queer coloring in the wake of aestheticists like Théophile Gautier, Walter Pater, and Wilde as well as their heirs among the Bloomsbury group.[38] In light of this narrative, it makes perfect sense why Marxists such as Jameson would fling suspicion toward what they see as the elitist tendencies of modern queer writers, artists, and intellectuals, who often theorize and practice, and thus come to figure and represent, what I am calling a "futilitarian" aesthetics, a word that can convey, among other things, a queer parody of the demand for utility (whether that demand comes from the Left or the Right, from progressive Marxists or reactionary capitalists).[39] There will always be a Jameson (or an Eagleton, a Bourdieu, or an Adorno or Horkheimer) around to demonstrate the complicity of such aestheticism with the pernicious forces of consumer capitalism, the culture industry, bourgeois individualism and elitism, and repressive "let them eat cake" aristocracy. Such claims, however, egregiously ignore a key point that Halperin limns so well: that gay male aestheticism's apparent elitism and self-indulgence may stem as much from sociopolitical inferiority, disempowerment, and abjection as from any kind of economic capital.[40]

These concerns may seem to take us far afield from the ostensible subject of this book, early modern literature, but I foreground them here because they have been central to this project from the very beginning. If my readings of early modern literature proceed here from any single axiomatic origin, it would be the recognition that literariness and queerness are often linked, as these various examples demonstrate, through the doxa of Western culture's hedonophobia: both are always open to the charges of self-indulgence and vanity; both are seen as distractions away from the aims of production and reproduction; and both activate defense mechanisms that justify their pleasures, but only at the cost of bringing them in line with the straight and narrow path toward virtuous ends. As Stephen Guy-Bray puts it, "Like sex, . . . texts are subjected to the calculus of profit and loss and are expected to lead to something, to be productive—not, indeed, to produce pleasure, since textual pleasure, like sexual pleasure, can only ever be a by-product of this process."[41] In the past decade, critics such as Guy-Bray have offered fascinating and important takes on the parallels that early modern English literary culture draws between textuality and sexuality, especially in their unproductive, futile, or asocial states.[42] One of my goals is to add to this conversation by considering the extent to which such parallels persist within the very theoretical and critical frameworks that we bring to the study of early modern literature in the first place. Central to such an investigation, both within and without early modern studies, is the ongoing force of queer theory itself, particularly in what has been characterized and criticized as its "ludic" strand.[43] Queer theory's engagement with, and indeed performance of, the vicissitudes of textuality *and* sexuality leave it vulnerable to the hedonophobia that structures homophobic animus and animosity as well.[44]

A large part of this story, too—as the next chapter will investigate in further detail—has to do with the messy inextricability of queer theory and deconstruction. As I will show, the latter has often been both attacked and defended in terms that paint it *as* queer—as engaged, that is, in unproductive, sterile, disseminative, narcissistic, and antisocial pleasures. In a 1992 interview with Derek Attridge, Derrida made the striking claim that deconstruction "perhaps has the effect, if not the mission, of liberating forbidden *jouissance*. . . . There is no efficient deconstruction without the greatest possible pleasure."[45] It is surprising to find Derrida here linking deconstruction so firmly to pleasure, even to the extent that he places them into a relationship of chiastic codependency: "So: no deconstruction without pleasure and no pleasure without deconstruction."[46] Such claims are surprising because the topic of pleasure never received the same close attention in Derrida's work that it enjoyed in the writings of his contemporaries, such as Lacan, Barthes, and Foucault. In the interview with Attridge, however, Derrida maintains that the question of pleasure accounts for the persistent attacks against deconstruction: "It is perhaps this *jouissance* which most irritates the all-out adversaries of 'deconstruction.' Who, moreover, blame those they call the 'deconstructionists' for depriving them of their habitual delectation in the reading of the great works or the rich treasures of tradition, and simultaneously for being too playful, for taking too much pleasure, for saying what they like for their own pleasure, etc."[47]

Bear in mind that this interview was conducted in 1992, one year before Derrida's *Specters of Marx* was published. Conducted, then, at a moment when his work had already begun to turn toward more explicitly political, ethical, and religious issues—justice, responsibility, hospitality, forgiveness, democracy, friendship, the *à venir* ("to come"), and a messianicity without messianism—the interview with Attridge is particularly notable in light of the shifts that Derrida's work began to take in relation, and likely in conscious response, to the kinds of attacks he identifies here. One could argue that, instead of owning up to the charges of excessive and disreputable *jouissance* levied against deconstructive thought, Derrida and others invested in pleasure and play were forced into a defensive and apologetic position that led them to play nice. In a short piece called "Art for Something's Sake," Barbara Johnson reflects on these turns in the trajectory of poststructuralist theory. Noting the degree to which literary theorists, including herself, were apprehended, especially in the wake of the revelation of Paul de Man's anti-Semitic wartime writings, by "a fear of forgetting reality," Johnson observes that critics "now act ashamed or guilty . . . if they are caught enjoying, analyzing, and *enjoying analyzing*, a literary structure for its own sake," despite the fact that such pleasure, Johnson acknowledges, "seem[s] to be the very enjoyment that would make someone choose literary studies in the first place."[48] Given its associations with queer and Continental excesses, which are always problematic from the viewpoint of Anglo-American gravitas, it is hardly surprising that the *jouissance* of literariness, whether in the form of literature or theory, would end up serving as a source of shame or guilt—especially in the United States, which Johnson elsewhere describes as "the land of ambivalence toward all pleasures that one is not giving up."[49]

Early modern England could also be characterized as just such a land of ambivalence toward undenounced and unrenounced pleasures, and one could theorize this connection between Renaissance England and the contemporary United States by linking it, in turn, to any number of ideological constructs. One such construct is the Protestant or Puritan work ethic, to take Max Weber's concept as an example. This overdetermined web of chiefly Calvinist values—with its emphasis on calling, vocation, profit, and an ascetic repudiation of idleness, leisure, play, and pleasure—took root in the Reformation, as Weber notes, and only intensified as English Puritans migrated to America, disseminating their celebration of productivity and profitability through the educational, political, financial, and spiritual institutions they formed in the colonies.[50] Such values, Weber hypothesizes, fed into the development of modern capitalism. I would surmise that they also fed into the institutionalization of Anglo-American literary criticism, which helps to explain why both early modern humanists and their contemporary counterparts display a revealing uneasiness toward the vanity of pleasure. And that uneasiness helps to explain why it seems that pleasure must always ultimately lose out in any dialectical contest with virtue.

Negative Dialectics

Andrew Marvell dramatizes just such a contest in his poem "A Dialogue, between the Resolved Soul and Created Pleasure."[51] Throughout the poem, the allegorical personification of Pleasure tempts the Soul with a series of vanities: food, pillows, perfumes, mirrors, music, gold, glory, knowledge. In the face of these "batteries of alluring sense" (47), the Soul repeatedly responds that a greater feast, however unknowable it may be from the vantage point of earthly life, awaits in heaven: "I sup above, and cannot stay/To bait so long upon the way" (17–18). Although the Soul admits the force of these temptations—"Had I but any time to lose/On this I would it all dispose" (41–42)—the poem concludes with a chorus that proclaims the unequivocal "triumph" of the "victorious Soul": "The world has not one pleasure more:/The rest does lie beyond the Pole,/And is thine everlasting store" (75–78). Using a pun straight out of *Hamlet*, Marvell's poem thus ends with a glance beyond its end at the "rest"—both the remainder and the repose—of pleasure to be found in the afterlife. Moreover, the patently didactic dimension of the poem, as embodied in and performed by the chorus, seems designed to leave the reader with the impression that the poem itself should not be catalogued among the vanities and temptations that its narrative force dialectically repudiates.

In the process of unfolding and resolving this simple allegorical conflict, Marvell's poem weaves together and condenses, as Frank Kermode and others have shown, a number of classical and Christian precedents: the choice of Hercules, the temptation of Christ, Saint Paul on Christian armor, the banquet of sense tradition.[52] With such authorities animating its narrative resolution, the poem's conclusion can hardly be considered a surprise. In the same way we can be quite sure that Guyon will capture Acrasia in Spenser's Legend of Temperance, that Caesar will defeat those self-indulgent hedonists Antony and Cleopatra in the Shakespeare play that bears their names, that the Lady will remain steadfast in the face of the temptations of Comus in Milton's *Maske at Ludlow Castle*, and that Christ will triumph over Satan and sacrifice himself for the sake of humankind's salvation in *Paradise Lost* and *Paradise Regained*, so too do we know that this allegorical story of a paradigmatic Resolved Soul must be resolved solely in the Soul's favor. We know how this narrative ends, if only because the narrative cannot end any other way. And it cannot end any other way due to the ideological suspicion toward pleasure that pervades Western culture in general and Renaissance culture in particular.

Over the course of Western history, there have been, to be sure, plenty of important exceptions to this general trend of hedonophobia. Any attempt to defend pleasure against attacks from puritanical moral camps could always draw on the examples and resources of Epicureanism, utilitarianism, aestheticism, and other hedonophile "isms." In all these cases, though, pleasure tends to be recuperated or redeemed as a good, a virtue, a value, or an end, a positive source and sign of fulfillment, happiness, and general well-being. "Whoever he might be," writes Lacan, "the traditional moralist always falls back into the rut of persuading us that pleasure is a good, that the path leading to good is blazed by pleasure."[53] Even Epicureanism admits only tempered or moderate pleasure as its goal, while utilitarianism, as its name indicates, makes pleasure into the ultimate object of utility; as for aestheticism, its celebration of art for art's sake is still a celebration *for something's* sake. From an important angle, then, these supposed exceptions to the rule end up only confirming the rule. The hedonophobe who chastises pleasure and the hedonophile who recuperates it share, despite their obvious differences, at least one key thing in common: both judge pleasure from the standpoint of positivity and cannot come face to face with it in the form of sheer negativity. As the example of Marvell's poem suggests, that negativity must always be recuperated—and if not recuperated, then wasted—in a dialectical fashion.

I mean "dialectical," then, in the sense of the concept as elaborated by Hegel and defined succinctly by Adorno: "achiev[ing] something positive by means of negation."[54] Dialectics designates and performs a temporal order that would be animated by what Hegel calls the sublation (*Aufhebung*) of negativity and that would culminate in the redemptive revelation of meaning, of Spirit (*Geist*).[55] Given this faith in the fantasy of redemption, the desire for transcendence, and the promise of plenitude, it is easy to see how the dialectic in Hegel's sense overlaps, mutatis mutandis, with the eschatological and messianic theologies developed over the course of millennia by the Abrahamic religions, especially, from Hegel's viewpoint, by Christianity in the wake of the Reformation. In both realms—Hegelian idealism and Abrahamic soteriology—the ideal of revelation and redemption entails a belief in just such a dialectical narrative, which aims to recuperate or reject whatever attempts to escape from or disrupt its progressive order (onward and upward, at any cost). This operation tends to be fueled by, and to refuel in turn, what Timothy Bewes calls "the idea that history's narratives inevitably converge upon a point of transparency."[56] The aesthetic realm, as Bewes suggests, and as we know from Sidney, Marvell, and many other Renaissance writers, is thoroughly implicated in this redemptive vision: "Art, like Christianity, bridges the gap between human inadequacy—the logic of the here and now—and the unknowable beyond, in a dialectically satisfactory way."[57]

That, at least, is how the engine of the dialectic is *supposed* to work. It has taken much of twentieth-century thought to redirect attention to the negativity that must always be sacrificed or recuperated within, because it can always potentially disrupt, the narrative economy of the dialectic.[58] Hence, Derrida calls attention to what he identifies, by way of Bataille, as the "blind spot of Hegelianism": namely, "the *point* at which destruction, suppression, death and sacrifice constitute so irreversible an expenditure, so radical a negativity—here we would have to say an expenditure and a negativity *without reserve*—that they can no longer be determined as negativity in a process or a system." This negativity "without reserve," Derrida goes on to explain, "can no longer permit itself to be converted into positivity, because it can no longer *collaborate* with the continuous linking-up of meaning, concept, time and truth in discourse." Following Bataille, Derrida associates such negativity with the sheer contingency—the chance, play, adventure, and risk of loss—that poetic discourse opens up in the form of a writing that "must assure us of nothing, must give us no certitude, no result, no profit. It is absolutely adventurous, is a chance and not a technique."[59]

It is a testament to the overwhelming power of dialectical recuperation that Derrida's early critique of such recuperation has *itself* been recuperated—mostly by Derrida's commentators, but also, one could argue, by Derrida himself. I have in mind the clichéd teleological narrative that values the ethical positivities of his later work over the negativity "without reserve" that his earlier work both theorized and performed. It is undeniable that Derrida's later interests in social justice all evince an ethical and political, if not wholly religious, turn in his work. It remains an open question, though, whether this turn to the "to come" inevitably leads Derrida to come *back* to the metaphysics of presence—of logos, of *parousia*, of teleological plenitude—that his earlier work had so trenchantly critiqued. On the one hand, Derrida's eschatological orientation can be distinguished, as Jonathan Gil Harris argues, from the logocentric biases of Hegelian teleology:

> For all the echoes of religious thought in Hegel's teleological vision of history, its final stage—the full self-identity, without contradiction, of Spirit—is different from the end as imagined by eschatology. In its explosive force, Derrida argues, eschatological time does not synthesize but shatters and hence pluralizes. . . . Derrida's eschatological time entails neither a Hegelian Aufhebung moving toward a final singularity nor a savior offering a final redemption. Rather, it moves, explosively and without end, toward heterogeneity.[60]

On the other hand, as Lee Edelman suggests, it may be premature to assume that Derrida's later work *doesn't* rely on conservative teleologocentric assumptions. Critiquing Derrida's unconditional affirmation of a "hope in the future,"[61] Edelman writes, "Even where that hope, conforming to the terms of Derrida's messianicity without messianism, identifies justice as the making of space for the event of the radically unknown, it presupposes our capacity to know in advance that justice will make itself known."[62] Derrida's affirmation of the *à venir* may announce its openness to heterogeneity and the absolute contingency of the unknown, but its very status *as an affirmation*—an affirmation that involves, moreover, an unequivocal imperative to justice—still ultimately closes deconstruction to anything but a reaffirmation of the revelation, and the survival, of a knowable good to come. As Edelman puts it, "When push comes to shove, . . . that good, even for one as committed as Derrida to a 'complication of the life/death opposition,' compels the choice of life over death, of a conservative rhetoric of futurism over real openness to an event, of a liberal version of messianicity ensnared in messianism's coils."[63]

Where the vast majority of Derrida's recent commentators have launched a concerted rescue mission to save him from the (charges of) nihilism and negativity to which deconstruction has always been susceptible, Edelman, by contrast, puts pressure on Derrida for pulling back from the radical implications toward which deconstruction could lead us. At stake here, though, I would suggest, are issues far more extensive than our attempt to process the twists and turns that form the path of Derrida's thought over the course of his career. Through Edelman's unremitting critique of the "conservative instinct to which [Derrida] finds himself bound,"[64] we can gain an oblique perspective on the messianic, utopic, eudemonic, and reparative tendencies pervasive throughout recent work in the humanities; we may begin to recognize, that is, how such tendencies are inescapably shadowed by the "absolutely adventurous" contingency that the early Derrida theorized. Such contingency, the lack of any guarantee that the aesthetic can ever successfully deliver the goods that it advertises, operates all over early modern and modern literary theory. More detailed analyses of these dynamics await us in the chapters to follow. For now, a close look at two short passages—one from George Herbert's *The Temple* and one from Stephen Greenblatt's *Marvelous Possessions*—can help us begin to see how the contingency of pleasure erupts from within even the most steadfast dialectical and redemptive visions of the aesthetic realm.

Contingencies of Pleasure

For centuries, it has been customary to read George Herbert as one of the most devoted of devotional poets, a pedagogically minded writer who composed poems expressly designed as instruments of atonement and salvation. Our understanding of Herbert's single-minded devotional intentions is complicated, however, as David Orvis demonstrates, by the fact that commentators in Herbert's own century and in the centuries since have failed to reach a consensus in identifying the doctrinal positions from which and for which he wrote.[65] Quite a few historicist, materialist, and queer critics, furthermore, have put some pressure on the conventional devotional portrait of the poet, demonstrating how Herbert, despite his almost obsessive devotion to the spiritual realm, does not and cannot forsake (and perhaps does not even desire to) the transitory vanity of the physical, the material, and the earthly.[66] Thanks to commonplace understandings of Saint Paul, Saint Augustine, and other authorities, the letter and the flesh will always be found lacking in relation to the spirit, but only by way of death (or a miraculous moment of translation and ascension, like that experienced by Enoch according to the Book of Genesis) can they be entirely, if ever, transcended.

However we factor these specific complications into the picture, it is nevertheless difficult to shed the overall impression that Herbert believes that such transcendence is possible and, more to the point, that poetry (or at least *his* poetry) is one of the best vehicles for achieving it. That belief clearly guides Herbert's explicit intentions, which get expressed most directly in the first stanza of "The Church-Porch," the long didactic poem that opens *The Temple*:

> Thou, whose sweet youth and early hopes enhance
> Thy rate and price, and mark thee for a treasure;
> Harken unto a Verser, who may chance
> Rhyme thee to good, and make a bait of pleasure.
>   A verse may find him, who a sermon flies,
>   And turn delight into a sacrifice.[67]

Ryan Netzley notes, in a rare close reading of this passage, that Herbert's claims here participate in that standard "tradition of instruction and delight stretching from Jonson and Sidney back to Horace."[68] Herbert's particular take on this tradition provides an especially acute glimpse of how pleasure functions, or is supposed to function, within the economy of poetic value: to make "a bait" of pleasure is, in effect, to abate it, to weaken its force by rendering it merely instrumental, turning it into a means rather than an end in itself. As Netzley comments about the last line in particular, "Transforming delight into sacrifice entails a basic alteration in the relationship between devotion and pleasure: not just using it as is, but transforming it into an offering to God. Whether delight is renounced as a sacrifice or offered up as a sacrifice, in both cases pleasure is the thing abandoned."[69]

From our standpoint, the ultimately conventional assertions about verse, pleasure, delight, and sacrifice cannot be characterized as the most surprising or striking aspects of this passage, however, at least when stacked up against the subtle, though not insignificant, way in which Herbert qualifies those statements: "Harken unto a Verser, who *may chance* / Rhyme thee to good." The word "may"—which Herbert repeats a mere two lines later ("A verse *may* find him, who a sermon flies")—injects a note of uncertainty into the stanza, raising the possibility that poets, despite their good intentions, may not be able to rhyme their readers to good, that the dynamic of poetic pleasure and utility may not function according to the neatly sacrificial economy by which it is supposed to operate. And the word "chance" suggests that even if everything does go according to plan, even if this economy does end up operating smoothly and effectively, its success may be the result of contingency, accident, and coincidence rather than intentional design or direct causality.

The qualifying dynamic at play in Herbert's stanza, whereby the intention of utility gets suspended by brief eruptions of contingency, uncertainty, and irony, is one we will see again and again in the work of early modern writers. But it is also a dynamic that gets played out in the work of modern humanists as well, a point I wish to illustrate by turning briefly to Greenblatt's *Marvelous Possessions*, his study of the rhetoric of wonder in New World discourse. Like so much of Greenblatt's classic work, *Marvelous Possessions* opens with an anecdote:

> When I was a child, my favorite books were *The Arabian Nights* and Richard Halliburton's *Book of Marvels*. The appeal of the former, even in what I assume was a grotesquely reduced version, lay in the primal power of storytelling. Some years ago, in the Djeema El Fnah in Marrakesh, I joined the charmed circle of listeners seated on the ground around the professional story-teller and attended uncomprehendingly to his long tale. In the peculiar reverie that comes with listening to a language one does not understand, hearing it as an alien music, knowing only that a tale is being told, I allowed my mind to wander and discovered that I was telling myself one of the stories from the Arabian Nights, the tale of Sinbad and the roc. If it is true, as Walter Benjamin writes, that every real story "contains, openly or covertly, something useful," then that tale . . . must have impressed itself upon my prepubescent imagination as containing something extremely useful, something I should never forget. The utility, in this particular case, has remained hidden from me, but I am reasonably confident that it will be someday revealed. And I remain possessed by stories and obsessed with their complex uses.[70]

Notice how quickly the demand for utility takes over what begins as a rather vivid description of the pleasurable "reverie" attached to "the primal power of storytelling," a pleasure initially detached even from any instance of comprehension or understanding. Even more remarkable than that, though, is how swiftly contingency takes over the demand for utility. No sooner does Greenblatt profess himself to be "reasonably confident" regarding the utility of this story than that confidence is undercut by an acutely noncommittal, passive, and even mystical or messianic assertion:

"it will be someday revealed." "Revealed" by whom or what? And when will that "someday" arrive? Like Herbert's "may chance," Greenblatt's phrasing throws into doubt the sure and stable economy of utility that the passage, at least initially, would otherwise seem to value, revealing that utility to be a matter of uncertainty—which is to say, a matter of faith.

The fact that we find a similar kind of dynamic at play in both Herbert's opening stanza and Greenblatt's opening paragraph could possibly seem surprising given the vast historical gulf that separates the two writers. Yet, as Robert Matz demonstrates, contemporary historicism's recapitulation of early modern humanism's assumptions regarding literary value is quite striking. Matz argues that New Historicism has taken up a very old tradition—the Horatian dictum so fundamental to Renaissance poets such as Sidney and Herbert—as the foundational premise of its project. "A Horatian poetics," Matz argues, "has enabled contemporary criticism's crossing between literature and history by helping to retain literature as a space of pleasure and play that nonetheless shapes political, social, and economic structures in the world of 'profit.'"[71] The question posed inadvertently by Herbert's and Greenblatt's texts is whether the "crossing" that Matz identifies is even possible, whether literary discourse, that is, like Hercules standing at the crossroads, could *ever* have it both ways, retaining a sense of pleasure and play, on the one hand, while also generating useful and virtuous profit, on the other. The volatile contingency of pleasure means that it can never be a reliable means to valuable ends and that the relationship between pleasure and profit can never be neatly reciprocal or dialectically balanced—however much, and however miraculously, it always manages to seem to be precisely that.

CHAPTER 2

Bonfire of the Vanities

Before coming here I read in Jones a kind of celebration of the sublime virtues of social pressure, without which our contemporaries, our fellow humans, would be vain, egotistical, sordid, sterile, etc. One is tempted to comment in the margin, "What are they but that?"

—JACQUES LACAN, *The Ethics of Psychoanalysis*

On Shrove Tuesday in 1497, supporters of the Dominican preacher Girolamo Savonarola sparked in Florence's Piazza della Signoria what has come to be known as the "bonfire of the vanities." A few years earlier, Savonarola had become republican leader of Florence after the French King Charles VIII's invasion of northern Italy led the city's populace to expel the Medici family, the de facto tyrants that had ruled Florence for over a century. In an attempt to purify the city of its particularly egregious sins, its reputation for extravagance and lax morals (among which, most infamously, was its relatively lenient attitude toward that most abominable vice of sodomy), Savonarola's followers erected in the piazza a wooden pyramid, sixty feet high and two hundred thirty feet in circumference, into which they threw, and in which they then burned, a vast collection of vanities, things collected from Florence's citizens that symbolized the frivolity and ultimate futility of earthly life. Among the objects thrown into the fire were "trinkets, obscene books such as Ovid and Boccaccio, dice, games of chance, harps, mirrors, masks, cosmetics and portraits of beautiful women, and other objects of luxury."[1]

In surveying this list, I begin with a deceptively simple question: what do mirrors and obscene books have in common that bound them together, so to speak, in the same fiery fate? The obvious answer to this question, at least from a religious perspective, is that both function as temptations to sin, particularly idolatry. Because they offer an unhealthy dose of illicit pleasure (self-love in the case of the mirror; a whole array of perversions in the case of obscene books), it is easy to see why Savonarola wanted to rid his adopted city of what he saw as their pernicious influence. I would suggest, however, that we miss a great deal of the importance of this question if we consider it solely from a religious perspective. The bonfire of the vanities was an event caught up in an intricately textured cultural network of not only religious but also philosophical, literary, political, economic, sexual, even mythological factors. That network, I suggest further, is hardly confined, historically or geographically, to Renaissance Florence. Rather, it informs Renaissance England's representations and performances of poetic and theatrical pleasure. It also informs, in often surprising and uncanny ways, those representations' more contemporary avatars.

In 1597, one hundred years after Savonarola's bonfire of the vanities, Shakespeare's *Richard II*, which represents the dethroning of a monarch on the charges of vanity and wastefulness, was first published in quarto. This chapter interprets the play as a bonfire of the vanities, as a text that attempts to purge its dramatic world of the futilitarian pleasures associated with Richard II and his queer followers. In making this argument, I intend to move beyond (though not entirely reject) the dominant critical focus on the political, ethical, legal, and religious issues raised by the play to direct attention to the nonproductive erotic and sensual pleasures for which King Richard and his councilors are vilified. My reading of *Richard II* thus builds on work by Mario DiGangi and Madhavi Menon on the play's queer eroticism,[2] but it branches out in several unexplored directions: it demonstrates the play's self-implication in the queer pleasures it scapegoats; it traces these dynamics through the remainder of the second tetralogy, the two parts of *Henry IV* and *Henry V*, which continue the narrative sequence begun in *Richard II*; and it considers how these issues have been uncannily replayed in the contemporary humanities, particularly in narratives about poststructuralist theory, which, like poetry in the early modern period, has been either attacked as self-indulgent or defended and redeemed as socially valuable. My broader goal, then, is to theorize more intensively the issue of pleasure in relation to the figure of vanity and to determine the implications of that relationship for both early modern and modern literary theory. Before turning to Shakespeare's play, I want to build upon the previous chapter's initial investigation into what makes pleasure, especially literary pleasure, so tricky and troublesome.

The Trouble with Pleasure

Perhaps the biggest obstacle to theorizing (let alone valorizing) pleasure is that it slides far too easily into the negative registers of irresponsibility, disengagement, hedonism, self-indulgence, self-abuse, quietism, passivity, narcissism, errancy, foolishness, superficiality, excess, waste, vulgarity, inconsequence, distractedness, irrelevance, irreverence, abandon, insufficiency, and incoherence. This list of epithets could, of course, go on. "There is something unseemly about pleasure," writes Laura Frost, "something too direct, selfish, nonrelational"—something detrimental, that is, to the stable forms of relationality on which collectivities and polities depend in order to ensure their form, function, and force.[3] Why else would the seventeenth-century poet Katherine Philips compose a poem called "Against Pleasure," in which she characterizes pleasure as "the empty bribe of yielding souls" and associates it with "the fruit of Sodom"?[4] Try as we might to redeem it within an economy of social value that would give it ethical currency, pleasure also tends to signal, if not effect, the absolute negation of value, exploding in the process the sublime foundations on which systems of value, of whatever political or economic stripe, can be constructed. Seen in this light, the capitalist or conservative insistence on profitability and productivity, on the one hand, and the Marxist or liberal insistence on activism and engagement, on the other, can no longer appear all that different from each other, at least to the extent that they *both* stand opposed to idle, pointless, and self-indulgent pleasures.

Consider, for example, J. Hillis Miller's presidential address at the 1986 Modern Language Association convention. At a time when New Historicism had taken hold of literary studies, at a time when both deconstructive theory and the backlash against it had reached a most vociferous high, at a time, therefore, when critics thought they were reconnecting with the material base located behind the veil of language, Miller offered a defense of theory, of reading, and of attention to language prior to the meaning it produces. Addressing the charge that deconstruction, in his words, "get[s] lost in the sterile meanderings of language playing with itself," Miller writes: "The word *sterile*, used in attacks from both sides as an epithet defining theory, carries a large sexual freight. The implication is that theory is narcissistic, even self-abusive. Theorists are impotent while the opponents of theory on both the left and the right are men and women of power.

They make things happen in the real world in a way whose model is procreation—either male or female reproduction."[5] Because the charges of sterility, narcissism, self-abuse, impotence, and a refusal to procreate and reproduce designate pleasures that are frequently attached to nonreproductive and, especially, nonheterosexual eroticism and style, it shouldn't be so difficult for us to recognize the periphrastic gymnastics by which Miller dares not name here the so-called love that dare not speak its name along with other unproductive sexualities.

In responding to these charges, however, Miller makes a defensive maneuver on behalf of his fellow deconstructors. "Neither Derrida nor de Man," he doesn't hesitate to point out, "has ever sequestered his enterprise from politics or history. Quite the reverse. Each has in somewhat different ways insisted all along that one cannot fail to be engaged in history and in political action. Both see humanistic study and literary theory as active interventions in history and politics."[6] Notice how Miller's defense instinctively and swiftly dissociates Jacques Derrida, Paul de Man, and deconstruction from the fey queerness of which they are accused by reassuring his auditors that theory "make[s] things happen in the real world." Whatever worries we may have had about deconstruction are assuaged by Miller's assurance that "language playing with itself" has a social use value after all because "one *cannot fail* to be engaged in history and in political action." It seems to me, however, that a deconstructive reading more perverse or queer—which is to say, more deconstructive—than Miller's would seek to question the ideological coercion that always grades such disengagement as a failure in the first place.

Of course, Miller is far from alone in making these kinds of defensive maneuvers.[7] Especially since the 1980s, such gestures constitute nothing less than common sense. This does not invalidate the valuable work carried out by a generation of intellectuals who, through a combination of bold vision and steadfast practice, expanded the academy, as well as the canon, beyond the narrow conservative boundaries in which they had been imprisoned for far too long. Rather than demean such advances, it is worth asking whether the logic behind them projects the structural *position* of de-meaning onto the very figures that seem to benefit from a progressive political agenda.[8]

The charges of narcissism—and the gender and sexual implications of such charges—have attended deconstruction, to be sure, for several decades. Writing in the early 1980s, Frank Lentricchia claims in *Criticism and Social Change*, for example, that deconstruction is "the best sign of all of where the American humanist intellectual stands today: feeling vaguely out of it, desiring change, but crushed, stifled, and enervated by the fear that the robust, active will may not succeed. . . . Politically, deconstruction translates into that passive kind of conservatism called quietism; it thereby plays into the hands of established power."[9] Writing nearly two decades later, David Scott Kastan argues in *Shakespeare after Theory* that "history functions as some apotropaic fetish to ward off our narcissism, or at least to prevent the premature imposition of present day interests and values. . . . To read Shakespeare historically would be to read the plays with a robust sense of their particularity and contingency."[10] The use of the word "robust" in both of these quotations should come as no surprise given the ground I've already covered, but it calls out for scrutiny nonetheless. The word appeals to a fantasy of straight male potency and entitlement that can only serve to demonize the "enervated" impotency or passivity explicitly figured, in these discussions, by the narcissism of theory, and obliquely figured by the narcissism of women and queers, gay men in particular. This is an impotence that must cower before the importance of effecting historical or political understanding, difference, and change.

These attacks against theory, like Miller's defense of it, therefore reveal the misogynistic and homophobic figures involved in the imperative to ideology critique. The assumptions evinced by Lentricchia's and Kastan's respective excoriations of theory could be traced back, in many ways, to the polemic advanced by *The German Ideology*, in which Karl Marx and Friedrich Engels oppose the passive, head-in-the-clouds abstractions of German idealism with a historical materialism that aims by contrast (and quite tellingly) to "set out from real, active men."[11] In invoking *The German Ideology* as an early expression of Lentricchia's and Kastan's resistance to (the queerness of) theory, one should probably bear in mind de Man's memorable assertion in "The Resistance to Theory": "Those who reproach literary theory for being oblivious to social and historical (that is to say ideological) reality are merely stating their fear at having their own ideological mystifications exposed by the tool they are trying to discredit. They are, in short, very poor readers of Marx's *German Ideology*."[12] Although de Man elsewhere projected that he would undertake the kind of critical reading of *The German Ideology* that he implicitly calls for here, his death in 1984 prevented him from doing so.[13] Such a reading would have to begin by interpreting *The German Ideology* against the grain of its explicit statements against idealism and theory, which have been rendered commonplace over the course of the twentieth century. Nevertheless, it is important to take seriously the commonplace reading of *The German Ideology* toward which a de Manian reading of the text would have most certainly been skeptical. Pulsating through twentieth-century critical thought, naturalized as a primary source of the energy that sustains intellectual and political vitality, such assumptions are no surprise at all when they appear in Lentricchia's and Kastan's polemics, condensed in the form of the word "robust."

Nor is it a surprise, then, that the same word pops up in the work of at least one conservative commentator to whom both Lentricchia and Kastan would likely be resolutely opposed—and who would surely return the favor by opposing Lentricchia and Kastan in turn. In his notorious reactionary manifesto from the era of the culture wars, *Tenured Radicals*, Roger Kimball writes an elegy for the fact that "until at least the early 1960s there was robust agreement about the intellectual and moral goals of a liberal arts education even if those goals seemed impossible to achieve."[14] The implicit difference between Lentricchia and Kastan, on the one hand, and Kimball, on the other, is that the former critics, or at least Lentricchia, might identify the 1960s as a paradise lost, while the latter would identify the same decade as the Fall. The difference between these radical and reactionary perspectives shouldn't obscure what demands to be called the "robust agreement" they share: a nostalgia for a prelapsarian robustness and a distaste for postlapsarian limpness, however or whenever they define the moment of lapse. In a perfect illustration of the nugget of wisdom that nothing unites warring parties so much as a common enemy, Lentricchia and Kimball direct their animosity toward the same figure: Paul de Man.[15]

As Barbara Johnson points out, the discovery in the late 1980s of de Man's collaborationist journalism from the early 1940s "has only intensified a fear of being politically suspect that started well before that."[16] Johnson, however, isn't specific about *when* such fears started. I do not wish to claim that the Renaissance marks such an origin. These fears of aesthetic and theoretical pleasure may be as old as Plato; moreover, it isn't their historical provenance that interests me but rather their figural or structural logic. The Renaissance does mark a moment when the potential vanity and futility of literary pleasure was the cause of particular worry because the fear of being politically suspect (simply by virtue of being a poet) was so intense. The strategies by which aesthetic pleasure was consequently determined continue to mirror, if not shape, our own fears of being politically suspect. Nowhere have these fears received more polemical airplay than in the so-called culture wars of the late 1980s and early 1990s. The effects of those debates over the value of humanities education still reverberate today and can be thrown into striking relief by considering briefly a belated entry to those wars: a collection of essays by Victor Davis Hanson, John Heath, and Bruce S. Thornton titled *Bonfire of the Humanities*.[17]

To the extent that it reproduces a litany of ill-informed, ill-supported, and illogical charges made more forcefully over a decade earlier by commentators such as Kimball, *Bonfire of the Humanities* seems hardly worthy of notice, never mind analysis. Yet the rhetoric with which Hanson, Heath, and Thornton attack the contemporary humanities deserves close attention in light of our discussion. According to the authors, the political correctness that has spread through the humanities, like a "cancer" (79), represents a "silly form of liberal guilt" (71) that is formally manifested, they claim, in the "ego-disease" (103) of leftist critics' narcissistic insistence on the first-person, the personal, and the autobiographical. Moreover, the authors rely on inflamed language that speaks directly to the web of intertextual links I've traced thus far. "The study of ancient Greek and Latin language and civilization," they write, "has been immolated in various bonfires lit by any number of modern Savonarolas, the ideologues of the multicultural and postmodern Left who wish to destroy the beauty and brilliance they cannot acknowledge or appreciate" (ix).

It doesn't necessarily take a deconstructive reader—although deconstruction certainly helps—to notice how the authors' invocation of the bonfire of the vanities ironically cuts against the stated intentions of the volume as a whole. For while this particular quote seeks to figure the liberal academic elite as a collection of "modern Savonarolas," and so to establish the populist credibility that the authors seek to maintain throughout, it is worth recalling that Savonarola was operating in the name of the people *against* the Florentine elite. So, too, do Hanson, Heath, and Thornton aim to stake a claim against what they see as the passively isolated and effete elitists who act as the Medicis of the contemporary academic Left. While the collection, therefore, attaches the name "Savonarola" to the elitist academic leftists who supposedly destroy the canon in book-burning bonfires, the authors' claim of speaking in the name of a healthy "academic populism" indirectly casts *them* as Savonarolas (x). This is an unstated point of comparison that the authors unwittingly reinforce by titling their collection *Bonfire of the Humanities*: the very title suggests that the authors' book is *itself* the kind of bonfire they otherwise wish to attribute to their opponents.

As this constellation of examples helps us to see, the general rhetoric with which critics tarnish theoretical work depends upon and regenerates a charged set of binary oppositions: populism versus narcissism, health versus disease, exteriority versus interiority, activity versus passivity, productivity versus sterility, union versus division, plenitude versus emptiness, meaning versus futility. Such binaries are inhospitable to any negative forms of being and knowing that are inhospitable to positive forms of identity and community. Moreover, this rhetorical network is as likely to inform so-called progressive work as it is to inform so-called conservative work. Indeed, progressive work, so called, can be seen as fundamentally regressive to the extent that it values healthy developmental narratives of progression over the supposedly unhealthy errancy of digression or transgression. It thereby reinforces the regressive ideological operations it supposedly seeks to counter. As Lee Edelman argues in "The Mirror and the Tank," "In our historical moment, it is easy to gain access to discursive authority by defining oneself, at least rhetorically, in opposition to narcissistic indulgences, by appropriating a resolutely aggressive, outwardly focused, and thus responsibly 'political' position that claims to speak both from and for a populist perspective and against the perspective of intellectuals, academics, and other 'special' interests."[18]

In the context of this particular essay, "our historical moment" means the 1980s and early 1990s: Edelman is anatomizing how the rhetoric of AIDS "activism"—insofar as it defines itself against the "passivity" (political and otherwise) of narcissistic and hedonistic gay men—mirrors, however unintentionally, homophobic constructions of same-sex desire. But Edelman could just as well be describing the plot of Shakespeare's *Richard II*, in which the self-styled populist Henry Bolingbroke does indeed gain access to discursive authority by defining himself in opposition to the narcissistic pleasures in which King Richard and his favorites, like poets and deconstructive and queer theorists, are said to indulge. The conflict between populism and narcissism in *Richard II* can therefore help us to critique the forms of hedonophobia that determine debates over the value of (modern) theory no less than debates over the value of (early modern) theater.

The Trouble with Richard

Writing a play about the deposition of Richard II at the hands of his cousin Henry Bolingbroke was a risky maneuver for Shakespeare. A few years prior, Shakespeare had composed four plays about the Wars of the Roses, the civil conflicts that took place between the Houses of York and Lancaster, which had rival claims to the throne. This first tetralogy—the three *Henry VI* plays and *Richard III*—concludes with the defeat of Richard III by Henry Tudor, who goes on to reign as King Henry VII and is, in fact, the grandfather of Elizabeth I. With *Richard II*, the two parts of *Henry IV*, and

Henry V—the second tetralogy more commonly known as the "Henriad"—Shakespeare writes the prequels to the Wars of the Roses plays. In doing so, he searches out the roots of English civil war and disorder, for Richard II's reign was, as Marjorie Garber puts it, "the beginning of the end of a certain idea of English unity."[19] The question, then, that *Richard II* poses is this: what were the forces that caused England to divide internally, to make "a shameful conquest of itself," as the character John of Gaunt, the Duke of Lancaster, declares in the play?[20] This is hardly a neutral question, though. Answering it, even simply asking it, requires Shakespeare to walk a political tightrope.

For over two hundred years prior to the events of *Richard II*, since the reign of Henry II, the crown had passed patrilineally, from father to eldest son, with only a couple of minor hiccups: once from brother (Richard I) to brother (John), and once from grandfather (Edward III) to grandson (Richard II). Bolingbroke's usurpation of the throne—the key event on which the action of *Richard II* pivots—disrupts this chain, a chain otherwise normally consolidated by what the Duke of York calls "fair sequence and succession" (2.1.199). In order to understand why this disruption is significant, we must recognize that the play depicts events that took place two hundred years prior to Shakespeare's own time. A current analogy would be someone writing a play or a film about the presidency of James Madison, except in Shakespeare's case the connection between the play's present context and its past content is much stronger because Elizabeth is a direct descendent of the historical figure on whom the character of John of Gaunt is based. The historical John of Gaunt was Elizabeth's great-great-great-great-grandfather, and Henry Bolingbroke is the half-brother of Elizabeth's great-great-great-grandfather.

This link puts Shakespeare in a profound double bind. On the one hand, because the Tudor dynasty descends from the House of Lancaster, and because Elizabeth's grandfather, Henry VII, deposed Richard III, Elizabeth's claim to the throne is based on the usurpation of it. In this regard, Shakespeare has to paint Bolingbroke's actions in a positive light. On the other hand, deposing a monarch (or even imagining the act of deposition) is an act of treason. In this regard, Shakespeare cannot endorse Bolingbroke's actions. In short, Shakespeare *has* to justify something he *cannot* justify: the deposition, and subsequent murder, of a monarch.

From a purely legal standpoint, the entire ideological dilemma is resolved in the first scene of act 4 when the Duke of York reports to Bolingbroke:

Great Duke of Lancaster, I come to thee
From plume-plucked Richard, who with willing soul
Adopts thee heir, and his high sceptre yields
To the possession of thy royal hand.
Ascend his throne, descending now from him,
And long live Henry, of that name the fourth!

(4.1.108–13)

Thus, Bolingbroke is adopted as Richard's legal heir. That way, what York earlier called "fair sequence and succession" can continue uninterrupted, and Bolingbroke's ascension to the throne can be viewed as legitimate. Such legitimation is prefigured even in act 1, in the repeated emphasis on Bolingbroke as Richard's "kin," for example. Or consider Bolingbroke's charge that Mowbray, the Duke of Norfolk, his rival in the first act, "is a traitor foul and dangerous/To God of heaven, King Richard and to me" (1.3.39–40). The succession of Bolingbroke's syntax inscribes him in a syntax of succession, reinforcing the ideology of divine right kingship by naturalizing a line that extends from God to Richard to himself. Even at the minute level of language, then, the play works toward establishing Bolingbroke as a figure of sequence and succession.

Yet it isn't enough to legitimize the usurper's act. Shakespeare also has to justify it. That is to say, the legal resolution to the dilemma is only part of the story; given the ongoing, unresolved significance that the play carried in Elizabethan England, there also has to be at the very least an attempt at an ethical resolution. The key to this ethics is the central polarity driving the action of the play: the characterological opposition between Richard and Bolingbroke.

If Bolingbroke is a figure of succession, Richard comes to be a figure of disruption. For one thing, Richard is a nongenitor; like Queen Elizabeth, he and his own queen, Isabel, have no heir. Although the second half of the play depicts in elegiac tones the affectionate relationship between Richard and Isabel, the play skirts around, and thereby generates, the sneaking suspicion that their relationship doesn't generate: that their relationship, in other words, generates only a gap in generative succession through which Bolingbroke is able to seize the throne. The play, though, doesn't simply present Richard as a nongenitor; it also pointedly portrays him as an antigenitor. York, for example, provides a list of Richard's crimes, among which is the bizarrely specific and arcane charge, taken from Holinshed, that Richard effected "the prevention of poor Bolingbroke/Against his marriage" (2.1.167–68). Such "prevention" is, of course, a royal prerogative, as it was for Queen Elizabeth in Shakespeare's own day. But when coupled with Richard's spilling of "kindred blood" more generally (2.1.182), Richard's hostility to genealogical stability becomes far more insidious than any royal prerogative would justify. It therefore comes as no surprise that Northumberland calls Richard a "most degenerate King" (2.1.262), for the word "degenerate" precisely encapsulates the problem with Richard.[21] Against this degeneracy, Leonard Tennenhouse writes, "Shakespeare makes the displaced and dispossessed Bullingbroke into the figure who rescues the principle of genealogy and links it to the law."[22]

More important, Richard's degeneracy gets figured, both within and without the play, as an indulgence in futilitarian pleasures.[23] In *Engendering a Nation*, their feminist study of the history plays, Jean Howard and Phyllis Rackin repeatedly emphasize this point in their brief discussion of *Richard II*. They write that Richard "wastes his kingdom's treasure by indulging in excessive luxuries"; that he "is addicted to luxurious pleasures"; that he "waste[s] the land's wealth in luxurious pleasures and courtly extravagance"; that he "wastes the land's wealth and honor on luxurious pleasures."[24] In the insistent repetition of this claim, the word "luxurious" stands out, for it is not a word that appears at all, in any of its forms, in the play. Here, the common definition of "luxurious" as wasteful and extravagant does capture, to some degree, Richard's crime, but it is also worth pointing out an early definition of "luxurious," now obsolete but current in Shakespeare's day, as "lascivious, lecherous, unchaste" (*OED*, s.v. "luxurious," *a.* 1). Howard and Rackin's discussion of Richard's "luxury" suggests, however accidentally or indirectly, the extent to which his crimes are as much sexual and erotic as they are economic and political. Indeed, the economic and the political charges may be a cover or screen for, or a mere effect of, the more occluded but nonetheless potent sexual crimes that lead to Richard's conviction and justify his deposition.[25]

In these various ways, Richard serves as a notable early modern instance of what Lee Edelman calls "*sinthom*osexuality," a portmanteau that grafts "homosexuality" to the Lacanian "sinthome." For Lacan, Edelman explains, the sinthome designates "a locus of enjoyment beyond the logic of interpretation," the site of *jouissance* through which the subject is at once constituted and undone.[26] On the one hand, insofar as it functions as "the knot that holds the subject together," the sinthome names "the node of senseless compulsion on which the subject's singularity depends."[27] On the other hand, insofar as it is intrinsically meaningless and carries "the force of a jouissance played out in the pulsions of the drive," the sinthome "unravels those fantasies by and within which the subject means"; it thus bespeaks the subject's "unthinkable implication in the Real," affording access to that senseless enjoyment "by which the subject finds itself driven beyond the logic of fantasy or desire."[28] By the neologism "*sinthomo*sexuality," then, Edelman links the meaningless sinthome to the homosexuality often figured, analogously, as "a mode of enjoyment at the social order's expense."[29] As "a figure for the subject's unthinkable implication in the Real as evinced by the meaningless jouissance made available through the sinthome,"[30] the *sinthomo*sexual serves the Symbolic order as a repository for the senseless pleasure that must be evacuated or abjected in order to sustain the fantasy of sociopolitical cohesion and ultimate redemption.

None of Edelman's primary examples of *sinthomo*sexuals—Ebenezer Scrooge, Silas Marner, Leonard in Alfred Hitchcock's *North by Northwest*, and the birds in Hitchcock's eponymous film—could be described as "gay" in modern identitarian terms, but all of them are recognizably *modern* characters and figures. Only in scattered references to Shakespeare does Edelman address the potential for an early modern version of *sinthomo*-sexuality; in a lengthy footnote on why our culture so rarely imagines female figures as *sinthomo*sexuals, for example, Edelman adduces Katherine, in *The Taming of the Shrew*, as a potentially "noteworthy counter-example."[31] Surely the meanings of what we would call *sinthomo*sexuality are inflected differently in the milieu of Elizabethan England, colored by constructions of status, politics, and theology pointedly distinct from our own supposedly bourgeois, democratic, and secular modernity. Nevertheless, what Katherine and Richard share with each other and with Edelman's more modern examples is an unremitting refusal of sociality and desire, a perverse fixation on excessive *jouissance* that both corrodes and, in the end, reinforces the foundations of social value.

To this brief list of *sinthomo*sexuals on the early modern stage one could also add Marlowe's Edward II and Gaveston, as well as Shakespeare's Malvolio, Angelo, Claudius, Iago, Macbeth and Lady Macbeth, Timon, Coriolanus, Antony and Cleopatra, and, from the realm of the histories, Richard III. Instead of submitting to communal law, all these characters indulge in futilitarian pleasures that must register, in the realm of the Symbolic, as profoundly narcissistic because they disrupt the meaning of sociality and the sociality of meaning. As Coppélia Kahn, comparing and contrasting Shakespeare's two Richards, writes, "Though Richard III is aggressive, cunning, and ruthless, while the other Richard is passive, naive, and impotent, both are narcissists unable to form or sustain bonds with others; they are fundamentally alone with themselves."[32] What does it mean to call Richard II a narcissist? Let me unfold some of the implications of this question by turning briefly to the locus classicus of narcissism for the Renaissance: the story of the beautiful, prideful Narcissus as recounted in the third book of Ovid's *Metamorphoses.*

Shortly after his birth, Narcissus's mother, Leirope, asks the blind prophet Tiresias if her son "should live to many yeares of age," to which Tiresias answers, "Yea full long, so that him selfe he does not know."[33] Years later, scorning the company of both men and women (Echo in particular), Narcissus stumbles across a pristine pool where he spies his own reflection, with which he falls vainly—in every sense of the word—in love. Frozen in a specular relation to the image of his face, he wastes away. Commonplace understandings of the Narcissus myth have tended to focus on the fact that he falls in love with an image of *himself*, but it is also important to consider how he falls in love with an *image* and, at least from his perspective for the first half of the tale, with an image of *another male*. These two details, the second more easily passed over than the first, are profoundly interrelated. To take the second detail first: until Narcissus realizes that the reflection is an image of himself, he has fallen in love with what he thinks is a fair youth specified as male: "It is but even a little droppe that keepes us two asunder./*He* would be had" (*Met.*, 3.565; my italics). This use of the third-person male pronoun comes a full forty-five lines after Narcissus first notices the image; in the interim, the narrator makes it abundantly clear to us that this is a pitiable example of *self*-love. The purpose of such moralizing is ostensibly to warn of the dangers of mistaking a sign for a referent, but that moralizing also functions to conceal the more intriguing homoeroticism that constitutes Narcissus's desire at first. In other words, the narrator's interventions correct two delusions. The first is the more general aesthetic delusion of confusing image and reality.[34] The second is the more specific, though less explicit, delusion of Narcissus falling in love with another male when he's actually fallen in love with himself.

In a brief discussion of Narcissus in *Persons and Things*, Barbara Johnson highlights the didactic impulses of Ovid's narrative voice, commenting that the narrator "make[s] sure we know right away that Narcissus is suffering from a delusion." "There is almost a taboo," Johnson goes on to say, "against sharing in that delusion, remaining in the space of desire, taking a shadow for a substance. Falling in love with a beautiful form, however, suggests more than emptiness: it suggests a realm of aesthetics."[35] Indeed, the language that Golding's translation uses to characterize the youth's delusion echoes descriptions, in antiquity as well as the Renaissance, of the seductive power of poetry: "He knowes not what it was he sawe. And yet the foolish elfe/Doth burne in ardent love thereof. The very selfsame thing/That doth bewitch and blinde his eyes, encreaseth all his sting" (*Met.*, 3.540–42). One might read the myth metatextually, then: just as Tiresias predicted, Narcissus's undoing comes when he knows himself, but only when he knows himself *as a signifier*—an image, a character, a sign, a figure locked within Ovid's text. The story of Narcissus taking pleasure in his own image can thus be read as an allegory for readers taking pleasure, perhaps even a narcissistic pleasure, in the very poem in which they are reading the story of Narcissus.

At the precise moment Narcissus realizes his delusion, he says, "It is my selfe I well perceyve, it is mine Image sure" (3.582). The comma splice here in Golding's translation helps to blur the distinction between "selfe" and "Image," a blurring that forms the basis of not just Narcissus's specific misapprehension, in all its fatal and futile queerness, but the misapprehension that forms the very basis of aesthetics as well. Kathryn Schwarz succinctly encapsulates this danger: "In failing to distinguish between other and self, Narcissus might lose himself entirely."[36] Small wonder, then, that the arc of the myth dramatizes the narrative logic whereby "vanity as narcissism," as Joseph Litvak puts it in a different context, "cannot help turning into vanity as futility."[37] Like those countless *sinthomo*sexuals in Tudor and Stuart drama who, depending on the genre, must be either reformed or deformed, subjected or abjected, lest they continue to block the teleological push toward the survival of the social order, Narcissus must be punished for spurning the company of others. According to the overdetermined logic that marks so many of Ovid's myths in the *Metamorphoses*, the act of rejecting companionship, society, and civilization *for* the self leads to the dissolution *of* the self, the one and only human attachment Narcissus has.

Yet insofar as Narcissus's delusion, as we have seen, is an inherently aesthetic one—that is, a delusion constitutive *of* the aesthetic—then Ovid's poem cannot help but be implicated in it as well. If the narrator, as Johnson writes, warns against "taking a shadow for a substance," that can only be because the act of taking a shadow for a substance can potentially lead to the opposite, complementary, and perhaps more insidious maneuver: taking a substance for a shadow. Both the dissolution of Narcissus into the abyss of pure futility and the redemption of that dissolution when Narcissus is memorialized in the form of a flower can be read as the poem's strategies for warding off its own potential fall from substance into shadow, an attempt to demonstrate that "the realm of aesthetics," to recall Johnson's words, constitutes something "*more* than emptiness." In an effort to resolve the ideological contradictions in which it is entangled and thus to avoid a similar fall into emptiness, *Richard II* displays much the same narrative arc as well, though without the aesthetic redemption that memorializes Narcissus. "To enter Richard II," writes Judith Brown, "is to enter negative space, a queer cavity of undoing."[38] To enter *Richard II*, the play, by contrast, is to enter *positive* space, insofar as the play projects vanity onto its eponymous character so as to avoid the futilitarian void into which he falls. Richard takes the fall so that the play, by means of that fall, can prove to be redemptively edifying and satisfying after all.

Throughout *Richard II*, Shakespeare figures the undoing of Richard's sovereignty as a violent act of despiritualization or desublimation, as if he were tossed into a bonfire of vanities. More specifically, such dissolution gets encapsulated in three key tropes: dust, the hollow crown, and the cracked mirror. When Richard, for example, realizes that he is doomed, he reduces his spiritual body—the more sublime of the king's two bodies—to the mere status of his material body:

Of comfort no man speak!
Let's talk of graves, of worms and epitaphs,
Make dust our paper and with rainy eyes
Write sorrow on the bosom of the earth.

(*R2*, 3.2.145–48)

The figure of dust pops up again in the final act of the play in the Duke of York's sketch of the now-deposed Richard's "rude" reception by the commoners of London. After the Duchess of York asks about the "rude misgoverned hands [that] from windows' tops/Threw dust and rubbish on King Richard's head," her husband reports that "No joyful tongue gave him his welcome home,/But dust was thrown upon his sacred head" (5.2.5–6, 29–30). This tableau, with its emphasis on Richard's "sacred head" (his crown, in more ways than one), indirectly confirms a proleptic vision Richard had articulated earlier: "I'll be buried in the King's highway,/Some way of common trade, where subjects' feet/May hourly trample on their sovereign's head" (3.3.155–57).

Lest we view this reduction of Richard to dust as unjust, it is important to recall that the play operates according to a narrative logic—similar to that which governs the myth of Narcissus—that requires us to view this as the correct and natural punishment for crimes Richard has committed. Consider the primary goal of the rebels, as expressed by Willoughby, one of Bolingbroke's supporters, in act 2: they aim to "redeem from broking pawn the blemished crown,/Wipe off the dust that hides our sceptre's gilt/And make high majesty look like itself" (2.1.293–95). The dirty despiritualization of the crown is not a tragedy that happens *to* Richard, but a tragedy already effected *by* Richard. Hence, it is insistently articulated by Richard, chiefly in the middle of act 3:

> For within the hollow crown
> That rounds the mortal temples of a king
> Keeps Death his court; and there the antic sits,
> Scoffing his state and grinning at his pomp,
> Allowing him a breath, a little scene,
> To monarchize, be feared and kill with looks,
> Infusing him with self and vain conceit
>
> (3.2.160–66)

The logic by which Richard expresses that for which he is responsible—his reduction of the crown to a "hollow" void—helps the play skirt around the issue of charging Bolingbroke with treason: even though Bolingbroke desublimates the crown's "high majesty" by seizing it, the play portrays him as redeeming it from Richard's debasement of it. Hence, Richard is made out to play a key role in the desublimation of the monarchy, if not directly then at least by giving his

> soul's consent
> T'undeck the pompous body of a king,
> Ma[king] Glory base and Sovereignty a slave,
> Proud Majesty a subject, State a peasant.
>
> (4.1.249–52)

Richard isn't reduced to nothing by forces of predation external to himself. Rather, like Narcissus, *he* is the means by which he is undone, split as subject and object, predator and prey. As John of Gaunt says, in a characteristically prophetic fashion, on his deathbed in act 2, "Light vanity, insatiate cormorant, / Consuming means, soon preys upon itself" (2.1.38–39).

Thus, when Richard, in act 4, calls for a mirror, explaining "that it may show me what a face I have, / Since it is *bankrupt* of his majesty" (4.1.266–67; my italics), we should hear an echo of Willoughby's earlier charge that "the King's grown *bankrupt* like a broken man," a charge for which Northumberland provides the natural, inevitable, forecasted retribution: "Reproach and dissolution hangeth over him" (2.1.257–58; my italics). The mirror scene literalizes what this earlier exchange figures: when Richard comes face-to-face with his vanity—his narcissism as well as the futility of his indulgence in useless pleasures—he confronts "a broken man" indeed and thus, not surprisingly, breaks the mirror. Charles Forker claims that the "solipsistic exhibitionism" of this scene can be read on two levels: "At one level the episode can be read as extravagant escapism, a means by which Richard narcissistically evades a reality he himself has invited. . . . But the mirror, as a reflector of truth (as well as of vanity), also allows the fallen King a moment of deeper insight into his own nature. . . . The brittleness of the glass symbolizes for Richard the fragility and impermanence of life itself and links up thematically with the 'hollow crown' speech of 3.2 with its effect of expanded consciousness and deepened self-perception" (36–38).

Notice the alacrity with which Forker attempts to sublimate the waste, the vanity and meaninglessness, of the first level of interpretation into the second level's production of "truth," "deeper insight," "expanded consciousness and deepened self-perception." Given the play's repeated association of Richard with that which is "vain," "hollow," and "nothing"—associations that reach a breaking point, literally and figuratively, in the mirror scene—I would claim, contra Forker, that the only truth the scene reveals is the truth with which Richard comes face-to-face: the truth that he has only ever defaced the truth, evacuating the signs and symbols of kingship, the very center around which his society revolves, of all their meaning and, in the process, dissolving himself, his self, into the void, the nothing, the meaningless *jouissance* in which he indulged like the classic narcissist or *sinthom*osexual he always was.

To claim, however, that the play's conflicts and tragedy are caused by Richard's vanity is to avoid the questions raised by the ideological dilemma that I addressed earlier: the play cannot vilify Bolingbroke, to be sure, but it also cannot wholly condemn Richard, given that the deposition of the king cannot entirely escape implications of sedition and treason. To solve this dilemma, or at least attempt to solve it, the play explicitly identifies a number of scapegoats—Richard's councilors: Bushy, Green, Bagot, and the Earl of Wiltshire—who are abjected so as to absolve Richard of some of the guilt that the play generates around his irresponsible pleasures.

Caterpillars of the Commonwealth

One of Bolingbroke's first actions upon returning to England from his banishment is to execute two of Richard's favorites: Bushy and Green. The charges that Bolingbroke levies against them have to do with what he identifies as their offenses against Richard:

> You have misled a prince, a royal king,
> A happy gentleman in blood and lineaments,
> By you unhappied and disfigured clean.
> You have in manner with your sinful hours

Made a divorce betwixt his queen and him,
Broke the possession of a royal bed
And stained the beauty of a fair queen's cheeks
With tears drawn from her eyes by your foul wrongs.

(*R2*, 3.1.8–15)

Notably, Bolingbroke condemns Bushy and Green for doing to Richard what Richard, as I pointed out earlier, was condemned for doing to Bolingbroke: they function as antigenitors, splitting up the happy heterosexual couple. Insofar as they "broke" up the royal bed, they can be viewed as a direct cause of Richard becoming a "broken man." The question of whether or not they have taken Queen Isabel's place in bed is an intriguing one, less for any determinate answer we can come up with than for the anxiety with which centuries' worth of criticism has ignored the possibility that they *might* have.[39] The rhetoric of *sinthom*osexuality is here displaced from Richard onto his favorites, in such a way that, like the scapegoats they are, or are made out to be, they are made to take some, if not all, of the blame.

But the charges don't end there. Bolingbroke continues by rebuking Bushy and Green for committing offenses against not only Richard but also himself:

Myself, a prince by fortune of my birth,
Near to the King in blood, and near in love
Till you did make him misinterpret me,
Have stooped my neck under your injuries
And sighed my English breath in foreign clouds,
Eating the bitter bread of banishment,
Whilst you have fed upon my signories,
Disparked my parks and felled my forest woods,
From my own windows torn my household coat,
Rased out my imprese, leaving me no sign
Save men's opinions and my living blood
To show the world I am a gentleman.

(3.1.16–27)

Once again the councilors are made to take the blame for offenses committed by Richard, whose performative command, we will recall, deprived Bolingbroke of his patrimony following Gaunt's death.[40] At the very least, they are blamed for carrying out Richard's actions to a significant degree: where Richard deprives Bolingbroke of the materials of his inheritance, Bushy and Green have deprived Bolingbroke of the signs and symbols of his signories.

Bolingbroke's accusation that Bushy and Green have "fed upon my signories" and "disparked my parks and felled my forest woods" means that their offenses are directed against the very land of England, as if they were pests who lay waste to the English nation-garden. Bolingbroke's charges are therefore inextricably linked with a network of images that are condensed, as if by centripetal force, in the play's emblematic core: the conversation, overheard by Queen Isabel and her ladies-in-waiting, that takes place between the gardener and his assistants. This exchange allegorically refigures the disfigurements associated with Richard and his councilors.

> GARDENER [*to one Man*]: Go bind thou up young dangling
> apricocks,
> Which, like unruly children, make their sire
> Stoop with oppression of their prodigal weight.
> Give some supportance to the bending twigs.
> [*to the other Man*]
> Go thou, and, like an executioner,
> Cut of the heads of too fast-growing sprays
> That look too lofty in our commonwealth.
> All must be even in our government.
> You thus employed, I will go root away
> The noisome weeds, which without profit suck
> The soil's fertility from wholesome flowers.
>
> I MAN: Why should we in the compass of a pale
> Keep law and form and due proportion,
> Showing, as in a model, our firm estate,
> When our sea-walled garden, the whole land,
> Is full of weeds, her fairest flowers choked up,
> Her fruit trees all unpruned, her hedges ruined,
> Her knots disordered and her wholesome herbs
> Swarming with caterpillars?
>
> GARDENER: Hold thy peace.
> He that hath suffered this disordered spring
> Hath now himself met with the fall of leaf.
> The weeds which his broad-spreading leaves did shelter,
> That seemed in eating him to hold him up,
> Are plucked up, root and all, by Bolingbroke—
> I mean the Earl of Wiltshire, Bushy, Green.
>
> (3.4.29–53)

To approach this conversation, first let me note how Richard's role in the wasting of England is far from unambiguous. Insofar as he "suffered this disordered spring," he is both the object and the subject, the victim and the perpetrator, for the verb "suffer" has a double meaning: either to "undergo, endure" or to "tolerate, allow" (*OED*, s.v. "suffer," v., I and II). That ambiguity, however, is resolved by the explicit identification of his councilors as the "weeds" and "caterpillars" that lay waste to the land, an identification that's prefigured in Bolingbroke's previous characterization of them as "caterpillars of the commonwealth, / Which I have sworn to weed and pluck away" (2.3.166–67).[41] And where Gaunt, as I pointed out, earlier figures Richard as an "insatiate cormorant" that "feeds upon itself" (2.1.38–39), here it is the councilors who "seemed in eating [Richard] to hold him up." By the end of the exchange, then, the insidious role of the councilors becomes clear: they assume the rhetorical position that the play had earlier attributed to Richard.[42] As Menon explains, the councilors "have clogged up King Richard's productivity and have, so to speak, sucked him dry."[43]

But why "caterpillars"? This may seem like an oddly specific, pedantic, or trivial question, but it's not for nothing that Shakespeare chooses this particular figure. As the larval forms of butterflies, caterpillars function as figures of immaturity, prematurity, and unripeness, associations that contrast with the garden scene's repetition of the words "whole" and "wholesome." That contrast, in turn, chiefly signals the disintegration of English unity that the play depicts and attributes first to Richard and then, by scapegoating displacement, to his favorites. Moreover, caterpillars are figures of rapaciousness; they're horticultural pests that feed and destroy. According to Karen Edwards, the figure is "appropriate for a furtive destroyer and devourer"; not surprisingly, caterpillars show up, as Edwards notes, in Milton's *Of Reformation* "when he calls the papacy 'a Caterpiller secretly gnawing at *Monarchy*.'"[44] Caterpillars, then, are like weeds: they stand in contrast to fertility and productivity and, as such, they conjure up associations that recall the connotatively sodomitical way in which Richard and his councilors stand against, and in the way of, *re*production as well as production. Because, as Edelman maintains, "the *sinthom*osexual has no privileged relation to any sex or sexuality—or even, indeed, to any species," caterpillars, like the titular birds of Hitchcock's film as analyzed in the last chapter of *No Future*, can be counted among the animal kingdom's primary *sinthom*osexuals.[45] Just as Hitchcock's birds lay waste to the meaningfulness that structures social cohesion, so too do Shakespeare's caterpillars come to figure the routine forces (Catholicism, sodomy) that threaten to unravel the very fabric of early modern England's social reality.

These associations help to explain why Bolingbroke refers to Richard's councilors not merely as caterpillars but as "caterpillars *of the commonwealth*." The word "common" reverberates throughout the play. Notice, for example, how the gardener refers to "our commonwealth," not "our kingdom," defining England as a property of the people rather than the monarch. Indeed, it is along the fault lines of this issue that the characterological opposition between Richard and Bolingbroke becomes most stark. From as early as the first act, Richard notes the populist support that Bolingbroke has: "Ourself and Bushy, Bagot here and Green / Observed his courtship to the common people" (*R2*, 1.4.23–24). That "*court*ship," compounded by what Richard, in the same speech, calls Bolingbroke's "humble and familiar *court*esy" (1.4.26), contrasts with the courtly, elitist disdain that Richard and his followers express toward what Bagot calls "the wavering commons" and what Bushy calls "the hateful commons" (2.2.128, 137). And the feeling, it seems, is mutual. Ross, one of Bolingbroke's supporters, notes that Richard "hath . . . pilled [the commons] with grievous taxes, / And quite lost their hearts" (2.1.246–47). As Forker notes in his annotation to this line, the word "pilled" "is cognate with modern 'pillage' and was associated through false etymology with 'caterpillars.'" All of this demonstrates how the futilitarian *jouissance* of Richard and his followers is profoundly antisocial and antipopulist in nature.

Yet the associations clustered around the epithet "caterpillars of the commonwealth" indict not only Richard II and his councilors but also *Richard II* itself. While searching the archive for other references to caterpillars (and commonwealths), I was surprised to find that the phrase appears on the title page of Stephen Gosson's 1579 antipoetic and antitheatrical tract, *The Schoole of Abuse*: *The Shoole of abuse, conteining a plesaunt inuective against poets, pipers, plaiers, jesters, and such like caterpillers of a commonwelth*. In his diatribe, Gosson writes that, if one were to "pul off the visard that Poets maske in," one would "disclose their reproach, bewray their wantonnesse, lament their follie," and that, because of this tendency among poets toward licentious vanity, it's "no marueyle [that] *Plato* shut them out of his Schoole, and banished them quite from his common wealth, as effeminate writers, vnprofitable members, and vtter enimies to vertue."[46] This language should sound familiar: it is as if Gosson were writing not about poets, players, and pipers, but about Richard, Bushy, and Green. Poetry and the theater were charged in Elizabethan England with the same kinds of wasteful pleasures for which Richard and his followers are indicted.

In that case, then, we can extend our analysis of Bushy, Bagot, and Green as scapegoats. These sodomitical flatterers, I've argued, draw off the charges of excessive vanity from Richard. But they also function as abject lightning rods in a different way, according to a logic outlined by D. A. Miller in reference to some modern *sinthomo*sexuals: "From Wilde's too-pretty Dorian Gray, to Hitchcock's anal murderers with their 'neat little touches,' to Fellini's affected fairies . . . examples abound of a homosexual or analogously queered figure meant to draw off the charges of excess and aberrance from the excessive and aberrant oeuvre under construction."[47] In a similar fashion, Shakespeare's play scapegoats those figures within the play that best represent, by analogy, the play's own disreputable pleasures.

Critics have by no means failed to consider the play's metapoetic dimensions, at least not to the extent that they've shied away from acknowledging its sodomitical subtext. Nevertheless, they tend to sublimate the play's poetic language, redeeming Richard and, by extension, the play itself from any irresponsible *jouissance*. Donovan Sherman, for example, argues that the queer futility, blankness, and nothingness with which Richard gets associated, particularly in the form of his ineffectively excessive theatricality, can be re-viewed and recuperated as a source of messianic promise, fulfillment, and revelation. As Sherman puts it, Richard "figures this nothingness, both within the play and outside it in its own existence as a performed text, as the promise of another order beyond his forces to demonstrate but that must be demonstrated nonetheless in an enactment that fulfills itself only by failing."[48] The play thus offers, for Sherman, a "reclamation of theatricality." "The theater we witness becomes meaningless," he writes, "but as a result, it catalyzes itself into the gap between one world and the next."[49] The dialectical recovery work that Sherman, like so many others before him, performs on both Richard and the play ultimately functions to re-cover—in the sense of repressing or covering up again—the unredeemably futilitarian pleasures with which Richard and his councilors, like poetry and the theater in Shakespeare's day, are associated.

Insofar as Sherman argues for the ultimate efficacy of Richard's apparently inefficacious performance, his reading repeats the most conventional claim about this play—namely, the judgment that Richard is a bad king but a great poet or performer, a mainstream reading of Richard that has been critiqued by Leonard Tennenhouse. "In actuality," Tennenhouse writes, "it is Henry IV rather than Richard in whom Shakespeare invests the power of the artist, not a power detached from matters political, that is, but the power to incorporate disruptive cultural elements within the official rituals of state."[50] Richard, I would add, lacks this power because he is himself a "disruptive" cultural element, narcissistically fixated on his own pleasure rather than the health of the commonwealth. The play characterizes Bolingbroke, by contrast, as the perfect Horatian poet. Upon Bolingbroke's return to England through the mountainous north, Northumberland praises him in such terms:

> These high wild hills and rough uneven ways
> Draws out our miles and makes them wearisome.
> And yet your fair discourse hath been as sugar,
> Making the hard way sweet and delectable.
> But I bethink me what a weary way
> From Ravenspurgh to Cotshall will be found
> In Ross and Willoughby, wanting your company,
> Which I protest hath very much beguiled
> The tediousness and process of my travel.
> But theirs is sweetened with the hope to have
> The present benefit which I possess.
>
> (*R2*, 2.3.4–14)

In contrast to the vain pleasures of Richard and his followers—pleasures that are, in the gardener's revealing phrase, "without profit"—Bolingbroke's use of pleasurable discourse generates a useful "benefit," alleviating the "hard way" in the way that the ideal poet, according to Horace and Sidney, is supposed to.

Richard, however, exemplifies both in his character and in his speech all the traits that Gosson, like other antitheatricalists of his day, attributed to bad (wasteful, indulgent, useless) poetry. That indulgence, moreover, makes his poetry "bad" in a different sense: it makes his efforts at sense-making nothing more than a failure. Nowhere is all this clearer than in the very speech that criticism has held up as Richard's most glorious piece of poetry: the lengthy soliloquy that he delivers in prison, which begins:

> I have been studying how I may compare
> This prison where I live unto the world;
> And, for because the world is populous
> And here is not a creature but myself,
> I cannot do it. Yet I'll hammer't out.
> My brain I'll prove the female to my soul,
> My soul the father, and these two beget

A generation of still-breeding thoughts;
And these same thoughts people this little world,
For no thought is contented.

(5.5.1–10)

We do not need to cast aside recognition of Shakespeare's poetic virtuosity to recognize that the speech is about the *lack* of poetic virtuosity. Although Menon doesn't address this monologue, it exemplifies her claim that "neither [Richard's] language nor his sexuality is metaphoric enough."[51] After all, the monologue opens with his admission that he cannot create a metaphor, that most basic of poetic tropes. Moreover, the terms he attempts to compare bear quite a bit of significance in this context: he cannot forge a comparison between the world and the solitary prison in which he resides. Given the narcissism and vanity that I've traced throughout this chapter, such failure to make sense makes a certain degree of sense: of course Richard cannot create a poetic link between his narcissistic self and the world; that has been his problem all along. His feeble attempt to "hammer't out" anyway—notably by recourse to the language of "generation"—merely calls further attention to the failure of the comparison.

At the end of the play, all Richard can do instead is to play with illusions without content, "thoughts" that are not "*content*ed." He is, in more than one sense, reduced to the "nothing" he always already was:

Thus play I in one person many people,
And none contented. Sometimes am I king;
Then treasons make me wish myself a beggar,
And so I am. Then crushing penury
Persuades me I was better when a king;
Then am I kinged again, and by and by
Think that I am unkinged by Bolingbroke,
And straight am nothing. But whate'er I be,
Nor I nor any man that but man is
With nothing shall be pleased till he be eased
With being nothing.

(5.5.31–41)

And yet we would be remiss in viewing this speech solely as an expression of Richard's personal narcissistic crisis. Just as Richard's councilors, those caterpillars of the commonwealth, are abjected so as to alleviate the blame directed toward their beloved king, so too must Richard II articulate his status as nothing, only with the effect of taking our suspicion off *Richard*

II—the suspicion, articulated so vehemently by Gosson with regard to theater in general, that the play, as such, is a caterpillar of the commonwealth as well, that it too takes pleasure in "being nothing."

Redeeming Hal

Not long after Richard is undone, the discursive materials that constitute his persona resurface in the guise of a character who doesn't appear at all in the play: Bolingbroke's son, Prince Hal, the future King Henry V. Toward the end of *Richard II*, after he has ascended to the throne, Henry IV, in a brief speech that functions, whether intentionally or not, as a nice teaser for the *Henry IV* plays, indicts the behavior of his "unthrifty son" in telling terms: Hal, according to Henry, "doth frequent/With unrestrained loose companions," a "dissolute" crew, and so amounts, thus far, to nothing more than a "young wanton and effeminate boy" (*R2*, 5.3.1–12). The remainder of the second tetralogy dramatizes the stakes, consequences, and redemption of Hal's "unrestrained" pleasure with lowly friends. The young prince's commitment to getting down and dirty with the commoners who haunt the taverns of Eastcheap cannot be problematic in itself, however. As we've seen, the ability to interact with and appeal to the "commons" constitutes a large part of Henry's success (and Hal's own future success, as represented in *Henry V*). Something else must be at work, or at play, in Hal's actions to render them "dissolute." Something more insidious must be factored in to explain why Hal's behavior aligns him more with Richard than with Henry.

The gluttony and petty thievery practiced by Hal's companions can help us reach an explanation, but only to a certain extent. More revealing is the language by which Henry, in *1 Henry IV*, censures his son when their long-anticipated and rehearsed confrontation takes center stage; Henry poses the following rhetorical question to his prodigal son:

> Could such inordinate and low desires,
> Such poor, such bare, such lewd, such mean attempts,
> Such barren pleasures, rude society,
> As thou art matched withal and grafted to,
> Accompany the greatness of thy blood,
> And hold their level with thy princely heart?
>
> (*1H4*, 3.2.12–17)

As this question moves toward its climax, the problem with Hal's pleasure becomes clear: the heir apparent has failed to live up to the sublime and stately expectations that his aristocratic, now royal, heritage demands of him. Before this general charge, though, Henry uses strikingly erotic terms to characterize the pleasure Hal practices. The *Norton Shakespeare* annotates the phrase "barren pleasures" as follows: "Unprofitable habits; nonreproductive erotic pursuits." Would it not be fair to say, then, that the language of sodomy, or *sinthom*osexuality, is clustered around Hal and his companions nearly as much as it was clustered around Richard and his companions?[52] In fact, the comparison between Richard and Hal is driven home by King Henry, in *2 Henry IV*, through a figure of speech familiar from *Richard II*: "Most subject is the fattest soil to weeds, / And [Hal], the noble image of my youth, / Is overspread with them" (*2H4*, 4.3.54–56).

What is instructive about the plays' treatment of Hal's misspent youth is that his indulgence in pleasure can be redeemed only when it is treated *as* instructive, when it is reinscribed, that is, as a means to more useful ends. In *2 Henry IV*, the Earl of Warwick defends Hal to Henry according to this logic of instructive utility:

> My gracious lord, you look beyond him quite.
> The Prince but studies his companions,
> Like a strange tongue, wherein, to gain the language,
> 'Tis needful that the most immodest word
> Be looked upon and learnt, which once attained,
> Your highness knows, comes to not further use
> But to be known and hated, so, like gross terms,
> The Prince will in the perfectness of time
> Cast off his followers, and their memory
> Shall as a pattern or a measure live
> By which his grace must mete the lives of other,
> Turning past evils to advantages.
>
> (4.3.67–78)

Commenting on this passage, Jonathan Goldberg points out that Warwick "speaks within the language of humanist pedagogy."[53] More specifically, the earl echoes those countless Reformation-era defenders of literature who insisted that aesthetic representations of disreputable pleasure on the page or on the stage are a pedagogical means of counteracting such pleasures in life, a way of gaining "advantages" from seemingly profitless activities. Henry is hardly convinced by this appeal to utility, though. "'Tis seldom," he says in response, "when the bee doth leave her comb / In the dead carrion" (4.3.79–80). A little later in the scene, when Henry, on his deathbed, awakens from a nap thinking that Hal has stolen the crown, he returns to the image of the bee in order to figure the futility of his own fatherly efforts:

> like the bee
> Culling from every flower the virtuous sweets,
> Our thighs packed with wax, our mouths with honey,
> We bring it to the hive; and, like the bees,
> Are murdered with our pains.
>
> (4.3.202–6)[54]

In the face of Henry's initial skepticism, however, Warwick's defensive appraisal comes true: ultimately Hal is redeemed and assumes the throne as Henry V. In the play that bears his royal name, the recently crowned Henry V receives a mocking gift of tennis balls from the haughty dauphin, the prince of France, to whose ambassador the king replies, "We understand [the dauphin] well, / How he comes o'er us with our wilder days, / Not measuring what *use* we made of them" (1.2.266–68; my italics).

The overall narrative arc of the second tetralogy therefore dramatizes what happens when pleasure is submitted to the demands of utility. The plays thus *ultimately* reinforce the ideology of socially useful ends to which vain pleasures must always, in "the perfectness of time," be submitted. Until Hal is redeemed, however, the plays are quite insistent about depicting what a nonteleological, futilitarian pleasure looks like. Consider, in this regard, the succinct formulation that King Henry uses in 2 *Henry IV* to forecast what *could* happen if Hal were not reformed, what *could* happen if abject pleasures were raised to the heights normally accorded to more reputable sublimities. The king's statement may also be taken as the insistent, though often disavowed, slogan of literature, including those forms of literature that go by the etymologically related names of "theater" and "theory": "Up, vanity! / Down, royal state!" (4.3.247–48).

In its attempts to grapple with the waves that deconstructive theory left in its wake, contemporary humanism has preferred to follow the example of the reformed Henry V, if not Savonarola. Avoiding the charge of excessive pleasure has become a matter of course, and the redemptive triumph of virtue over vanity has become the ideological narrative we reinforce. As Litvak states, "Even the academy's theoretical interlude of the seventies and eighties, its encounter with a more or less French 'playfulness,' seems to have left its most enduring legacy by congealing into a corpus of prestigious rationales for the practices of virtue and rigor that would have prevailed in American literary studies anyway."[55] We can see this tendency especially in the now commonplace dialectical, teleological, allegorical, and messianic narrative that sublimates the self-indulgent early work of theorists like Derrida by arguing that it anticipates the ethical turn or political turn or even religious turn exemplified by these theorists' late work. What is this if not a blockbuster adaptation of the conversion narrative staged by the second tetralogy, featuring Derrida in the starring role as the redeemed Prince Hal? As comforting as it may be, however, this narrative comes with many costs, not the least of which is that the imperative to ideological gravity has the tendency, as we have seen, to unleash antifeminist and homophobic energies. Furthermore, the very act of defending, justifying, recuperating, and redeeming vanity produces a tricky double bind, ceding far too much ground to the values of utility and virtue.

How, then, can we break out of this double bind? To a great degree, we can't. Barbara Johnson has suggested that the "sense of urgency" with which deconstructive criticism undoes systems of value "cannot help but imply that the critiquing of value systems is itself a valuable activity."[56] If, however, the critiquing of value systems is itself valuable, then one must recognize that its value cannot be located in the same sphere as the value of value itself. If you read the stuttering repetitions of this last sentence only with difficulty, then you've already understood its point: the critique of value redoubles value in a way that doesn't *simply* reproduce or augment it but, rather, spins us into the complicated twists and turns of irony. And while the invocation of value may be inevitable, even desirable, we should try as hard as possible not to fall back on it as soon as we try to interrogate it. In the various venues where I presented this argument, the first question I was almost always asked, almost always immediately, was some version of the following: "Can't the lack of value be a form of value?" Of course it can; I am not trying to assert otherwise. I am simply trying to question why we always feel the need to ask this question, why we feel so uncomfortable with the negation of value. The absolute negation of value may be impossible, but that impossibility does not make it any less of a crucial theoretical and critical question. Indeed, it is all the more crucial *because* it is impossible.

CHAPTER 3

Art for Nothing's Sake

I have no other resource but this *irony*:
to speak of the "nothing to say."

—ROLAND BARTHES, *Camera Lucida*

For the Renaissance, poetry's futilitarian impulses were pushed to the extreme by the mode of writing known as romance, which posed a problem for early modern writers because it produced an excess of pleasure over instruction. Or so its critics firmly alleged. In his *Education of a Christian Woman* (1523), for example, the humanist Juan Luis Vives condemned the dangers of reading romance. After cataloguing over a dozen titles of such texts, from the *Amadís de Gaula* to the *Decameron*, Vives launches his attack in the following manner: "All these books were written by idle, unoccupied, ignorant men, the slaves of vice and filth. I wonder what it is that delights us in these books unless it be that we are attracted by indecency. Learning is not to be expected from authors who never saw even a shadow of learning. As for their storytelling, what pleasure is to be derived from the things they invent, full of lies and stupidity?"[1]

Vives goes on to enumerate examples of such "lies and stupidity"—heroes who single-handedly kill twenty men, fabulous treasures that no real ship could possibly carry—but it is important to pause on the rhetorical question he asks. Given the context of his condemnation as well as the standard of "learning" to which he holds fiction, the answer to his question is fairly transparent: *no* pleasure should be derived from the fictions that idle, unoccupied, ignorant writers invent. Considering, however, that Vives and other humanists of his time and kind were hardly successful in halting the production of romances in Renaissance Europe, it is tempting to read his question in the literal sense. What pleasure *is* to be derived from the fictions that poets invent? What *is* it that delights us in these books?

In Catholic Italy, Ludovico Ariosto's sprawling *Orlando furioso* provided the flashpoint for conflicts over romance. Ariosto's error, as Patricia Parker summarizes the debates, "was to come too close to the *dulce* side of the famous Horatian dictum, to succumb to the attractions of diverting fable over the essential, if perhaps less interesting, moral kernel."[2] When translated into a Protestant English context, the potential dangers of romance become more acute and, in order to be tempered, must be tampered. Sir John Harington's 1591 translation of *Orlando furioso* provides a case in point. In translating Ariosto's romance, Harington trims down the unwieldy and errant plot, eliminates authorial intrusions, and includes an allegorical key that moralizes the text. These maneuvers can be read together as an attempt to reform (which is, of course, a loaded word in this context) the poem's romance errors for an English Protestant audience.[3] In all its loose errancy, romance provides an extreme case of what early modern writers found so problematic about the pleasurable means that poetry employs in order to work its unpredictable effects. It is no surprise, then, that Renaissance writers should wish to subordinate those means to virtuous ends.

What *is* surprising is that contemporary critics perform similar maneuvers. In recent years, there has been no shortage of studies on Renaissance romance; critics working from a wide variety of intellectual perspectives have analyzed romance in relation to an even wider variety of contexts, topics, and themes: gender, religion, race, empire, economics, the print marketplace, theories of the contract, even disease. For all their topical variability, the one premise these studies tend to share is that romance provides a useful tool for thinking through, if not resolving, epistemological and ethical questions and tensions.[4] So persistently has this assumption been reproduced that it has become less an *idée reçue* than an *idée fixe*. For that reason alone, it demands to be called into question, especially because it exemplifies larger critical trends in the wake of New Historicism. "Attention to form," writes Benedict Robinson in his study of romance and Islam, for instance, "does not distract from recognition of the historical productivity of a literary text but enables a more complex and wide-ranging sense of the text's engagement with history."[5] But why, one might ask, are literary critics still so committed to the notion that literature *is and ought to be* productive and engaged? This approach seems preferable to the belief that literature passively reflects or registers preexisting social issues and historical realities, and it seems more in line with early modern views of poetry's rhetorical agency. But what if poetry's detractors were right? What happens, in short, when pleasure and utility come into extreme conflict with each other?

One answer is that Thomas Nashe happens. As the enfant terrible of late Elizabethan literature, Nashe has always proven to be difficult to assimilate into the canons of humanism—even more so than those other bad boys of the times, his friends and collaborators Christopher Marlowe, Robert Greene, and Ben Jonson. If making sense of Nashe's writings has long been an exercise in futility, that can only be because his excessive style reveals the limits of the demand for utility, a demand that contemporary critics, no less than Renaissance writers, adhere to and value. In this regard, we might recall at the outset C. S. Lewis's often-quoted assessment of him: "In a certain sense of the word 'say,' if asked what Nashe 'says,' we should have to reply, 'Nothing.'"[6] In the main sense of the word "say," Lewis is completely wrong: all too often, Nashe has too much to say. Yet in the economy of Elizabethan rhetoric and poetics, having too much to say can easily amount to having nothing to say; hyperproductivity and unproductivity end up representing two sides of the same worthless coin. Lewis's appraisal points to the ways in which Nashe's style leaves him open to the charge of a writerly vein so vain that it offers, in the end, "nothing" of value.

In the past several decades, critics have developed two general strategies for dealing with Nashe's futilitarian aesthetic. The first was to portray him as a Bakhtinian or Derridean *avant la lettre*, detaching him from his time by deeming him, and thus redeeming him, as being ahead of his time.[7] In direct response to this more theoretical mode of reading, recent critics have "reject[ed] high theory and anachronism," in the words of Steve Mentz, with the aim of resituating Nashe within the context of Renaissance humanism and the literary marketplace of Elizabethan England.[8] However opposed their methods may be, these two approaches can be seen as aimed toward a similar end: rescuing Nashe from the accusation of having "nothing" to say. While theoretically minded critics revalorize that "nothing" by viewing it as a positive strategy, a deliberately transgressive affront to the logocentric or monological values promoted in the early modern period as well as now, historicist critics have tended implicitly to refute the charge altogether by demonstrating the myriad ways in which Nashe has *something* to say. In what may be taken as a still-paradigmatic statement, Lorna Hutson, for example, claims that the "apparent shapelessness" of

Nashe's writing, its "lack of continuity and coherence, might function as a politically and morally significant aesthetic in its own right."[9]

My own argument is directed, at least heuristically, against this sort of recuperative gesture, which tends to underlie all scholarship on Nashe (not to mention literary studies more generally) regardless of whether it takes a more theoretical or more historicist approach to Nashe's style. Where critics like Hutson stake their arguments on the wager that Nashe's futilitarian aesthetic "might" be productive and significant, this chapter explores the inverse possibility implicit in Hutson's hesitant language: that Nashe's writing might *not* be so easily recuperable.[10] As tempting as it has nearly always been to view and celebrate Nashe as an avant-garde rhetorical renegade, I want to take seriously the risks he courted, and the high prices he paid, for engaging in such an unconventional style of writing.[11] By reading some particularly inscrutable and intractable passages in Nashe's writing, my goal will be to demonstrate the necessity—but also, it is necessary to add, the virtual impossibility—of *not* redeeming or recuperating the pleasure of Nashe's writing within humanist systems of aesthetic, ethical, and social value.

As a way into Nashe's outrageous and outlandish work, I would first like to look closely at a text on the opposite end of the spectrum, a more restrained and normative example of Renaissance English humanist writing: Roger Ascham's 1570 educational handbook, *The Scholemaster*. No two Elizabethan writers could appear more different than Ascham and Nashe. Ascham, on the one hand, was a high-minded authority on education, childhood tutor to the Tudor queen; his subject matter consisted of pedagogical strategies for reading and translating the great books of antiquity. Nashe, on the other hand, was the most notoriously prodigal of Renaissance writers; the salacious topics of his writing included brothels, dildos, masturbation, rape, drunken intemperance, horrific violence and torture, and the disreputable cities of Catholic Italy. Ascham enjoyed positive relations with his patrons, including the supreme patron in all the land, Queen Elizabeth, who, on hearing news of his death, reportedly said, "I would rather have cast £10,000 in the sea than parted with my Ascham."[12] Nashe, by contrast, went to his grave a poor man, cursing his misfortune. The pattern of dissimilarity also extends to their respective styles of writing: where Ascham, for the most part, writes with a didactic sobriety characteristic of a man of his profession and surroundings, Nashe's style can be characterized as a slight and scintillating semiotic soup that provides not even the slightest scintilla or soupçon of semantic, sociocultural, or spiritual significance.

Given these stark contrasts, one can be forgiven for seeking out any common ground the two men occupy. Any similarities to be found between such different Elizabethan writers may reveal something unexpected, though fundamental, about the environment in which they wrote and about the limits of humanism. It cannot be insignificant, for instance, that Ascham and Nashe share an alma mater: St. John's College, Cambridge.[13] Beyond, however, this mere biographical correspondence, it is worth noting that both men are frequently cited for their hostile attitudes toward romance. In Ascham's *The Scholemaster* and in Nashe's *The Unfortunate Traveller*, both writers attempt to project the errors and vagaries of romance onto Italy in general and Rome in particular by censuring those Italianate Englishmen who fall victim to the enchantments of Circe, the classical figure that emblematizes the potential degeneration caused by romance's futilitarian pleasures. Taking these explicit statements at face value, critics have generally read these texts as Protestant humanist diatribes against the romance of travel abroad, especially to Catholic Rome. Yet what seem, at first glance, to be polemics against romance turn out, ironically enough, to take the form of the kinds of errant pleasures against which the stated arguments are directed. Indeed, it is precisely such irony—its forms and its stakes—that this chapter seeks to investigate.

Pleasure, Pastime, Papistry

On December 10, 1563, while the plague raged in London, a group of Elizabethan statesmen gathered at Windsor Castle in the private chamber of Sir William Cecil, Lord Burghley, England's secretary of state and chief advisor to Queen Elizabeth. At dinner, Lord Burghley reported that a number of students had run away from Eton because they feared being beaten. This comment soon sparked a provocative debate among the dinner guests about the role of pleasure versus punishment in the schoolroom. Among those in attendance was Roger Ascham, who reports that he would have kept quiet among these great men had Lord Burghley not asked him to voice his expert opinion on the matter: that pleasure and love, not fear and punishment, entice children to learning. After dinner, Ascham retired to the queen's chamber to read Greek with her and was soon approached by Sir Richard Sackville, treasurer of the exchequer; the two men continued the evening's conversation, and the treasurer requested that Ascham put into writing his advice about the education of young gentlemen, particularly for Sackville's grandson Robert.

So began, and so begins, Ascham's *The Scholemaster*.[14] In opening his handbook with this anecdote, Ascham clearly aims to establish his schoolmasterly credentials by anchoring his text to courtly, political figures invested with authority that far surpasses his own. The scene depicted might seem, then, to be nothing more than a spectacle of opportunistic name-dropping, of the kind one might expect from a writer caught, like all writers of his day, in a patronage economy. Yet the anecdote serves a further, and just as obvious, function for Ascham: it anchors his text in the real, or at the very least produces what Joel Fineman, writing of the genre of the anecdote in terms that recall Roland Barthes, calls "the effect of the real."[15] The conjunction of power and realism serves to signify to Ascham's readers in advance that *The Scholemaster* is no idle or inane, no prodigal or improvident, work. It is, in short, not poetry—and certainly not romance.

Whatever textual authority is generated by the realism of this anecdote is simultaneously shorn, however, by the sharp ironic cut of a remarkable, though perhaps unintentional, intertextual echo. A group of nobles gather in a magnificent country estate while plague devastates the city, and the discussion that occurs subsequently authorizes (the) text: this is the story, more specifically the frame story, of Boccaccio's *Decameron*, which exemplifies, as it did for Vives, the kind of idle, pleasurable, sprawling, and errant romance text that Renaissance humanists found so problematic. Its implicit cameo at the beginning of *The Scholemaster* (to say nothing yet of its explicit cameos) is therefore noteworthy because it helps to put pressure on the standard critical view of Ascham as a fiercely Protestant schoolmaster opposed to reading romance—and especially Italian romances like the *Decameron*.[16] As I will argue, the place of romance and pleasure in *The Scholemaster* is far less simple or certain than this conventional reading of Ascham has long implied.

Consider, for instance, another anecdote in which Ascham interacts with a notable figure of the times; I refer to his conversation with Lady Jane Grey:

> Her parents, the duke and the duchess, with all the household, gentlemen and gentlewomen, were hunting in the park. I found her in her chamber reading *Phaedon Platonis* [i.e., Plato's *Phaedo*] in Greek, and that with as much delight as some gentleman would read a merry tale in Boccaccio. After salutation and duty done, with some other talk, I asked her why she would lose such pastime in the park. Smiling she answered me, "Iwis, all their sport in the park is but a shadow to that

> pleasure that I find in Plato. Alas, good folk, they never felt what true pleasure meant."
>
> (35–36)

The whole point of this anecdote—and, one might add, the whole point of *The Scholemaster*—is to establish a preference for learning by reading over learning by experience. As Lady Grey says to Ascham (or so Ascham reports), "And thus my book hath been so much my pleasure, and bringeth daily to me more pleasure and more, that in respect of it all other pleasures in deed be but trifles and troubles unto me" (36). Among these trifles and troubles is surely the mere pastime of hunting. And by calling the aristocratic pastime of hunting a "shadow" of the "true" pleasure to be found in Plato, Lady Grey performs a patently Platonic gesture. But what of that other Platonic shadow, the "merry tale in Boccaccio"? If the passage trivializes aristocratic pastimes in relation to true Platonic pleasure, then what are we to make of the rhetoric of equivalence with which Ascham compares Plato to Boccaccio? If Lady Grey reads the *Phaedo* with "as much" pleasure as one would read a tale from Boccaccio, then on what epistemological grounds can one distinguish true pleasure from false pleasure?

Pleasure, for Ascham, is the means by which the pupil will not only be allured to education, but also thereby gain the judgment to distinguish honest pleasure from dishonest pleasure. Pleasure is thus the means by which one gains the ability to figure out whether pleasure can ever be a valid and valuable means in the first place. This kind of circular slippage, implicit throughout *The Scholemaster*, evinces what Melanie Ord calls "a certain ambivalence in Ascham's project," such that the word "pleasure" itself is, in Ord's astute estimation, a "leaky signifier" in Ascham's text.[17] Ascham, for example, prefaces his anecdote about Lady Jane Grey by claiming that it "may be heard with some pleasure and followed with more profit" (35). This typical Horatian comment should come as no surprise: pleasure and profit are so often linked in Renaissance writing that Ascham may be seen as merely rehearsing common sense. But there's something peculiar about Ascham's particular use of this commonplace: namely, the phrase "and followed," which can imply either causality or contingency. That is, the sentence can be interpreted to mean that profit is *caused* by pleasure—and thus, as Renaissance humanism would have it, that pleasure is the means to the end of profit—or that profit simply comes after pleasure in a noncausal sequence. The contingency implied in this second reading, which disjoins pleasure and profit from a tidy ends-oriented economy, shadows the Horatian dialectic on which Ascham bases his argument.[18]

To be sure, Ascham hardly stands opposed to pleasure *tout court*—and that is, in fact, a large part of the problem that pleasure poses in his text. Later in the text he defends his arguments against potential charges of austerity and asceticism: "And I do not mean by all this my talk that young gentlemen should always be poring on a book, and by using good studies should lose honest pleasure and haunt no good pastime. . . . I was never either Stoic in doctrine or Anabaptist in religion, to mislike a merry, pleasant, and playful nature, if no outrage be committed against law, measure, and good order" (52). Despite the subjunctive qualification tacked on, as if parenthetically, to the end of this last sentence, Ascham gives no *clear* indication of how to distinguish "honest pleasure" and "good pastime" from the kinds of pastimes and pleasures with which he associates Boccaccio and hunting.

The intricacies involved in Ascham's take on pleasure get concentrated in one of the text's most frequently cited passages: his discussion of Arthurian romances. After he specifically indicts books translated from Italian into English (about which I will shortly have more to say), Ascham denounces a past time when reading such romances for pleasure was an English pastime:

> In our forefathers' time, when papistry as a standing pool covered and overflowed all England, few books were read in our tongue, saving certain books of chivalry, as they said, for pastime and pleasure, which, as some say, were made in monasteries by idle monks or wanton canons; as one for example, *Morte Darthur*, the whole pleasure of which book standeth in two special points—in open manslaughter and bold bawdry; in which book those be counted the noblest knights that do kill most men without any quarrel and commit foulest adulteries by subtlest shifts: as Sir Lancelot with the wife of King Arthur his master, Sir Tristram with the wife of King Mark his uncle, sir Lamorak with the wife of King Lot that was his own aunt. This is good stuff for wise men to laugh at or honest men to take pleasure at. Yet I know when God's Bible was banished the court and *Morte Darthur* received into the prince's chamber. What toys the daily reading of such a book may work in the will of a young gentleman or a young maid that liveth wealthily and idly, wise men can judge and honest men do pity.
>
> (68–69)

The polemical vehemence of Ascham's attack should not keep us from realizing that his arguments are mostly unoriginal. Scholars ranging from Arthur Ferguson to Alex Davis offer comprehensive surveys of what Davis calls "the war between 'the humanists' and 'chivalry.'"[19] In the context of such a war, Ascham clearly stands on the side of the humanists, offering a reiteration of attacks made earlier in the century by More, Erasmus, and Vives, who charged chivalric romance with disrupting humanism's goal: the cultivation of wholesome, virtuous, socially responsible human subjects. Before capitulating to this understanding of Ascham's condemnation, though, it would be helpful to pause on the passage to see if its rhetorical somersaults can be completely explained by the polarized structure that the notion of a "war" necessarily implies.[20]

Ascham's main charge of "open manslaughter and bold bawdry" gives the impression that the problem with romance lies in its content: it is the *representation* of violence and cupidity, of murder and adultery, that will "work" "toys" "in the will of a young gentleman or a young maid." But what makes Ascham's young gentleman and young maid particularly susceptible to such toys isn't merely their tender juvenescence, but the fact that they "liveth wealthily and idly." "The fear of idleness," writes Shannon Miller, "took multiple forms in sixteenth-century England."[21] According to Miller, "idleness signifies nonaction," but also becomes, in this period, "a metaphor encompassing a wide range of threats to England: no New World involvement, no religious conversions, no sexual reproduction."[22] One should also specifically consider the charge of idleness in relation to the other adverb to which Ascham links it: "wealthily." Robert Matz, drawing on the work of Lawrence Stone on the crisis of the aristocracy, informs us that "humanist education was intended to reduce the idleness of the aristocracy and to emphasize the importance of aristocratic service to the state."[23] As Matz (writing about early modern England) and Virginia Krause (writing about early modern France) have, in different ways, helped us to see, Renaissance aristocrats defined themselves in a contradictory relationship to idleness—accepting it, on the one hand, as a sign of noble leisure and rejecting it, on the other hand, as a sign of wasted time.[24] When read, though, in terms of what Max Weber calls the Protestant work ethic, the culture's suspicion of idleness becomes less ambivalent. "According to God's unambiguously revealed will," Weber emphatically asserts, "it is *only* action, not idleness and indulgence, that serves to increase his glory. *Wasting time* is therefore the first and most serious of all sins."[25] In idle hands, then, the idylls of romance may easily constitute idols that distract readers from the proper pursuit of virtuous action and spiritual truth, from one's calling and thus from nothing less than salvation itself; hence Ascham's reference to a time "when God's Bible was banished the court and *Morte Darthur* received into the prince's chamber."

But the text is even more specific about the problem with romance. The charge of idleness is attached not only to the young aristocratic gentlemen and ladies who live "wealthily and idly," but also to the "idle monks" who, "as some say," according to Ascham, wrote these romances in the first place. Why does Catholicism enter this discussion? Why does Ascham associate the Arthurian romances native to Britain with papistry? In order to address these questions, it is necessary to retrace the errant course of Ascham's argument, an errancy that is far from incidental, I hope to show, in what is, after all, a polemic *against* the errancy of travel and romance.

The Enchantments of Circe

The context for Ascham's attack against romance, as I've noted, is the danger of learning by experience. In this context, the phrase "learning by experience" may even be considered too oxymoronic: as Jeff Dolven explains, in the early modern period, "experience was often invoked as the opposite of school, associated with debauchery and travel to the Catholic south."[26] Nowhere is such an invocation more vivid than in the following passage from *The Scholemaster*:

> Learning teacheth more in one year than experience in twenty, and learning teacheth safely, when experience maketh more miserable than wise. He hazardeth sore that waxeth wise by experience. An unhappy master he is that is made cunning by many shipwrecks; a miserable merchant, that is neither rich nor wise but after some bankrupts. It is costly wisdom that is bought by experience. We know by experience itself that it is a marvelous pain to find out but a short way by long wandering.
>
> (50)

The governing figure of this passage—the shipwreck—echoes an earlier moment in the text in which Ascham uses the ship as a figure for self-government: "But nobility governed by learning and wisdom is indeed most like a fair ship, having tide and wind at will, under the rule of a skillful master, when contrariwise a ship carried, yea, with the highest tide and greatest wind, lacking a skillful master, most commonly doth either sink itself upon sands or break itself upon rocks. And even so, how many have been either drowned in vain pleasure or overwhelmed by stout willfulness, the histories of England be able to afford overmany examples unto us" (41).

It might be useful to interpret the language of hazards, shipwrecks, and wandering as contextual references to the instability of commercial ventures at sea. Even if Ascham may not have had literal experiences of shipwrecks in mind while constructing his rant against experience, he at least draws on a long-standing emblematic tradition that figures self-discipline as a well-helmed ship. For a counterexample of this trope, recall Phaedria's "litle Gondelay" in book 2 of *The Faerie Queene*, a "shallow ship" that wanders the Idle Lake "withouten oare or Pilot it to guide."[27] Certainly the horror that Ascham imagines is akin to the horror that Spenser imagines: that of a ship, and therefore a gentleman, always at risk of running off course.

These contextual paths are by no means unrelated to romance, but the route of Ascham's own argumentation leads us to consider more specific frames of reference. From his general condemnation of learning by experience, Ascham is carried into an intense denunciation of travel to Italy in particular. What is most pertinent is that he uses the *Odyssey*, the paradigmatic romance text, as a framework for his discussion: "Yet if a gentleman will needs travel into Italy, he shall do well to look on the life of the wisest traveler that ever traveled hither, set out by the wisest writer that ever spake with tongue (God's doctrine only excepted), and that is Ulysses in Homer" (61). Ascham thus deploys the travels of romance as an allegory for the romance of travel. In the first place, the *Odyssey* provides a local habitation and name for the general language of shipwreck and "long wandering." Within Ascham's rhetorical constellation, moreover, the *Odyssey* supplies an array of figures for the dangers that Ascham writes against: the Cyclops, Dame Calypso, the Sirens, Scylla and Charybdis, and, above all, "the enchantments of Circe," which serve repeatedly in the subsequent discussion as a trope for Italian sin.

Most important, the *Odyssey* furnishes Ascham with classical images of the best *defenses* against Circean pleasures. He admits that Ulysses would have "run headlong into overmany jeopardies . . . if Pallas had not always governed him, if he had not used to stop his ears with wax, to bind himself to the mast of his ship, to feed daily upon that sweet herb *moly* . . . given unto him by Mercury to avoid all the enchantments of Circe" (63). Of course, Ascham the Christian cannot rest contentedly with this locus classicus of askesis. Like all good humanists he supplements his classical allegory with biblical allegoresis. After identifying moly as an effective defense, he writes of the herb, "Whereby the divine poet Homer meant covertly (as wise and godly men do judge) that love of honesty and hatred of ill which David more plainly doth call the fear of God, the only remedy against all enchantments of sin" (63). The word "whereby" indicates that reconciling the classical and Christian traditions is as easy as fashioning a grammatical transition.

Less easy to reconcile is the schism *within* Christianity between Protestantism and Catholicism. Now, it is not even remotely surprising that an Elizabethan diatribe against travel to Italy would be colored by complaints against Catholicism. As a matter of fact, there may be localized historical reasons for the intensity of Ascham's attack: although Ascham died in 1568 before he could finish *The Scholemaster* (his wife posthumously published the incomplete text in 1570), it was written in the midst of escalating tension between England and Rome, tension that culminated in the Northern Rebellion of 1569 and Pope Pius V's excommunication of Queen Elizabeth in 1570. Such information gives credence to Ryan J. Stark's claim that *The Scholemaster* "ought to be understood as one part of the larger Protestant effort to dissociate England from Rome."[28] Yet it is important to remember that Catholicism enters Ascham's text not in direct reference to Italy or Rome but through the indirect mediation of Arthurian romance, which would seem to associate England with, rather than dissociate it from, Rome.

Our reading thus far still hasn't accounted for this complication because we've been working in merely spatial terms, casting the ideological tensions of *The Scholemaster*, in the same way Stark does, as stark oppositions between England and Italy, London and Rome. Such a reading, while not entirely erroneous, omits a small but not unimportant detail. The passage in which Ascham attacks Arthurian romance begins, we will recall, with a key *temporal* signpost: "In our forefathers' time, when papistry as a standing pool covered and overflowed all England." Let me juxtapose this demarcation between past England and contemporary England to an earlier moment in the text when Ascham carefully distinguishes between "old" Italy and "present" Italy: there was a time, he admits, "when Italy and Rome have been, to the great good of us that now live, the best breeders and bringers-up of the worthiest men. . . . But now that time is gone and, though the place remain, yet the old and present manners do differ as far as black and white, as virtue and vice" (60–61). A superimposition of the temporal and spatial axes of Ascham's schema yields four quadrants: present England, past England, present Italy, and past Italy. The correlation between romance and Catholicism serves as a means of connecting England's Catholic past with Italy's Catholic present. And establishing *that* connection allows Ascham to resolve, on a symbolic level, the contradiction of turning to ancient pagan texts as instruments of humanist education. Plato may be a pagan, the implication seems to be, but at least he's not a papist like Petrarch.

As we soon find out, though, Ascham's attack against Arthurian legend functions not, or not only, as an elaborate system for resolving Elizabethan England's contradictory relationship to classical/Catholic Rome; rather, it serves primarily as a rhetorical way station, a pawn in an attempt to set up a hyperbolic comparison with books translated out of Italy: "And yet ten *Morte Darthurs* do not the tenth part so much harm as one of these books made in Italy and translated in England" (69). In addition, Ascham doesn't unequivocally celebrate the authority of classical pagan texts. We have seen how Homer and Plato, at earlier moments in the text, occupy a position of privilege set against the licentious vanity of texts by Boccaccio or Malory, but the two anchors of the ancient Greek canon now pale in comparison to "God's word." After attacking Italianate Englishmen for "willingly" and "freely say[ing] their minds to the open contempt of God and all godliness both in living and doctrine," Ascham writes, "And how? I will express how, not by a fable of Homer nor by the philosophy of Plato, but by a plain truth of God's word" (70). Because of their mediated nature, neither "fable" nor "philosophy" can supply the transparent signifier or transcendental signified guaranteed by scriptural authority.

But the "plain truth of God's word" is not, for Ascham, the last word. Like so many homilists and defenders of the faith who resort (by what forces, we can only speculate) to paralepsis, Ascham, after quoting Psalm 14, is compelled to mention precisely the kinds of mediated texts he has just cast out from his discourse in favor of Scripture: the Italianate Englishmen, in his words, "have in more reverence the *Triumphs* of Petrarch than the Genesis of Moses; they make more account of Tully's *Offices* than St. Paul's Epistles, of a tale in Boccaccio than a story of the Bible. Then they count as fables the holy mysteries of Christian religion" (70). At first the real danger seems, for Ascham, to be to read Petrarch, Cicero, and Boccaccio *in place of* the Bible. But then the problem is to read the Bible *as if it were* a text by Petrarch, Cicero, or Boccaccio, or even Homer or Plato—which is to say, as if it were a fable or a fiction. A lot hinges on how we read the "then" in the phrase "Then they count as fables": like the phrase "and followed" that I discussed earlier, "then" can convey mere consecution, but it can also establish a causal chain. In the second case, reading romance is a means, but not a means to virtuous profit; instead, it serves as a means to reading *religion* as a romance, a means, that is, to atheism.

Is atheism, then, the ultimate object of Ascham's scorn? According to Ascham, Italianate Englishmen

> boldly laugh to scorn both Protestant and papist. They care for no Scripture; they make no count of general councils; they contemn the consent of the church; they pass for no doctors; they mock the Pope; they rail on Luther; they allow neither side; they like none but only themselves; the mark they shoot at, the end they look for, the heaven they desire, is only their own present pleasure and private profit; whereby they plainly declare of whose school, or what religion, they be; that is, epicures in living and ἄθεοι [atheists] in doctrine.
>
> (71)

Considering the virulent anti-Catholic rhetoric of this section of *The Scholemaster*, one cannot help but be struck by the juxtaposition of "Protestant and papist," of "Pope" and "Luther," in the same sentences. Ascham has now imagined a third term against which *both* Catholicism and Protestantism are able to establish their common Christian ground: the narcissistic atheists or epicures who "like none but only themselves" and aim only for "present pleasure and private profit," wasting time in a manner that makes no allowances for, no investment in, either the civic realm or eternal life. But just when we think that Ascham has finally fixed the object of his disparagement, he returns to his vehement scorn for Catholicism, sniping that "Christ's true religion set no sure footing where the Pope hath any jurisdiction" (73).

In these various ways—these crooked, errant ways—*The Scholemaster* produces the impression of a writer eternally in pursuit of a protean foe always just beyond his grasp. Ascham's contempt both is and is not directed to pleasure, is and is not directed to romance, is and is not directed to Italy, to Rome, to Catholicism, to experience, to atheism. By pursuing a negative path, by attempting to grasp what a virtuous education is *not*, Ascham warps his project beyond repair. The text wanders to the extent that Ascham himself, at the conclusion to part 1, indicts his waywardness: "And thus far have I wandered from my first purpose of teaching a child, yet not altogether out of the way, because this whole talk hath tended to the only advancement of truth in religion and honesty of living." This self-indictment is only partial; Ascham subsequently insists that his wandering "hath been wholly within the compass" of his subject (and the word "compass" is no casual figure of speech in the context of what is mainly a discussion about travel). He then expresses an assured desire to get completely back on track: "But to my matter. As I began plainly and simply with my young scholar, so will I not leave him, God willing, until I have brought him a perfect scholar out of the school and placed him in the university to become a fit student for logic and rhetoric, and so after to physic, law, or divinity, as aptness of nature, advice of friends and God's disposition shall lead him" (75).

Despite Ascham's claims for an ordered discourse, the specter of errancy proves difficult to exorcise. After the first part of the text ends, Ascham abruptly moves to the more pragmatic and methodical discussion of the instruction of Latin. Yet even in part 2, in the midst of his more technically pedagogical argument, Ascham must repeatedly remind himself to stay on track. For example, after characterizing imitation as a "large and wide" topic because "all the works of nature in a manner be examples for art to follow," he writes, "but to our purpose. All languages, both learned and mother tongues, be gotten, and gotten only, by imitation" (114). As one might expect, the subsequent discussion wanders from the topic of imitation into a general discussion of rudeness of learning and God's providence, so much so that Ascham reminds himself "to return to imitation again" (116). If the second half of *The Scholemaster* is supposed to correct the errancy of the first part's indictment of errancy, then it can hardly be characterized as an effective corrective. In fact, because the text's organizational signposts are frequently phrased in passive terms, the reader is led to believe that the text is writing itself: "In this place, or I proceed farther, I will now declare by whose authority *I am led*" (82; my italics); "By this small mention of Cambridge *I am carried* into three imaginations" (132; my italics). It's as if *The Scholemaster* were animated, in spite of Ascham's best intentions, by the same kinds of forces—romance, pleasure, errancy—that it rails against. It's as if Ascham, Elizabethan England's most vehement critic of romance, had written an endless romance.

Irony beyond Intention

Ascham's waywardness, his frequent interruptions of the order of his discourse, and his disavowal of authorial agency all point to a disjunction between what his text says and what it does. On the face of it, such a tension could never be characterized as particularly shocking. For the Renaissance in particular, though, it taps into deep fears about the potential futility of literature. According to Alex Davis, "The portrait of the reader of romance painted by many Renaissance authors is . . . an image of the humanistic nightmare: of books that gain mastery over their readers."[29] The errancy of Ascham's text paints the portrait of a similar nightmare: of a book that gains mastery over its *writer*. In this regard, it is worth recalling Roland Barthes's claim that the pleasure of the text "can very well take the form of a drift [*dérive*]." "*Drifting*," Barthes goes on to add, "occurs whenever *I do not respect the whole*, and whenever, by dint of seeming driven about by language's illusions, seductions, and intimidations, like a cork on the waves [*comme un buchon sur la vague*], I remain motionless, pivoting on the *intractable* bliss that binds me to the text (to the world)."[30] Bearing in mind that *vague*, the French word for "wave," bears the etymological connotation of wandering, we might be compelled to say that the kind of d(é)rive of which Barthes speaks betrays the vagaries of a wavelike compulsion—a compulsion to err as much as a compulsion to repeat—that leads texts like *The Scholemaster* to tread the primrose path of vagrancy.

Given the frequency and evident self-consciousness with which Ascham succumbs to this compulsion, it might be claimed that his digressions signal not a text that has run out of control but, rather, a text very much in control—a text that, like Stanley Fish's *Paradise Lost*, intentionally goes astray for dialectically didactic reasons, ironically and tactically deploying romance pleasures with the aim of annulling them. If it is easy to highlight moments in Renaissance texts, particularly romance texts, when the writer appears to take pleasure in error—moments when the narrative runs around and awry, wandering beyond the bounds of decorum into territories connected to the main narrative thread by the flimsiest of associations—the burden of proof works in such a way that it is far less easy to argue that the writer is indulging in, never mind succumbing to, pleasure for pleasure's sake. The temptation, as well as the ability, to sublimate error to a purposeful—a self-consciously ironic—end is just far too strong.[31] Consider, as a brief example, one of the only studies to discuss explicitly the period's rhetoric of digression: Anne Cotterill's *Digressive Voices in Early Modern English Literature*, which announces, at its very beginning, its intention to examine "the intellectual and imaginative pleasures of narrative wandering."[32] "Traditionally," Cotterill writes, "the practice of digression has been linked to the capture of a listener's desire for forbidden pleasure: the delight in escape from time's inexorable forward movement and in passion's transport out of time."[33] In her readings of seventeenth-century writers such as John Donne, Andrew Marvell, Thomas Browne, John Milton, and John Dryden, Cotterill is certainly attentive to the pleasures of digressive moments. And yet for these writers, according to her analysis, these structures of escape and evasion ultimately have a purposeful social function—granted, a function that deconstructs the foundational dichotomies on which the social is based, but one that is nevertheless "turned *outward* for purposes of self-defence and self-portraiture."[34]

Even if we grant the validity of this reading for later, seventeenth-century writers, it applies less easily to writers like Ascham, who contradictorily rely on the pleasurable means *least* suited to their purposeful ends. Furthermore, insofar as it relocates the ironic contradictions of the text within an economy of purpose determined by either authorial volition or cultural forces or a combination of both, this kind of interpretation stands guilty of committing the intentional fallacy. It might be better to take a lead instead from Paul de Man's attempt to locate irony apart from—insofar as it permanently disrupts—self-conscious intent or purpose. Admittedly, it may seem strange to seek in de Man's reflections on irony a working theory of textual pleasure. "De Man's work," Fredric Jameson puts it (not entirely unfairly), "is unique among that of modern critics and theorists in its ascetic repudiation of pleasure, desire, and the intoxication of the sensory."[35] More directly ethical, political, phenomenological, and psychoanalytic treatments of pleasure abound in the poststructuralist archive, and it would therefore, no doubt, be more prudent and productive to turn instead, for instance, to Michel Foucault, Jacques Lacan, or Gilles Deleuze. Nevertheless, de Man's reflections on the machinery of irony—including his steadfast resistance to recuperative gestures, his relentless critique of dialectical thinking and the soporific platitudes of aesthetic ideology, and his emphasis on textual patterns that exceed or escape intentionality and control—can help us release pleasure from the claims of purposefulness and the ends-oriented standards by which it is often measured and against which it offers some degree of pushback.

In the midst of his lecture "The Concept of Irony," de Man focuses on a short chapter in Friedrich Schlegel's incomplete novel, *Lucinde*. According to de Man, the fragment "reads like a philosophical treatise or argument," but, he hastens to add, "it doesn't take a very perverse mind, only a slightly perverse one, to see that what is actually being described is not a philosophical argument at all but is—well, how should I put it?—a reflection on the very physical questions involved in sexual intercourse."[36] It would likely be as fruitful as it is tempting to read the chaste hesitation ("how should I put it?") with which de Man names sexual pleasure as the seedy underbelly of the Schlegel passage, or to think about his invocation of perversion as the critical perspective necessary to bring this irony into relief.[37] But here I wish merely to highlight the theoretical implications that he draws from his reading of the passage: "There seems to be a particular threat emanating from this double relationship in the writing, which is not just a double code. It's not just that there is a philosophical code and then another code describing sexual activities. These two codes are radically incompatible with each other. They interrupt, they disrupt, each other in such a fundamental way that this very possibility of disruption represents a threat to all assumptions one has about what a text should be."[38] De Man goes on to argue that critical thought defuses the "particular threat" of irony by recourse to three maneuvers: first, by reducing irony "to an aesthetic practice or artistic device, . . . an artistic effect, something a text does for aesthetic reasons, to heighten or diversify the aesthetic appeal"; second, by reducing irony "to a dialectic of the self as a reflexive structure . . . within which the self looks at itself from a certain distance"; and third, by "insert[ing] ironic moments or ironic structures into a dialectic of history."[39]

De Man's subsequent analysis calls these three maneuvers into question by viewing irony as a function of the contingent machinery of language, not of aesthetic value, self-reflexivity, or history. "Words have a way of saying things," de Man says, "which are not at all what you want them to say. You are writing a splendid and coherent philosophical argument but, lo and behold, you are describing sexual intercourse. Or you are writing a fine compliment for somebody and without your knowledge, just because words have a way of doing things, it's sheer insult and obscenity that you are really saying."[40] Or, as in the case of Ascham's *The Scholemaster*, you are outlining an educational plan that you claim is "straight, plain, and easy" but that takes the form of the kind of perverse wandering, the kind of going "ever out of the way," that your plan is designed to counteract (79). In order to think further about this kind of ironic split, let me now turn to the work of Thomas Nashe, who, like Ascham, relies on excessive or perverse textual pleasure even as he appears to heap a mass of words against it.

Bable Bookmungers

Nashe, according to Jonathan Crewe, began his career by "identifying himself explicitly with the dogmas and values enshrined in Ascham's *The Schoolmaster*."[41] This identification is especially evident in Nashe's first major text, his 1589 misogynistic rant, *The Anatomie of Absurditie*, in which he launches his own attack against what he calls the "bable bookemungers" who produce romances, those who "endeauor," as he puts it, "to repaire the ruinous wals of *Venus* Court, to restore to the worlde that forgotten Legendary licence of lying, to imitate a fresh the fantasticall dreames of those exiled Abbie-lubbers, from whose idle pens proceeded those worne out impressions of the feyned no where acts, of Arthur of the rounde table, Arthur of little Brittaine, sir Tristram," and so on, "with infinite others" (1:11). The canon of Arthurian legends, the association with Catholicism ("exiled Abbie-lubbers"), the accusations of illicit, feminine desire ("Venus Court") and idleness: all these features of antiromance discourse are commonplace to the point of being clichés, familiar from *The Scholemaster*.[42]

When this passage has been addressed in scholarship on Nashe or on romance, critics have indeed cited it as a particularly bald example of anti-romance sentiment on the order of Ascham's text.[43] If, however, we more closely read this passage for its style, rather than simply cite it for its content, we can catch sight of a form of writing less austere than Ascham's, however didactic Nashe's diatribe seems to strive to be. Take the phrases "bable bookemungers" and "Legendary licence of lying," for instance. In *The Arte of English Poesy* (a text published, as it happens, in the same year as *The Anatomie of Absurditie*), George Puttenham claims that alliteration becomes a vice when a poet "takes too much delight to fill his verse with words beginning all with a letter." Granted, Puttenham goes on to assert that alliteration "doth not ill but prettily becomes the meter."[44] In Nashe's case, though, where the alliteration appears in prose, not verse, it especially exceeds any useful or purposeful telos to which it might be directed. Beyond being merely an instance of Nashe's dalliance with the vogue for patterned euphuistic writing established by his fellow University Wit and anti-Martinist, John Lyly, it exemplifies what Crewe calls "a linguistic excess surpassing any functional explanation, any acceptable rationale, or any power of repression."[45]

This is not to say that functional signification plays no role over the course of Nashe's sentence. Surely the meanings of the signifier "bable," for instance, convey some significance. "To babble," according to the *OED*, is to talk incoherently, childishly, excessively, and inopportunely, and, in a transitive sense, to "repeat or utter" something "with meaningless iteration."[46] The *OED* also informs us that the word "bauble"—as in a mere toy—was frequently spelled, in the early modern period, as "bable." And especially considering Barthes's characterization of the text of pleasure as a *Babel heureuse*—a "sanctioned Babel," as Richard Miller translates the phrase, or, even better, a "fortunate Babel" (like a *felix culpa*, or fortunate fall)—it would also be difficult to ignore how Nashe's "bable" plays on the homonym "Babel," which designates, of course, the Judeo-Christian myth of linguistic incoherence.[47] Thus, the word "bable" *means* meaninglessness and thus generates meaning above, or after, all.

Yet even if the various signifieds attached to "bable" make sense in light of Nashe's attempt to cast romance as senseless, we should not cast aside the possibility that the *signifier* "bable" imposes itself more on the basis of sound than of sense—not only because it alliterates with the first letter of "bookemungers," but also because the two *b*s within "bable" stutteringly echo each other. Insofar as it distracts or drives the reader's attention to the materiality of the letter that killeth at the potential expense of the spirit, the sense, that giveth life, alliteration, like a necromancer who interrupts the progress of a knight's quest, disrupts the orderly flow of meaning normally guaranteed by what Barthes calls "the sacred armature of syntax."[48] Or, to put the point in a slightly different way, sound partially deprives Nashe's sentence of sense (and soundness) as that sentence stumbles over alliterative hurdles on its way to making a point.[49]

Curiously enough, neither is *The Scholemaster* immune to this sort of alliterative play, what Lacan would call the "instance" or "insistence" of the letter. In the "Preface to the Reader," Ascham recalls his follow-up talk with Sir Richard Sackville in the following terms: "We passed from children and came to young men, namely, gentlemen. We talked of their too much *l*iberty to *l*ive as they *l*ust; of their *l*etting *l*oose too soon to overmuch experience of ill" (8; my italics). While such petty indulgences ought to be allowed in so august an educational authority as Ascham, the stakes are higher in the case of Nashe, who has always been seen, in a way Ascham never has been seen, as a particularly prodigal writer. In Nashe's alliterative play, we can see him indulging in the kind of stylistic and rhetorical virtuosity—a virtuosity of excessive pleasure, of "too much delight," as Puttenham phrases it—with which subsequent readers, C. S. Lewis chief among them, would associate him. We can see, that is, the pleasure of the text, *even as* that pleasure is subordinated to didactic ends that resemble Ascham's: namely, an attack against the very dangers of idle poetic pleasures. In her study *Thomas Nashe in Context*, Hutson notes how Nashe "abandon[ed] the protestant-humanist notion of reading for profit . . . at the very beginning of his career, even while he was busy sifting the provident profits of poetry from its licentious abuses in the didactic *Anatomie of Abuses* [*sic*]."[50] However much Hutson may overstate the case—however impossible the abandonment of "reading for profit" may, in fact, ultimately be—it would not be a stretch to say that Nashe comes closer than any other Elizabethan writer to approaching the asymptote of absolute futility.[51] In reading Nashe, generations of critics have struggled to grasp, and so to come to grips with, what Crewe identifies as "the phenomenon of an unreduced excess of 'rhetoric.'"[52] After Nashe's themes have been catalogued, after his content has been paraphrased, after his logic has been parsed, after his irony has been ironed and, in the process, straightened out, there remains a residue of superficial superfluity, a rhetorical surplus exemplified in one form, as we have seen, by the rapid-fire bursts of functionless and valueless alliteration in *The Anatomie of Absurditie*.

This kind of futile excess has always put critics in a double bind. As Crewe writes, "The defense of rhetoric as an opposing and putatively superior *principle* to that of logic is liable to degenerate into transparent bluster or to become a defense of the palpably indefensible—the defense, for example, of irrational excess, of logical incoherence, of narcissistic display, of violence, and of injustice."[53] With Crewe's observation in hand, I would now like to turn to Nashe's picaresque adventure tale, *The Unfortunate Traveller*, which could easily be characterized as a text precisely *about* irrational excess, logical incoherence, narcissistic display, violence, and injustice. Because *The Unfortunate Traveller* thematizes at the level of content the prodigality that Nashe's style enacts at the level of form, it can therefore provide us with a better view of the perversity, as well as the costs, of Nashe's improvident and indulgent futilitarian commitments.

Nashe's Text Machine

The Unfortunate Traveller recounts the misadventures of its narrator-protagonist-antihero, Jack Wilton, as he wanders the Continent, meeting the key figures of early sixteenth-century humanism—Thomas More, Desiderius Erasmus, Cornelius Agrippa, and Henry Howard, the Earl of Surrey—along the way. A little over halfway through the narrative, Nashe inscribes Surrey in a stereotypical chivalric romance tournament that evokes not only those found in Sir Philip Sidney's *Arcadia*, as Katherine Duncan-Jones demonstrates,[54] but also allegorical set pieces such as the parade of the Seven Deadly Sins in Spenser's House of Pride. Jack offers the reader an elaborate description of Surrey's armor and regalia, the centerpiece of which is a "rough-plumed silver plush, in full proportion and shape of an estrich," or ostrich, on his horse. In a meta-allegorical moment, Jack interprets the significance of these tournament ornaments as follows:

> The morall of the whole is this, that as the estrich, the most burning sighted bird of all others, insomuch as the female of them hatcheth not her egs by couering them, but by the effectual rayes of her eyes, as he, I say, outstrippeth the nimblest trippers of his feathered condition in footmanship, onely spurd on with the needle quickening goad vnder

> his side, so he, no less burning sighted than the estrich, spurde on to the race of honor by the sweet rayes of his mistres eyes, perswaded himselfe he should outstrip all other in running to the goale of glorie, onely animated and incited by hir excellence. And as the estrich will eate yron, swallow anie hard mettall whatsoeuer, so woulde he refuse no iron aduenture, no hard taske whatsoeuer, to sit in the grace of so fayre a commander.
>
> (2:273)

In spite of the spate of critical interest that *The Unfortunate Traveller* continues to command in Nashe studies, this is one of the few passages in the text that critics decline to ponder, let alone mention. Indeed, we have to rewind the clock of literary critical history a good number of decades in order to reach a moment when scholars *did* pay attention to this bit of text. Even then, though, the meaning of this passage is generally determined by an act of displacement, by viewing it as a source for a more valuable textual matter: the crux posed by Vernon's description to Hotspur, in *1 Henry IV*, of Prince Hal and his comrades: "All furnished, all in arms, / All plumed like ostriches" (4.1.97–98).[55] Identifying this passage as a potential source for Shakespeare, though, only helps us understand Shakespeare; it hardly brings us any closer to figuring out what tricks Nashe may be up to.

Critics' lack of interest in reading the meaning of this passage "in itself" or "on its own terms," as we like to say, may be a displaced textual effect, then, of the way in which the passage itself performs resistance to the act of reading meaning out of something. Were we in a romance on the order of *The Faerie Queene* or the *Arcadia*, we could reasonably expect here a pithy maxim, a sententia or adage fit for a commonplace book, that sums up the profitable precept to be learned from Surrey's allegorically significant armor, ornaments, and trappings, but Nashe inserts only a rambling sentence, a perfect instance of what Renaissance humanists might identify as the fault of indecorousness, that swallows up whatever point is to be made, such that the only point the sentence ever seems to reach is the period mark that brings it to its arbitrary conclusion. And just when we think the conclusion has finally been reached, Nashe extends the point beyond the bounds of the sentence, attaching *another* sentence by a flimsy conjunction, an added sentence, we should add, that adds very little to the already paltry and shaky moral content conveyed by the previous sentence.

From here it would be easy to move on to speculate about the significance of this lack of significance—to view it, for instance, as part of Nashe's general contempt for acts of interpretation made by those whom he derides, in *Lenten Stuffe*, as "mice-eyed decipherers and calculaters vppon characters" (3:218), or to view it as a more specific send-up of the always strained attempts to fuse the pleasures of romance to the lessons of allegory in the works of Sidney and Spenser. Indeed, one could even cite Spenser himself here, for ostriches make a cameo appearance in book 2 of *The Faerie Queene*, among the description of the villains who assail Alma's castle in canto 11:

> a grysie rablement,
> Some mouth'd like greedy Oystriges, some faste
> Like loathly Toades, some fashioned in the waste
> Like swine; for so deformed is luxury,
> Surfeat, misdiet, and unthriftie waste,
> Vaine feastes, and ydle superfluity.
>
> (2.11.12)

"Surfeat, misdiet, and unthriftie waste,/Vaine feastes, and ydle superfluity": this description could be applied quite easily to Nashe's writing. It would be easy too, then, for me to claim in conclusion that the ostriches of Spenser's romance help give meaning to the apparent meaninglessness of the ostriches of Nashe's antiromance.

Yet any reader of Nashe would be remiss in taking this interpretive route. The question the text seems to ask of us instead is whether we might—and, if not, why we wouldn't—view the irrelevance of this passage as mere irrelevance. It is important to recognize, of course, that there is nothing "mere" about irrelevance; pure irrelevance may be impossible, for even irrelevance, as we have seen, can be dialectically recuperated as a form of relevance. The interpretation of irrelevance may be a useful way of sidestepping or suppressing the potential irrelevance of interpretation. Yet, as Jeff Dolven demonstrates, the potential pleasures and dangers of irrelevance should not be so quickly dismissed or repressed, especially where Renaissance romance is concerned. His primary example is Britomart, Spenser's Knight of Chastity, lost in a daze before the idol of Cupid in the House of Busirane; as Dolven argues, this odd pause in the allegory shows Britomart indulging in "spectatorial self-pleasuring (rather than study or moral-making). She is a hedonist of what ought to be a merely propaedeutic thrill."[56] Following Dolven's compelling reading, I want to suggest that Nashe teases his readers to indulge in the kind of irrelevant hedonism that Britomart briefly experiences before the demand for relevance restores the linearity of her allegorical quest. What Spenser's poem represents, Nashe's work frequently performs. Nashe's writing unapologetically jumps into the gap that Spenser, according to Dolven's reading, exposes within the project of humanism.

While the bulk of *The Unfortunate Traveller* represents Jack's misadventures on the European continent, the opening episodes of the narrative establish both the thematic tenor of Jack's tale and also the narrative vehicle: Jack narrates a series of plots, taken out of the jest book tradition, that implicitly reflects back on how narrative plots work in the first place. In the first plot, Jack directs his trickster energies toward a "Lord of misrule" (2:210), an ale dealer in the English camp, for whom he constructs a "holiday lye" that serves no other purpose than to generate pleasure, to make the other men in the camp "merrie . . . manie a Winters euening after" (2:216). The lie runs as follows: Jack begins by flattering the ale dealer "with a long circumstaunce" (2:211), thus enticing him with a dilated discourse; that enticement is so effective that, when the tapster barges in, the ale dealer "was readie," Jack reports, "to haue stricken his tapster for interrupting him in attention of this his so much desired relation, but for feare of displeasing mee hee moderated his furie. . . . Well, at his earnest importunitie, after I had moistned my lippes to make my lie run glibbe to his iourneie's end, forward I went as followeth" (2:212). Jack then begins to say that he happened to overhear the king and the royal advisors speaking about the ale dealer; the knowledge of what they said, however, Jack further withholds, a lacuna graphically marked in the text by a series of interruptions: "it was," Jack says to the man, "priuily informed (no villains to these priuie informers) that you, euen you that I now speake to, had—(Oh, would I had no tong to tell the rest; by this drinke it grieues me so I am not able to repeate it)" (2:212–13). To the reader, Jack then says, "Now was my dronken Lord readie to hang himselfe for the ende of the full point" (2:213).

In this opening episode Jack thus plays with an excess of pleasure—a ton of will, one might call it, keeping Jack's last name in mind—that simultaneously flames and frustrates the lord's desire for satisfactory narrative fulfillment. As Jack's meta-plot plays with the frustration of narrative satisfaction, it exemplifies in miniature the decisively antiteleological drive—a death drive, in a way, given the fact that the lord is "readie to hang himselfe" for such satisfaction—associated with romance, particularly in its Ariostan strand. *The Unfortunate Traveller* as a whole also wanders into Ariostan territory by way of frequent narrative interruptions.[57] Like Ascham's signals to his readers that he is or is not on track, Nashe's interruptions, through his narrator, call attention to the text's circumlocutory straying. "[Just] a little neerer to the matter & the purpose," Jack says toward the beginning of the narrative (2:207), but over the course of *The Unfortunate Traveller* one increasingly receives the impression that the tale is wandering further and further from a matter and a purpose that do not exist in the first place.

There is, in fact, a rhetorical term that designates both the digressiveness of the text and Jack's narrative interruptions. "Parabasis" refers to the moment in Greek Old Comedy when the chorus punctures the drama's illusion by addressing the audience directly, but it is also more broadly a term for digression. In fact, it is the term that Puttenham uses in *The Arte of English Poesy* to name digression, a term that he translates into English as "the Straggler."[58] Not incidentally, parabasis is also the term that de Man uses to characterize irony. "Parabasis," de Man says in "The Concept of Irony," "is the interruption of a discourse by a shift in rhetorical register. It's what you would get in [Lawrence] Sterne, precisely, the constant interruption of the narrative illusion by intrusion."[59] In the parabasis of irony one may find, as de Man suggests, "a machine there, a text machine, an implacable determination and a total arbitrariness . . . which inhabits words on the level of the play of the signifier, which undoes any consistency of lines, and which undoes the reflexive and dialectical model, both of which are, as you know, the basis of any narration."[60] The interruptions of *The Unfortunate Traveller* enact precisely the kind of disruptions that de Man associates with ironic parabasis; every time Jack calls attention to the text's attempts *not* to stray, he threatens to stall the text's progress, the "consistency" of its narrative "lines."

With the image of de Man's "text machine" in mind, it is an opportune moment to turn to the most famous set piece in *The Unfortunate Traveller*, the passage that describes what we might call Nashe's text machine: the mechanical summer banqueting house that Jack encounters while roaming through Rome.

> I sawe a summer banketting house belonging to a merchaunt, that was the meruaile of the world, & could not be matcht except God should make another paradise. It was builte round of greene marble like a Theater with-out: within there was a heauen and earth comprehended both vnder one roofe; the heauen was a cleere ouerhanging vault of christall, wherein the Sunne and Moone and each visible Starre had his true similitude, shine, scituation, and motion, and, by what enwrapped arte I cannot conceiue, these spheares in their proper orbes obserued their circular wheelinges and turnings, making a certaine kinde of soft angelical murmering musicke in their often windings & going about; which musick the philosophers say in the true heauen, by reason of the grosenes of our senses, we are not capable of. . . . On the wel clothed boughs of this conspiracie of pine trees against the resembled Sun

> beames, were pearcht as many sortes of shrill breasted birdes as the Summer hath allowed for singing men in hir siluane chapels. Who though they were bodies without soules, and sweete resembled substances without sense, yet by the mathematicall experimentes of long siluer pipes secretlye inrinded in the intrailes of the boughs whereon they sat, and vndiscerneablie conuaid vnder their bellies into their small throats sloaping, they whistled and freely carold theyr naturall field note.
>
> (2:282–83)

In approaching this lengthy and difficult passage, which actually continues for a couple more pages, we should first note that the mechanics by which the summer banqueting house operates may have specific referents. As Jonathan Sawday points out in *Engines of the Imagination: Renaissance Culture and the Rise of the Machine*, early modern travel writers such as Fynes Moryson supplied descriptions of the complex hydraulics of pleasure gardens in Italy, descriptions from which Nashe is clearly drawing for his own, albeit fictional, description. "To populate such theaters of what Nashe termed 'soul-exalting objects,'" Sawday writes, "Renaissance designers became skilled in creating bestiaries of moving mechanical animals and figures." According to Sawday, these mechanical figures served primarily an ornamental function, of "adorn[ing] the tables of the wealthy," but they also had a political purpose insofar as they "could be considered as a form of clockwork diplomacy, designed to impress the recipient with the technological prowess of the culture able to produce such an artefact."[61]

As much as Nashe's banqueting house may derive some of its significance from these material and political machines, one shouldn't let that fact distract from what Nashe takes great pains to stress: the banqueting house is more a figural topos than a literal one. Beyond simply representing, through its literal dimension, the latest in Renaissance technology, the banqueting house figures the most ancient of symbolic sites. It is like the garden of Eden, as Jack tells us, "counterfeited in that liknes that Adam lorded [over] before his fall" (2:283). And according to a sentence that evokes Sir Philip Sidney's *Defence of Poesy*, the banqueting house re-creates the Ovidian golden age: "Such a golden age, such a good age, such an honest age was set forth in this banketting house" (2:285).[62]

If the banqueting house is composed of thoroughly familiar classical and biblical tropes—the privileged, sublime tropes of high humanism—it can also be read as a *mise en abyme* of romance, which has prompted several critics to invoke implicit intertexts. Julian Yates, for example, associates the banqueting house with Reynaldo's fountain in Ariosto's *Orlando furioso*.[63] In summarizing readings of this passage, Steve Mentz tellingly writes, "Criticism remains divided about whether this house is Nashe's ideal or his version of the Bower of Bliss."[64] The text itself is explicit about another intertextual referent, one that, as we've seen, frequently animates and orients English humanist attacks on romance (including Nashe's own attack in *The Anatomie of Absurditie*): "A wide vast spacious roome [the banqueting house] was, such as we would conceit prince Arthurs hall to be, where he feasted all his knights of the round table together euerie penticost" (2:283). Though less obvious and central than the biblical and classical references, the Ariostan, Spenserian, and Arthurian echoes work together to figure the banqueting house as a conventional romance topos.

From the moment when the Earl of Surrey arrives on the scene, *The Unfortunate Traveller* swerves into the orbit of romance, allegorized here, as if in direct response to Ascham, as a tour of Catholic Italy. The final third of the text marshals a series of genres—from the tragedies of Heraclide and Cutwolfe to the banished English earl's Aschamesque lecture about the dangers of travel abroad—in order to reform the text, and its narrator and readers, following its tempting, pleasurable, *de*forming digressions into romance. As the last bit of romance before these reforming genres, the summer banqueting house represents romance in its purest form, a moment of perfect *otium* before the text revs up its well-oiled ascetic machinery in an attempt to counteract the stalling effects of its ironic aesthetics. As stylistically overindulgent as it is symbolically overdetermined, the passage says a whole lot about very little. Indeed, it functions as a kind of narrative parabasis, an interruption of the narrative's flow.

Even still, critics have recoiled from considering the passage in these kinds of terms. Channeling twentieth-century condemnations of *l'art pour l'art*, Alexander Leggatt, for example, maintains that the description of the summer banqueting house is "not . . . simply a piece of 'fine writing' indulged in for its own sake."[65] Yet attention should be paid to how long Nashe lingers over the description, which runs on for several pages. Indeed, the only descriptive passages in the text that run longer are those of the tournament scene and the rape of Heraclide, but in these cases the purposes of the descriptions are clear: witty satire in the case of the former, horrific tragedy in the case of the latter. By contrast, the purpose of the summer banqueting house description is far less clear. If it is not written, as Leggatt says, "for its own sake," then for what's sake *is* it written? What is its meaning, function, and use? Following Leggatt, critics often interpret the banqueting house in opposition to the plague-ridden Italian society that surrounds it.[66] Seeing no such contrast, Jessica Wolfe argues that the banqueting house serves to satirize Italian "artifice," its hydraulic machinery symbolizing Italian machinations.[67] Despite superficial differences, these two interpretations share the assumption that Nashe, like Ascham, is invested in condemning the Italians.

One might be inclined to reinforce that assumption were it not for certain assertions in the paragraph that immediately follows Jack's description of the banqueting house:

> O *Rome*, if thou hast in thee such soul-exalting obiects [as the banqueting house], what a thing is heauen in comparison of thee, of which *Mercators* globe is a perfecter modell than thou art? Yet this I must saie to the shame of vs protestants; if good workes may merite heauen, they doe them, we talke of them. Whether supersticion or no makes them vnprofitable seruants, that let pulpits decide; but there you shall haue the brauest ladies, in gownes of beaten golde, washing pilgrimes & poore souldiers feete, and doing nothing, they and their waiting maides, all the yeare long, but making shirts and bands for them against they come by in distresse. Their hospitals are more lyke noble mens houses than otherwise; so richly furnished, cleane kept, and hot perfumed, that a souldier would thinke it a sufficient recompence for all his trauell and his wounds, to haue such a heauenly retyring place. For the Pope and his pontificalibus I will not deale with; onely I will dilate vnto you what happened whilest I was in *Rome*.
>
> (2:285–86)

From this paragraph, Jack proceeds to narrate the plague that fell down on Rome during the "vehement hot summer when [he] was a soiourner there." Critics generally pass over this paragraph, though, in order to focus on the plague itself, which marks the beginning of an escalating series of violent episodes in Italy before Jack returns, in conclusion, to Henry VIII's ambit. Leggatt, for example, refers to this paragraph as a merely "brief interlude," a marginal status that he reinforces by relegating the phrase to a parenthetical space in his reading: "The fact that Nashe moves (with only a brief interlude) from the garden to a startling description of the plague would seem to indicate that the contrast is intentional."[68]

Why does this "brief interlude" receive such short shrift? For one thing, Jack's praise of the Italians undermines any "contrast" between England and Rome, or between inside and outside, that common sense dictates we must draw. One's uncertainty in relation to this passage increases still insofar as it is difficult to tell whether or not the irony of Jack's praise is *itself* ironic. The situation can only be resolved in a circular fashion, by recourse to the very opposition between England and Italy that the first degree of irony—the irony of Jack's praise of the Italians—calls into question. Whether or not Nashe intends his readers to take Jack's praise at face value is beside the point: even if the passage aims for blame by way of praise, it does so by way of praise to the extent that the only explicit blame here is directed to "the shame of vs protestants."[69] Evoking the possibility that "good workes may merite heauen"—Calvinist theology, we will recall, emphatically asserts that good works *do not* merit heaven—Jack lauds the social and spiritual efficacy of the Roman Catholic matrons, the "brauest ladies, in gownes of beaten golde," who wash the feet of pilgrims and soldiers in "richly furnished" hospitals. One should be careful, however, of reaching the conclusion that Jack, in praising such civic engagement, endorses some quasi-Horatian view of aesthetics. The passage establishes no causal relation between the gilt ornament of the ladies' gowns and their good social works; the latter may very well take place in spite of the former. More important, the aesthetics of the summer banqueting house—as well as the aesthetics of Rome, and romance, more generally—do not lead *Jack* to perform such charitable actions. In talking about these actions rather than doing them, Jack reduplicates the shame of "vs" Protestants.

This passage, so easily passed over, therefore makes it difficult to localize Jack's—and much less Nashe's—position in relation to Rome. One cannot be so sure, in other words, that the text is *simply* invested in condemning the seductively romantic extravagancies of Rome. On the one hand, Jack ironically praises the Catholic ladies who perform good social works regardless of their indulgence in extravagant and pleasurable vanity. On the other hand, that irony could be read as ironic—probably should, in fact, be read as ironic, at least as long as one wishes to operate within a dichotomous scheme that pits England against Italy. From a contextual perspective, it would be perverse to argue that Nashe is secretly pro-Catholic, but from a textual perspective such an argument would not be completely out of the question.[70] The conflict between these two positions cannot be sublated or resolved in any dialectically stable manner. The text machine that is the summer banqueting house extends its pulsating ironic effects across the perverse Italian romance landscape of *The Unfortunate Traveller*, compromising any stable moral one might try to glean from such a prodigal text—especially, as we will soon see, at those moments when the text puts on a dazzling display of heavy-handed moralizing.

Endless Prodigality

After Jack surveys the summer banqueting house, he finds himself, as I noted earlier, in the midst of a particularly vicious plague, so he takes refuge in the home of the Roman matron Heraclide. While Jack is there, two bandits—Esdras, a Spaniard, and Bartol, an Italian—break into the house and rape Heraclide before stealing away with the house's riches. Heraclide, in the tradition of Lucrece, consequently commits suicide. As if witnessing this horrific tragedy weren't punishment enough for Jack's knavery, what he calls his own "purgatorie" begins only when Heraclide's husband, hitherto passed out because, presumably, of the plague, wakes up: finding his wife "defiled and massacred," and Jack locked in a bedroom with "rapier vnsheathed," the husband draws the logical conclusion that Jack committed the rape (2:295). Jack is thus led to prison and from there to be hanged—until "a banisht English Earle" arrives, *ex machina*, to save the day, by reporting that he had happened to overhear "one *Bartoll*, an *Italian*, greeuously wounded and bloodie," confess the rape of Heraclide (2:296). As a result of the earl's testimony, Jack's execution is stayed. "To the banisht Earle I came to render thankes," Jack tells us, "when thus he examined and schoold me" (2:297).

As Jack's extemporal schoolmaster, the banished earl takes a page or two out of Ascham's *The Scholemaster*, launching a lengthy diatribe against the dangers of traveling in foreign countries. Reinforcing his arguments with reference to Icarus, Cain, the Israelites in Egypt, and the parable of the prodigal son, the earl attempts to draw, as starkly as possible, the kind of opposition between England and abroad that the text elsewhere ironically blurs. In addition, his arguments against travel turn primarily on the issue of perverse pleasure. Asserting that "nought but lasciuiousnesse is to be learned" in places such as Italy (2:297), the earl goes on to claim that from such sites a traveler will receive a bad education in "the art of atheisme, the art of epicurising, the art of whoring, the art of poysoning, the art of Sodomitrie" (2:301).[71] The earl rehearses all the standard sixteenth-century stereotypes about not only the Italians but also the French, the Spanish, the Danish, and the Dutch, before concluding his lecture to Jack with a succinct statement of the value of "home": "Let no man for anie transitorie pleasure sell away the inheritance he hath of breathing in the place where hee was borne. Get thee home, my yong lad, laye thy bones peaceably in the sepulcher of thy fathers, waxe olde in ouerlooking thy grounds, be at hand to close the eyes of thy kinred. The diuel and I am desperate, he of being restored to heauen, I of being recalled home" (2:302–3).

The length of this sermon, the amount of space Nashe devotes to it, might lead us to the conclusion that it is meant to be taken seriously—intended, that is, to be an elaborate resolution to the text's ambivalent position regarding the issue of the harmful pleasures of places such as Rome. The speech's span, in that case, suits its social sobriety. But in a text that elsewhere satirizes bloated orators and orations—Jack's caricaturization of the humanists at Wittenberg provides a particularly hilarious and memorable example (2:246–49)—the very lengthiness of the banished earl's speech might lead us to the opposite conclusion: that the opinions it expresses are expressly *not* to be taken seriously.[72] Moreover, surely the unequivocal value that the earl attaches to home in opposition to Rome must be considered in relation to the fact that he himself was banished from England, for reasons the text never divulges: "I am a banisht exile from my country," the earl says, "though nere linked in consanguinitie to the best: an Earle borne by birth, but a beggar now as thou seest. These manie years in *Italy* have I liued an outlaw" (2:302). The fact that the earl speaks from a position of abject experience might make him more of an authority on the abjectness of experience. Yet perhaps the clearest indication that the earl's sermon is to be taken as a lampoon can be gleaned from Jack's reaction of indifference, if not open hostility, to the lesson: "Heeres a stir, thought I to my selfe after I was set at libertie, that is worse than an vpbraiding lesson after a britching" (2:303).

Let me juxtapose this quotation to Jack's reaction, earlier in the text, to Surrey's account of being bewitched by his paramour, Geraldine: "Not a little was I delighted with this vnexpected loue storie, especially from a mouth out of which was nought wont to march but sterne precepts of grauetie & modestie. I sweare vnto you I thought his companie the better by a thousand crownes, because hee had discarded those nice tearmes of chastitie and continencie" (2:245). The Earl of Surrey relates a tale of bewitchment and Circean enchantment and travel to Italy—relates, that is, a romance; Jack responds with patent pleasure. The unnamed banished earl presents a long winded diatribe *against* bewitchment, Circean enchantments, and travel to Italy; Jack responds with indifference. The counterpoetics modeled in the text seems to operate, then, according to a simple principle: whereas delight without didacticism succeeds, didacticism without delight fails.

Such a formula should not, however, be taken to mean that the text's ambivalence can be resolved squarely on the side of hedonism and vanity. In other words, just because Jack disregards the banished earl's heavy-handed advice doesn't mean that the text does. The narrative events of the rest of *The Unfortunate Traveller* could be read as Jack's punishments for not taking the earl's lecture seriously. Just as the text pushes Surrey into the tournament arena, and so into the generic arena of romance, it causes Jack to fall, literally as well as figuratively, into the violent realm of revenge tragedy, as if the text were taking revenge *on* its protagonist. After departing from the earl, Jack wanders Rome in search of his courtesan, Diamante, and by chance (which is to say, by the text's narrative machinery) he falls into the cellar door of a house owned by a Jew named Zadoch. If the anti-Semitic portrait of Zadoch were not indication enough that Jack has fallen into a Marlovian drama, Nashe presents the threat of dismemberment (Zadoch sells Jack to Doctor Zacharie, who intends to use him for an anatomy), machinations in and around the Vatican, and, as the text's set piece *de la resistance*, the ghastly executions of Zadoch as well as of a man named Cutwolfe, who had gruesomely killed Esdras, the man who raped Heraclide. After this heavy load of tragic events, *The Unfortunate Traveller* concludes, rather hastily, in the following manner:

> Vnsearchable is the booke of our destinies. One murder begetteth another: was neuer yet bloud-shed barren from the beginning of the world to this daie. Mortifiedly abiected and danted was I with this truculent tragedie of *Cutwolfe* and *Esdras*. To such straight life did it thence forward incite me that ere I went out of *Bolognia* I married my curtizan, performed many almes deedes; and hasted so fast out of the *Sodom* of *Italy*, that within fortie daies I arriued at the king of *Englands* campe twixt *Ardes* and *Guines* in *France*, where he with great triumphs met and entertained the Emperour and the French king, and feasted many daies. And so as my storie began with the king at *Turnay* and *Turwin*, I thinke meete here to end it with the king at *Ardes* and *Guines*. All the conclusiue epilogue I wil make is this; that if herein I haue pleased anie, it shall animat me to more paines in this kind.
>
> Otherwise I will swear vpon an English Chronicle
> neuer to bee out-landish Chronicler more
> while I liue. Farewell as many
> as wish me well.
>
> (2:327–28)

If the banished earl's lecture was not enough to reform Jack—if it had been, Jack would have returned to England, and the text would have thus concluded at that point—then it is obvious that "the truculent tragedy of *Cutwolfe* and *Esdras*" *is* enough. Not only does the text return Jack to King Henry's purview; it also reorients him to the telos of compulsory heterosexuality and marriage, the telos of what Nashe, in a phrase that has more uncanny resonance for us than it could have had for him, calls the "straight life."

Has Jack learned his lesson, then? Has the reader? What is that lesson? These are questions that cannot be answered easily. The text, to be sure, ends with a clear moral: "Vnsearchable is the booke of our destinies. One murder begetteth another: was neuer yet bloud-shed barren from the beginning of the world to this daie." Moreover, the circularity of the tale's narrative arc ("as my storie began with the king at *Turnay* and *Turwin*, I thinke meete here to end it with the king at *Ardes* and *Guines*") might lead us to consider *The Unfortunate Traveller* as a typical prodigal son story, with its pattern of departure and return, of repentance after a literally and figuratively "outlandish" period of license and licentiousness.[73] Unlike *The Faerie Queene* or the revised *Arcadia* or even *The Scholemaster*, *The Unfortunate Traveller* is not an unfinished text.

At the same time, though, the text's "conclusiue epilogue" is too hasty, too tacked-on to be taken straight—almost as if it were a parenthetical aside, a supplement or appendix to a narrative that has failed to prepare the way for it.[74] Yes, the text ends. And yes, it ends by rejecting the excesses of romance, travel, and hedonism. This rejection takes the form of abjection, or projection, a displacement of these excesses onto "the *Sodom* of *Italy*." To emphasize the ending, however, is to provide only a partial picture of *The Unfortunate Traveller*, of what I've traced, throughout this chapter, as a radically incompatible ironic doubling between the pleasurable means and apparently virtuous ends of the text. Yet to make even this claim is still to operate under the assumption that the containment of pleasure *is* the "end" of the text—its goal or function as well as its conclusion. Is it, though? "All the conclusiue epilogue I wil make is this; that if herein I haue pleased anie, it shall animat me to more paines in this kind." This statement is difficult to interpret, phrased as it is in the uncertainty of a conditional statement. Yet the fulcrum on which this conditional pivots is clearly the notion of pleasure—a reader's pleasure, no less, that will generate more text beyond the closed system that this very statement seeks to effect. By way of pleasure, the ending of the text contradictorily opens up the text.

Virtuosity without Virtue

As we have seen, Nashe's futilitarian texts fail to practice what, according to the demands of humanism, they must preach, a point too easily overlooked if we pay attention only to what Nashe must preach, if we therefore fail to pay attention to the rhetorical operations and stylistic textures of his texts, independent of the stated intentions, thematic content, and commonsensical meanings and morals that can be paraphrased and summarized with facility. As Hutson asserts, the humanist "need to inculcate responsible social attitudes through literature produced a schematically pre-fabricated or compendious style of discourse which could not but frustrate a writer whose special talent was, as was Nashe's, for improvisation."[75] Yet a close analysis of Nashe's style exposes less a difference between Nashe and humanism than a difference within humanism itself: a tension, enacted throughout Nashe's work, between the humanist program of pedagogical profitability and the propensity for prodigal play that was a necessary by-product of the humanists' simultaneous emphasis on pleasure. Although pleasure is a necessary element for the production of utility and moral instruction, the very use of pleasure as a means for valuable ends introduces an element of volatile contingency that provides no assurance that the values of humanism will ever be entirely or successfully reinforced.

One could therefore say about Nashe's self-indulgent style what D. A. Miller claims about the self-indulgent style of Federico Fellini's *8 1/2* (1963): on the one hand, it is "so profoundly antisocial that it doesn't let us envision revolution or even social change. It offers only the practice of irrelevance, sustained with—and even like—a vengeance. Far from arguing or apologizing for this irrelevance, his style simply puts it before our eyes. Its only 'reason' is the self-evident pleasure we take in it"; on the other hand, "style, in this sense, is also a rare thing. Most styles are simply not powerful enough to achieve social negation even momentarily. And if they are, they tend either to dialecticize it as the ruse of redemption after all, or to trivialize it as so much detailing on a winsome niche brand."[76] In a similar fashion, it is precisely because the pleasure of Nashe's style is *so* unstable—so prodigal, outlandish, and ironic—that we feel the temptation to redeem, recuperate, or sublimate his writing by reinscribing it within a dialectical economy that would ensure its relevance and utility.

Hence, Georgia Brown argues that writers of the 1590s replaced the older humanist defense of literature—that poetry expresses moral and political values—with a newer model that reveled in poetic prodigality. This "new kind of defense," Brown claims, "does not deny the traditional association of literature with the trivial and transgressive, but *capitalizes* upon it to uncover the paradoxical *value* of marginality, error, ornamentality and excess."[77] In the context of this model, Nashe is Brown's exemplary writer: she claims that "while Nashe was associated with the unbridled excesses of satirical wit, he was also the personification of a particular kind of literariness, of an easy and highly *productive* relationship with words."[78] It may be true that Nashe, like other writers of the 1590s, aimed to find "value in the valueless," as Brown puts it, in order to assert authorial autonomy, authority, and originality.[79] But to adopt such an aim as the end of our readings would be to commit the intentional fallacy, to rely on an under-theorized Romantic notion of authorial individuality, and to overlook the fact that, from the perspective of Elizabethan literary culture, Nashe's style was anything *but* "productive."

Indeed, the literary market of Elizabethan England was not so kind to Nashe, a point that Brown's study glosses over. After claiming that critics have inaccurately painted a portrait of Nashe as a victim of the patronage system, she writes in a brief footnote, "This is not to deny that Nashe led an increasingly precarious existence towards the end of his career."[80] While the content of Brown's footnote may not altogether deny the difficulties Nashe faced, its very status *as* a footnote problematically minimizes those difficulties. If Nashe, as Hutson writes, "abandon[ed] the protestant-humanist notion of reading for profit,"[81] he also seems to have abandoned any notion of writing for profit—or rather, that notion abandoned him, as the name of his alter ego, "Pierce Penniless," suggests. Here is Nashe, in the early text that bears his alter ego's name, depicting his indigence:

> But all in vaine, I sate up late and rose earely, contended with the cold, and conuersed with scarcitie: for all my labours turned to losse, my vulgar Muse was despised and neglected, my paines not rewarded, or slightly rewarded, and I my selfe (in prime of my best wit) laide open to pouertie. Whereupon (in a malecontent humour) I accursed my fortune, raild on my patrones, bit my pen, and ragde in all parts like a mad man.
>
> (1:157)

Even if this bleak self-portrait offers nothing more than an embellished performance intended to elicit sympathy from his readers and money from his potential patrons—for as far as we know, this depiction may or may not correspond to the actual reality of Nashe's *experience* of his poverty at this early stage in his career—it nonetheless reveals quite a bit about how struggling writers saw themselves within a literary economy based on utility, profit, and instruction. Nashe can be in the "prime" of his "best wit," but that primacy functions in inverse proportion to his ability to produce anything of value. All his "labours" turn to "losse"; his virtuosity has no virtue; and his efforts end up being "all in vaine."

Given the self-portrait Nashe paints in its pages, *Pierce Penniless* ironically ended up being one of his most successful texts, but only if one restricts the metric for judging that success to the fact that three editions were printed within a few months after its initial publication, with two more in the following few years; Nashe himself later referred to it as "most saleable" (3:35). By other metrics, however, *Pierce Penniless* proved to be counterproductive. Its viciously biting attack on Richard Harvey helped spark Nashe's lengthy war with Richard's brother Gabriel, while its allegory of the fox and the bear also seems to have gotten Nashe into trouble, having been (mis)interpreted as a satirical criticism of one of the most powerful men in England, Sir Philip Sidney's uncle Robert Dudley, the Earl of Leicester.[82] Over the next several years, Nashe seems to have run through several patrons—Ferdinando Stanley, Lord Strange; Henry Wriothesley, the Earl of Southampton; and the Carey family—losing their favor almost as quickly as he gained it. And no less an authority than John Whitgift, the Archbishop of Canterbury—who had hired Nashe and his fellow University Wits to defend the Church of England against the anonymous Puritan writer Martin Marprelate, and for whom Nashe seems to have written his entertainment *Summer's Last Will and Testament* while he was Whitgift's guest at the archepiscopal summer palace—came down hard on his erstwhile foot soldier by outlawing both Nashe's and Harvey's texts in the infamous Bishops' Ban of 1599. Things only got worse when *The Isle of Dogs*, Nashe's lost theatrical collaboration with Ben Jonson, landed the two in hot water, causing Jonson to be thrown in jail while Nashe fled London for the coast at Yarmouth, where he wrote his final completed text, the mock-encomium *Lenten Stuffe*. Within a year or two after the publication of *Lenten Stuffe*, Nashe was dead; the circumstances surrounding his death remain a mystery.

It is not, then, that Nashe necessarily found value in the valueless, but that he dwelled, or saw himself as dwelling, in the negation of value at all costs. More specifically, that negation entailed an explicit rejection of the Horatian dictum that poetry should produce a profitable, productive, and useful pleasure. The most explicit emblem of that refusal can be found on the title page of *Have with You to Saffron Walden*, Nashe's mock biography of Gabriel Harvey and the final entry in their years-long quarrel. Beneath the title, we read the following words: "The Mott or Posie, in stead of *Omne tulit punctum:/Pacis fiducia nunquam./As much as to say, as* I sayd I would speake with/him." As I pointed out in Chapter 1, many writers of the period included on their title pages, as the "mott" (motto) or "posie" (emblem) for their work, the quintessential line from Horace: *Omne tulit punctum qui miscuit dulci utili* ("He who combines the sweet and useful wins every vote"). Nashe "in stead" discards this commonplace in favor of another motto, *Pacis fiducia nunquam*, which is part of a line in Ovid's *Tristia*: *Pax tamen interdum, pacis fiducia nunquam est* (5.2.71) ("There's peace at times, but reliance on peace, as such, never").[83] Against the simplistic pacifications of the Horatian dictum, Nashe poses as the principle of his writing the unremitting unreliability of peace. Against the demand to generate a productive and profitable pleasure, Nashe indulges in an enjoyment beyond the pleasure principle, a delight in playful antagonism and contingency that got him into trouble again and again. *Pacis fiducia nunquam*: never more than here should we remember that the phrase Nashe takes as the motto for *Have with You* was composed by Ovid as part of a lamentation written while he was in exile, having been banished to the Black Sea, by the Emperor Augustus, for a song and an error.[84]

Nashe's relentlessly futilitarian writings thus evince not only the limits of humanism but also the steep price that must be paid by any writer who strives for, if not reaches, those limits. In the ongoing trial of writing that Plato instigated and that the Renaissance raised to a fever pitch, Nashe, like Ovid before him, faces some of the heaviest charges. Nashe scholars, it seems to me, feel the constant pressure to act as his defense team. The task, then, as I see it, is to let the defense rest. Resisting the temptation to apologize for Nashe, to save him, and to justify the pleasurable excesses of his writing is no easy task; indeed, it may very well be impossible given that any writing on Nashe automatically, necessarily legitimizes him. But it is important to try, if for no other reason than Nashe himself is not only unapologetic in his futilitarian commitments, but also attuned to the potential ridiculousness or self-defeating effects of the very logic of apology itself: "If I in the beginning of my Book should haue come off with a long Apologie to excuse my selfe, it were all one as if a theefe, going to steale a horse, should deuise by the waie as he went, what to speake when he came at the gallows" (1:241). Nashe, it should be noted, has no moral investment in condemning the stealing of the horse. His skepticism is directly only against the horse thief's premature composing of final words for the gallows. The implication here is that the act of apologizing thus puts the cart before the horse. The question remains whether we can get off our high horse long enough to put that horse out to pasture.

CHAPTER 4

Spenser's Unhappy Ends

> This signifier of little, this discourse that doesn't amount to much, is like all ghosts: errant. It rolls this way and that like someone who has lost his way, who doesn't know where he is going, having strayed from the correct path, the right direction, the rule of rectitude, the norm; but also like someone who has lost his rights, an outlaw, a pervert, a bad seed, a vagrant, an adventurer, a bum.
>
> —JACQUES DERRIDA, *Dissemination*

Edmund Spenser, wrote William Butler Yeats, always loved "the journey more than its end . . . and the tale less than its telling."[1] In our current critical climate, so far removed from Yeats's moment, endorsing such a reading of Spenser means opening oneself to the charge of anachronism, of projecting backward onto the Renaissance a post-Romantic or modernist aestheticism that values art for art's sake. As Jane Grogan reminds us in her pedagogical reading of *The Faerie Queene*, the poem "takes its place in a tradition of English writing which strove to transmit the *utile* by means of the *dulce* without concealing its didactic agenda or selling out to the surface pleasures of the text."[2] Yeats's bifurcation of the journey and its end, of the tale's telling and the tale itself, hardly squares well with this "tradition of English writing," the mainstream of Renaissance humanism. Certainly one only has to mention Spenser's statements of intention in his "Letter to Raleigh"—specifically his often-quoted assertion that the "generall intention and end" of *The Faerie Queene* is to "fashion a gentleman or noble person in vertuous and gentle discipline"[3]—in order to argue that Spenser was more concerned with the "end" than Yeats would have us believe.

Despite a number of attempts to call into question the terms of the "Letter to Raleigh"—an ongoing project to which this chapter, especially later, offers a contribution—it is safe to say that invocations of intention, such as that which Grogan provides, pervade Spenser criticism in general, which seems all too willing to commit the intentional fallacy and thus to operate in the face of *la mort de l'auteur*. Even Stephen Greenblatt's *Renaissance Self-Fashioning*—the founding text of New Historicism, which has guided the direction that Spenser studies, and early modern studies in general, has taken in the last few decades—circumscribes its reading of *The Faerie Queene* within the bounds of what it calls Spenser's "stated intention."[4] According to Greenblatt's rendition of that intention, Spenser must construct a "distinction," precarious though it may be, "between a pleasure that serves some useful purpose, some virtuous end, and a pleasure that does not." This virtuous end, this "agency of purposeful direction," according to Greenblatt, is "expressed in *The Faerie Queene* as a whole by the idea of the *quest*" and is directed, heteronormatively, toward a "sexuality found in the power of love to inspire virtuous action and ultimately, with the sanctification of marriage, in the generation of offspring." The kind of generation of which Greenblatt speaks "restores the sense of linear progression to an experience that threatens to turn in upon itself, reveling"—like Narcissus, or like a Wildean aesthete, the implication seems to be—"in its own exquisite beauty." Without this restorative generation, one is left with a more insidious pleasure that "serves as its own end, that claims to be self-justifying rather than instrumental, purposeless rather than generative," a pleasure that is therefore "immoderate and must be destroyed," says Greenblatt, "lest it undermine the power that Spenser worships."[5]

Although Greenblatt's argument was published over thirty years ago, the degree to which critics have felt, and continue to feel, the need to scrutinize and interrogate his reading of the tension between pleasure and discipline in *The Faerie Queene* reveals just how difficult it is to dislodge his interpretation of the poem.[6] Perhaps that difficulty is an effect (or a cause) of the fact that when scholars have critiqued Greenblatt's discussion, they have tended to do so on the very textual site on which Greenblatt develops his claims: the Legend of Temperance. This focus on book 2 makes more than a little sense; Spenser's account of the virtue of temperance explicitly thematizes and allegorizes the questions raised by Greenblatt's discussion as well as by the "Letter to Raleigh." After all, the Legend of Temperance is, as Joseph Campana describes it, the "part of *The Faerie Queene* most explicitly concerned with the validity of aesthetic and sexual enjoyment," and it "features extraordinary figures of excessive pleasure."[7] Building on the late work of Michel Foucault—the Foucault of *The History of Sexuality* rather than the Foucault of *Discipline and Punish* preferred by earlier New Historicists—critics like Campana and Jonathan Goldberg have used the Legend of Temperance to call into question the repressive version of Spenser offered by Greenblatt (and, before him, C. S. Lewis). In doing so, however, they have also followed Foucault in seeking to redeem pleasure as a viable and valuable ethical category, claiming that Spenser's explicit representations of pleasure in the second book of *The Faerie Queene*, like Foucault's discussions of pleasure in the second volume of *The History of Sexuality*, provide "lessons in the uses of pleasure," as Campana, invoking Foucault's title, puts it.[8] Although these scholars reject Greenblatt's argument that Spenser subordinates pleasure to heteronormative ends, they nonetheless join company with Greenblatt in arguing, however implicitly, that Spenser's poem redirects pleasure toward redemptive ends more generally.

In an effort to put pressure on both the strictly disciplinary Spenser proffered by critics such as Greenblatt and the more liberated, liberating Spenser preferred by the critics who have critiqued him, I want to depart, in a manner of speaking, from book 2 in order to redirect our critical gaze from the 1590 *Faerie Queene* to the 1596 *Faerie Queene*, the second edition that added the final three completed books (the Legends of Friendship, Justice, and Courtesy), revised the ending of the Legend of Chastity, and was notably printed without the "Letter to Raleigh." If the 1590 edition of Spenser's romance can be read in Foucauldian terms as "a project in askesis," or self-discipline, as Goldberg persuasively shows,[9] then the 1596 edition can be read as a project in the ironic undoing of askesis. This chapter also departs from Foucauldian readings of Spenserian pleasure in another way: it demonstrates how this irony has everything to do with the very *forms* of romance, not just the themes of pleasure and discipline so blatant in book 2 and in recent criticism on the subject.

More than three decades have passed since Patricia Parker highlighted romance's tendency toward errancy and dilation.[10] Despite a profusion of studies on romance since the beginning of the twenty-first century, the perversity of that errancy has gone largely unexplored. It is worth revisiting such questions in light of attempts by queer theorists, both within and without early modern studies, to consider how pleasure often exceeds any use value toward which it must be aimed. In a sense, romance harnesses for early modern England its own version of what Roland Barthes calls "the pleasure potential of a perversion"; Barthes himself has in mind homosexuality and hashish ("the two H.'s," as he memorably calls them) when he writes that perversion "produces a *more*: I am more sensitive, more perceptive, more loquacious, more amused, etc."[11] The pleasure that perversion produces constitutes wasteful excess that cannot be redeemed in any economically useful way; it is an instance of hyperproductivity that can only be considered unproductive because it bursts the bounds of any normal aim toward which it might be directed. Perversions, as Sigmund Freud famously defines them in the *Three Essays on the Theory of Sexuality*, involve, like romance, both spatial and temporal errancy: they are "sexual activities which either (a) extend, in an anatomical sense, beyond the regions of the body that are designed for sexual union, or (b) linger over the intermediate relations to the sexual object which should normally be traversed rapidly on the path towards the final sexual aim [i.e., reproduction]."[12] To the extent that romance wanders, it cannot be wholly assimilated to useful ends, in the same way perversion, according to Freud, confounds the aims of reproduction. Along these lines, sexual perversion can be correlated with the kind of textual perversion by which romance stalls the narrative push toward valued and valuable ends.[13]

In order to explore these issues, I want to focus my attention in particular on book 6 of *The Faerie Queene*, the Legend of Courtesy, where Spenser's didactic aims unravel and romance errancy subsumes the ethical substance and disciplinary teleology of his plot. Grogan grants this point in her book on Spenser, but for her it is the virtue of courtesy itself, rather than romance, which effects that unraveling. Indeed, as Grogan states, romance "is not necessarily anathema to didactic poetics, particularly one as flexible and sensible as Spenser's."[14] Building on the work of Jeff Dolven, my overarching claim is that romance, especially in the Legend of Courtesy, is not necessarily *hospitable* to didactic poetics either.[15] Through its emphasis on contingency over causality, errancy over linearity, and misconduct over askesis, the Legend of Courtesy deeply qualifies the virtuous standards according to which Renaissance theorists measured the value of poetry. Exploring the legend's pleasure principle can therefore help us question the ends-oriented economy to which literature seems so often to be tied. Yet if book 6 prevents us from adhering to a strictly utilitarian and instrumental view of aesthetic pleasure, neither does it allow us to view Spenser as intentionally or unequivocally embracing pointless, polymorphously perverse pleasures. The sense of disillusionment, passivity, contingency, and failure that saturates the Legend of Courtesy's representational and formal design suspends any desire we might have to view Spenser either as a heteronormative, industrious Puritan, or as a queerly hedonistic Epicurean.

At the outset, it is worth noting that critics, editors, and teachers tend to overlook the Legend of Courtesy. This may be because the other legends of *The Faerie Queene* engage the more favored themes of early modern studies: religion in the Legend of Holiness, embodiment in the Legend of Temperance, gender in the Legend of Chastity, friendship and sexuality in the Legend of Friendship, and law and colonialism in the Legend of Justice. Courtesy and the court, while formerly central to early New Historicism, are no longer major preoccupations; in fact, early New Historicists have frequently been criticized for their interest in court politics.[16] Yet the resistance to reading the Legend of Courtesy may be more than simply a thematic or topical resistance. The Legend of Courtesy not only betrays ambivalence toward the virtue of courtesy—the point on which most scholars agree—but also puts extreme pressure on poetry's reputed ability to supply *any* "vertuous and gentle discipline." As we will see, the legend's extreme digressiveness and errancy—the false starts, wrong ways, and dead ends of its narrative structure—fundamentally contribute to its ironic suspension of Spenser's narrative intention to inculcate self-discipline. The resistance to reading book 6 may therefore be a resistance to reading the ambivalent pleasure that romance takes in error.

Unredemptive Romance

In the Legend of Courtesy, the fulfillment of Spenser's intention indeed proves difficult to achieve. Calidore, the Knight of Courtesy, serves as the moral example by which the legend attempts to fashion its readers in the ways of the titular virtue he personifies, but he famously drops out for nearly half the narrative. When the narration returns to him at long last, after following various narrative paths into digressions that lead nowhere, the reader learns that the knight has been sojourning all the while in the realm of pastoral *otium*, attracted by the charms of the damsel Pastorella. And when Calidore finally returns to his proper journey, he fails to keep the Blatant Beast, whose capture constitutes the objective of the legend's quest, under wraps. If Calidore, as the Legend of Courtesy's exemplary hero, emblematizes the object of the legend's instruction, then it is to be expected that the reader, upon finishing the legend, will have learned nothing of value. I will return to Calidore and the topic of his truancy, around which much critical debate has been generated, later in this chapter. For now, he must drop out of my own narrative nearly as abruptly as he drops out of Spenser's (I write "nearly" because I have at least signaled Calidore's departure, whereas Spenser significantly offers no such signal).

My immediate interest is directed toward one of the digressive subplots that take place during Calidore's absence from the narrative. This subplot is worth examining carefully because, despite initial appearances, it unravels the ideology of intention and action on which the forward momentum of the romance quest depends.

The middle cantos of the Legend of Courtesy follow, for the most part, the misfortunes of the knight Calepine and his lady, Serena, after the Blatant Beast bites her. Calepine, with Serena on his horse, travels in search of aid for her and is subsequently attacked and wounded by the profoundly discourteous knight Turpine. In the wake of these unfortunate events, the couple is rescued by a Salvage Man who is able to cure Calepine's wounds but not Serena's. One day when Calepine is strong enough, he leaves the Salvage Man's abode in order to take fresh air. Spenser is careful to note that the knight, as he enters the wood, is "unarm'd, as fearing neither foe nor frend,/And without sword his person to defend"; suddenly a "cruell Beare" barges out of the forest, bearing an infant "betwixt his bloodie iawes, besprinckled all with gore" (6.4.17). Calepine pursues the bear, defeats it, and rescues the bloodied infant but then quickly realizes that he is lost in the dense forest. "All that day in wandring vainely he did spend" until he comes upon a woman, Matilda, who is crying and complaining about fate and fortune (6.4.25). At Calepine's urging, Matilda reveals the "cause" of her "griefe" (6.4.33): she is the wife of Sir Bruin, who recently conquered and seized lands from a giant named Cormoraunt, but while this victory assures their "prosperitie," as Matilda puts it, they have not been blessed with "posteritie" (6.4.31), without which the lands will fall back into Cormoraunt's hands and Sir Bruin into ruin. Matilda does express a glimmer of hope, however:

> Yet was it sayd, there should to [Sir Bruin] a sonne
> *Be gotten, not begotten*, which should drinke
> And dry vp all the water, which doth ronne
> In the next brooke, by whom that feend shold be fordonne.
>
> (6.4.32)

Putting two and two together, Calepine neatly fulfills the prophecy by offering to Matilda the infant he rescued. Spenser seems to resolve the subplot as follows:

> Right glad was *Calepine* to be so rid
> Of his young charge, whereof he skilled nought:
> Ne she lesse glad; for she so wisely did,

> And with her husband vnder hand so wrought,
> That when that infant vnto him she brought,
> She made him thinke it surely was his owne,
> And it in goodly thewes so well vpbrought,
> That it became a famous knight well knowne
> And did right noble deedes, the which elswhere are showne.
>
> (6.4.38)

Setting aside for a moment the question of where those "right noble deedes" are "elswhere" shown (surely not in *The Faerie Queene*, for this is the first and last time we encounter Matilda and Sir Bruin and their only "gotten, not begotten" son), the first observation we can make about this episode is that it seems to offer, in a legend with so many loose threads, a happy ending.

Along these lines, the episode can be read as the manifestation of a particular version or understanding of romance: as an end-oriented, wish-fulfillment narrative that revolves around the miraculous recovery of displaced origins and disrupted genealogies. This redemptive reading of romance, this reading of romance *as* redemptive, forms the basis of Northrop Frye's discussions of the mode, and it constitutes romance's most recognizable avatar in contemporary criticism.[17] The narratives that follow this pattern of loss–wandering–recovery derive from the Hellenistic prose fiction of Heliodorus and others, so popular among Elizabethan writers.[18] In *The Secular Scripture*, Northrop Frye offers a catalogue of the narrative devices common to these redemptive romances: "In the Greek romances we find stories of mysterious birth, oracular prophecies about the future contortions of the plot, foster parents, adventures which involve capture by pirates, narrow escapes from death, recognition of the true identity of the hero and his eventual marriage with the heroine."[19] These narrative conventions are also recognizable as the discursive materials out of which works of dramatic tragicomedy—Shakespeare's late plays, for example—are constructed. The problematic conflation of romance with tragicomedy has no doubt reinforced a view of romance as an "end-determined" fiction, to cite Steve Mentz's use of Frank Kermode's term.[20] Yet the word "romance" was used most often in Renaissance England and Italy to refer to the expansive, digressive medieval and Italian verse poems so problematic for early modern pedagogues. Spenser's use of romance, especially in books 4, 5, and 6, draws more from these precursors—Ariosto chief among them—and from the less easily resolved contortions of *their* plots than from the coherently ended

Heliodoran paradigm so perfectly suited for popular prose fiction and for the two-hours' traffic of the stage.

Nevertheless, the episode of Matilda and Sir Bruin may be seen to exemplify the neatly resolved redemptive romance. And indeed, many critics have offered just such a reading of their story. Even Jonathan Goldberg's brief deconstructive reading of the episode in his earlier study *Endlesse Worke* highlights its neatly redemptive circularity, which operates by way of a fortuitous pun: the child passes from "beare" to "Bruin" (a name which means "brown bear") and is thus Sir Bruin's "fitting heir," as Goldberg puts it. "Matilde," he writes, "demonstrates that a child—one's own child—can be gotten even if it is not begotten."[21] Echoing Matilda's own language of "prosperitie," Humphrey Tonkin, in his study of the Legend of Courtesy, reveals just what is at stake in such narratives: "stories of the *enfance* of heroes, like Tristram and Matilda's babe, bring promise of future prosperity and social order."[22] At stake in this "promise of future prosperity and social order" is nothing less than what Lee Edelman characterizes as "the promissory note, the guarantee of futurity," the ideology of what he calls "reproductive futurism" as condensed in the figure of the Child.[23] This is the very stuff of redemptive romance, particularly as manifested on the Jacobean stage. One might, for example, briefly compare the role that Matilda and Sir Bruin's son plays in Spenser's miniromance to the function played by Mamillius, Hermione and Leontes's son, at the beginning of Shakespeare's *The Winter's Tale*. The chief difference between these two figures is that Mamillius's death, among other events, veers Shakespeare's play toward tragedy, whereas the life of Matilda and Sir Bruin's son ensures a happy ending. That very difference, however, reinforces the same ideological structure; Matilda and Sir Bruin's son "stands," like Mamillius in the words of Leonard Tennenhouse, "as the living symbol of the genealogical principle."[24] Redemptive romances such as these strive to redeem precisely this principle—what Edelman elsewhere calls "the fetishistic prestige of origin, genealogy, telos"[25]—and thus the survival of the social order and the hope of the future.

In addition, Matilda and Sir Bruin's story is graced with a happy ending not only in the colloquial sense of the word "happy," but also in a more literal, or etymological, sense, to the extent that it repeatedly emphasizes the machinery of good fortune, or hap, that produces it. This emphasis on providential fortune is another key feature of redemptive romance. Mentz, for instance, documents its centrality to the Heliodoran paradigm, and Spenser seems in this episode to be drawing on such models.[26] Fortune has the uncanny tendency to pop up whenever the narrative force of the episode breaks through whatever impasses momentarily preclude the move toward a point or end, as it does when Calepine's seemingly endless wandering finally brings him out of the forest: "Him selfe out of the forest he did wynd,/And by good fortune the plaine champion wonne" (6.4.26); or as it does when Calepine hands the baby over to Matilda: "Lo how good fortune doth to you present/This little babe, of sweete and louely face" (6.4.35). These references to fortune establish that there is a divinity that not only shapes our ends but also shapes our ends in the right direction, toward a happy ending. This recourse to fortune and providence as explanations for the episode's narrative structure is therefore animated, to a large degree, by the poem itself. But such explanations can only carry us so far. Matilda and Sir Bruin's story is resolved, thanks to providence, with a happy ending; if that is the case, though, then why does Spenser, at the moment when the bear shows up with the baby betwixt its jaws, introduce this strand of plot by characterizing it as "An hard aduenture with vnhappie end" (6.4.17)?

When Calepine arrives with babe in tow, he certainly provides an expedient resolution, as if he were a *deus ex machina*, to Matilda and Sir Bruin's story. Yet the resolution to their story is not the resolution to *his* story. It is necessary, then, to identify and schematize, as in a Venn diagram, two overlapping but no less distinct narrative arcs in this subplot: one is Calepine's, the other is Sir Bruin and Matilda's. Calepine's story is not as fortunate as the Bruins'; he is now lost, without armor, far away from his love Serena. After resolving the Bruins' story, Calepine, like Calidore, drops out of the narrative and is not reunited with Serena until several cantos later. At this point Serena has been captured by members of a Salvage Nation and is about to be cannibalistically sacrificed by them when Calepine again arrives on the scene. The poem does emphasize the role that fortune plays in reuniting the two lovers:

Now mote ye vnderstand that to this groue
Sir *Calepine* by chaunce, more then by choyce,
The selfe same euening fortune hether droue,
As he to seeke *Serena* through the woods did roue

(6.8.46)

But that reunion is (1) ironically futile, in that Calepine does not at first recognize Serena, and (2) indefinitely deferred, in that the two are never shown again despite Spenser's promise of a future continuation of their story:

So all that night to him vnknowen she past.
But day, that discouer bad and good,

> Ensewing, made her knowen to him at last:
> The end whereof Ile keepe vntill another cast.
>
> (6.8.51)

At this point canto 8 ends and the narrative returns, finally, to Calidore, never to revisit the unresolved reunion of Calepine and Serena. The recognition scene by which Serena would, in Heliodorus or Sidney or late Shakespeare, be "made knowen" to Calepine does not appear in Spenser's poem. In fact, not only does it not appear, but Spenser's narratorial intrusion at the end of the canto, precisely by promising such an ending, also draws attention to the fact that it does not appear. Calepine, then, is resolutely deprived of the kind of happy resolution bestowed upon the Bruins and characteristic of redemptive romance.

Then again, *is* the Bruins' narrative as happy, resolved, and redemptive as a first-glance reading of it would suggest? As Parker proposes, the episode "is virtually a parody of the fortunate coincidence," offering "a *reductio ad absurdum* of the romance tale and its almost perfect circular form."[27] Yet even without any intimation of parody, certain features of the story's design might also lead us to suspect the neatness of its redemptive logic. As is the case with the incompleteness of Calepine and Serena's tale, Spenser's cryptic glance at the possible continuation of the Bruins' story—the fact that the child's subsequent knightly deeds are "elswhere" shown—functions as a loose thread that never gets tied back into the sort of coherency one might expect from a redemptive romance such as this. One might plunder the prophetic dimension of the episode for a supply of at least some degree of that missing coherency. But while the prophecy, *qua* prophecy, reinforces the sense of fortune or providence guiding the events of the episode, the very terms of the prophecy qualify such explanations: "Yet was it sayd, there should to [Sir Bruin] a sonne/*Be gotten, not begotten.*" The contingency of "be gotten" opens up a gap—figuratively as well as literally (that is, at the level of the letter)—within the order of causality implied by "begotten." The phrase thereby denies the Bruins any agency in their own subplot, insofar as the child is "gotten" *to* them rather than "begotten" *by* them. If genealogy functions to secure reference to a locatable origin, the prophecy's emphasis on the contingency of that genealogy—however much that contingency may be animated by fortune or providence—reminds the reader that the child has no origin. Yet the prophecy also denies Calepine's agency in the scene insofar as the passive-voice construction erases him as the subject who "gets" the baby to the Bruins. In a legend that repeatedly emphasizes the active practice of courtesy, the way in which "The gentle minde by gentle *deeds* is knowne" (6.3.1; my italics), it is notable that this episode would emphasize that its story is something over which Calepine has little control.

I claimed earlier that the Bruins' tale turns on the survival of the social order. That survival depends on two important factors: first, the Bruins must act as if their heir were "begotten" rather than merely "gotten" (Spenser makes a point of stressing how Matilda makes Sir Bruin think the son is his own, and how they raise it as if it were their own child); second, the Bruins must inculcate askesis by using good pedagogy to raise their heir in "goodly thewes," or good manners.[28] We have just seen how the prophecy ironically disrupts the success of the first of these factors. But the poem takes great pains to stress that divine providence has a hand in assuring the second factor. Speaking of the kinds of foundlings so typical of redemptive romance, Calepine, upon handing the baby over to Matilda, says, "Therefore some thought, that those braue imps were / Here by the Gods, and fed with heauenly sap, / That made them grow so high t'all honorable hap" (6.4.36); this interpretation of the foundling narrative is readily accepted by Matilda: "The Ladie hearkening to his sensefull speach, / Found nothing that he said, vnmeet nor geason, / Having oft seene it tryde, as he did teach" (6.4.37). One assumes that the reader of *The Faerie Queene* is supposed to accept this interpretation as well, that Calepine's "teach[ing]" of Matilda is the means for teaching the reader to understand divine providence as a causal explanation for the success of askesis despite the lack of any clear origin or genealogy. Maybe so, but that interpretation is belied by the hesitancy with which Calepine introduces his redemptive reading of the scene: only a vague "some" thought that foundlings were "fed with heauenly sap." It is also belied by the passive constructions that mark the lead-up to his interpretation:

> And certes it hath oftentimes *bene seene*,
> That of the like, whose linage was vnknowne,
> More braue and noble knights *haue raysed beene*,
> As their victorious deedes haue often showen,
> Being with fame through many Nations blowen,
> Then those, which *haue bene dandled* in the lap.
>
> (6.4.36; my italics)

The lack of any agents for these verbs suggests a fictional universe in which contingency and mere circumstance replace the forms of action, intention, origin, and cause that elsewhere animate the heroic means and redemptive ends of chivalric romance.

Interestingly enough, the untethering of story and origin *in* the story of Sir Bruin and Matilda's adopted son also extends, by an uncanny coincidence, to *the story itself*. Tonkin notes that the episode is "curious primarily because it is such a strange mixture of materials, for which no single source has ever been found, nor is it likely to be found."[29] It is as if the subplot were itself an orphan, with unknown and unknowable provenance, adopted by Spenser. That fact, though, has by no means discouraged other critics from hunting for a source. In one of the few readings of the Bruins' mini-romance, Brian C. Lockey observes that "the episode alludes directly to the Old English families in Ireland," where Spenser wrote *The Faerie Queene* while serving as a colonial administrator.[30] In fact, in *A View of the Present State of Ireland*, his notorious tract on the English colonization of Ireland, Spenser makes mention, as Lockey notes, of a family called the Fitz-Ursulas ("Sons of Bears"). This echo functions as the key with which Lockey unlocks what he views as the political-allegorical significance of the episode, leading him to argue that the "Bruins, like the Fitz-Ursulas, are menaced by the impinging forces of Irish 'degeneracy,' in this case symbolized by the giant [Cormoraunt]."[31] We might notice how Lockey's attempt to locate a historical source, and thus a useful symbolic meaning, for the episode gets inscribed as a symptomatic oxymoron: "alludes directly." If an allusion is, per definition, a "covert, implied, or indirect reference" (*OED*, *s.v. "allusion,"* I.4), how could a text ever allude *directly*? My point here is not to invalidate Lockey's symbolic reading, which seems more or less plausible as far as it goes, but rather to stress how the episode itself seems to replicate the undoing of origins upon which its narrative and thematic content pivots. The contingency with which the episode ironizes askesis, pedagogy, and providence—all of which depend on an ideology of intention, source, and design—leads me to agree with Clare Regan Kinney when she states that she "cannot agree with those readers who equate the fortune of Book VI with the providence that guides events in Book I. . . . Indeed, in [book 6], the supposition that causality is at the mercy of blind chance is wholly congruent with the breakdown of moral cause and effect in a universe where the [Blatant] Beast savages innocent and guilty alike and injury is not necessarily the result of a fall into error."[32] Through its structures of contingency and passivity, the episode of Sir Bruin and Matilda provides, on every level, a strong countercurrent to the providential logic of redemption that seems, at first glance, to overdetermine not only the subplot but also *The Faerie Queene* in general.

Inaction Heroes

When considered from the perspective of dominant Renaissance ideologies, the passivity inherent in Calepine's adventures and, by extension, in

Spenser's poem itself can only be viewed in a negative light. Action is one of the primary standards by which the value of both the writing and the reading of poetry were established. When poetry is denigrated, it is denigrated as passive; when poetry is defended, it is defended as active; in both cases, then, passivity gets denigrated. Thus, when Sir Philip Sidney begins his *Defence of Poesy* with a characteristically humble dismissal of poetry, he casts both his vocation and his defense of that vocation in passive, accidental terms: "I will give you a nearer example of myself, who (I know not *by what mischance*) in these my not old years and idlest times *having slipped* into the title of a poet, *am provoked* to say something unto you in the defence of that my *unelected* vocation."[33] Whereas the situation of Sidney's *Defence* is thus written in terms of passivity, the logical argument of his defense stresses poetry's activity. All of Sidney's major statements about poetry take the same grammatical form: "poetry" and/or "poets" as the subject, followed by an active verb ("grow," "goeth," "deliver," "bestow," "imitate to teach and delight," "range," "move men," and "make them know"). The action of these activities is condensed in the very etymology of the word "poetry": *poiein*, "to make."

Sidney's strongest defense of the value of poetry rests on its ability to inspire noble action in its readers. Shortly after claiming that the "final end" of all learning is "to lead and draw us to as high a perfection as our degenerate souls, made worse by their clayey lodgings, can be capable of," Sidney asserts that "the ending end of all earthy learning" is "virtuous action" and goes on to establish poetry as the mode in which such action is best imitated.[34] How does this insistence on action work out in a given literary text? To illustrate how Sidney seems to practice, or at least model, in his fiction what he preaches in his *Defence*, I would now like to digress briefly in order to consider an early episode in the revised edition of his own romance, *The Countess of Pembroke's Arcadia*.

While staying in the house of Kalander, Musidorus, going by the name of Palladius (the name by which I will refer to him), is puzzled when his host suddenly changes countenance after receiving some sort of startling information from a servant. Kalander retreats into his study and leaves Palladius in the hands of his household staff. Palladius asks one of Kalander's stewards to explain this abrupt shift in behavior, and the steward fulfills this request by explaining how the neighboring warring Helots have captured Kalander's son, Clitophon. The tale that the steward tells sounds like a romance fiction to the extreme. A valorous young man, Argalus, comes to Arcadia and befriends Clitophon. Argalus falls in love with Clitophon's cousin, the beautiful Parthenia, but she is already betrothed to a proud, vehement man named Demagorus. When Parthenia chooses Argalus over him, Demagorus disfigures her by throwing poison all over her face; Demagorus is promptly banished, and he joins up with the Helots. The noble Argalus accepts Parthenia despite the loss of her beauty, but she flees in shame; Argalus, seeking to be revenged against Demagorus, goes in disguise among the Helots but is soon captured and held prisoner. Clitophon, attempting to rescue his good friend, is also captured. Thus, Palladius is brought up to date, and the steward ends with the following words: "I have delivered all I understand touching the loss of my lord's son, and the cause thereof: which though it was not necessary to Clitophon's case to be so particularly old, yet the strangeness of it made me think it would not be unpleasant unto you." Here Sidney gives us a chapter break; the next chapter begins: "Palladius thanked [the steward] greatly for it, being even passionately delighted with hearing so strange an accident of a knight so famous over the world as Argalus, with whom he had himself a long desire to meet: so had fame poured a noble emulation in him towards him."[35]

Demonstrating the Horatian dictum at its best, its most effective, this episode models in miniature how the incitement to action should properly work by means of a pleasurable tale. The "strange accident" of the steward's mini-romance stirs Palladius's passions but directs that "passionate delight" toward a virtuous end: it reinforces the "noble emulation" that Palladius feels for Argalus, recalling Sidney's arguments in the *Defence* that the poet will "bestow a Cyrus upon the world to make many Cyruses," and that the poet "nameth Cyrus and Aeneas no other way than to show what men of their fames, fortunes, and estates should do," for who, asks Sidney, "readeth Aeneas carrying old Anchises on his back, that wisheth not it were his fortune to perform so excellent an act"?[36] In Sidney's universe the contemporary phrase "action hero" would be redundant, for heroism *is* action. Indeed, the steward's romance inspires Palladius to assemble an army and rescue Argalus and Clitophon from the Helots' evil clutches. The episode can thus be read as the *Arcadia*'s set of instructions for reader response: Sidney's readers are taught to respond to his romance in the same way Palladius responds to the steward's romance. The proper reaction is action.

And yet the move from pleasurable tale to virtuous action in this episode is not as easy or direct as it may first appear. The fact that the move is stretched across a chapter break highlights a contingent disjunction, rather than a causal link, between the pleasure of the story and the effective profit of Palladius's action. In making this claim, I do not intend to suggest that immediate continuity is the only way of establishing causality. Rather, my point is that this kind of discontinuity is a prime way of instantiating contingency. Writing of Jane Austen's *Emma*, but in terms that apply to the materiality of any text divided into sections, chapters, or cantos, D. A. Miller asserts that "the hurdle of a chapter break, . . . like a fade-to-black in film, executes as strong an internal disconnect as the Novel has at its disposal."[37] Sidney's metaromance hesitates in this black hole, the space-time discontinuum between the telling of the tale and the response to the tale—between the tale's end and the actualization of its ends. Granted, the Horatian effect logically, as well as narratologically, succeeds across and despite the disruptiveness of this ironic split, but the split itself reveals the contingency of that success. The void or gap at the heart of the *Arcadia*'s metaromance reveals the fragility of the Horatian dictum's ends-oriented economy. The pause in the text belies the cause of the text. In the process, it rends asunder what the Horatian dictum tries so hard to render: an easy, seamless passage from poetics to ethics.

The Legend of Courtesy, as we have already begun to see, is even bolder than the *Arcadia* about opening up and locating itself within the gap between poetics and ethics. Suggesting that the link between the aesthetic and the ascetic is contingent and accidental at best, as is the case in the Matilda/Calepine subplot, the legend provides a perverse or oblique glance at the ethical system undergirding Renaissance humanist poetics. Such a reading, however, must inevitably confront the abiding question of Spenser's intentions. That is to say, the poet is quite explicit about the ethical aims and dimensions of his text, and critics have frequently used those statements of intention as a way of controlling the kinds of readings one may offer of *The Faerie Queene*. At this point, then, I would like to return from the *Arcadia* to *The Faerie Queene* in order to show how the very forms of romance—specifically, its tendency toward digression and dilation—confound Spenser's intentions.

Intermeddled Accidents

Critics have long recognized that the Legend of Courtesy poses a number of problems with regard to what Grogan calls Spenser's "didactic poetics." Yet it is striking that virtually all these critics, working from wildly varying perspectives, feel obligated to explain away those problems by appealing to some notion of intention. Responding, for example, to J. C. Maxwell's critique of Calidore's truancy, Harry Berger Jr., in a landmark essay, observes the inconclusive and unresolved nature of most of the legend's episodes. But he goes on to stress that Spenser, in writing a legend with so many loose threads, "intended a poetic effect: he *shows* poetry facing the actual world to cope with the difficult social problems of slander and courtesy, but he *knows* poetry's true work and pleasure require detachment rather than involvement." "Thus," writes Berger, "the apparent inattention Maxwell notes seems deliberate."[38] More recently, Douglas A. Northrop has noted that "the Legend of Courtesy is notable for its discontinuity." But he, too, stresses that such discontinuities "create the very tone and character of the book; they are clearly intentional."[39] Critics have anchored the wanderings and uncertainties of the Legend of Courtesy if not to a generalized notion of authorial intention, then at least to some kind of historical, moral, or philosophical cause: Fortune, pastoral, courtesy, Queen Elizabeth, Sir Walter Raleigh, Ireland, Calvinist theology, and, above all, the vision of the Graces in canto 10, are all topics favored by critics who seek to reorient Spenser's poetics to a definable origin and telos.

The issue here is that Spenser is one of the few early modern poets whose intentions are so explicit. The poet makes a cameo appearance in Lodowick Bryskett's *A Discourse on Civill Life*, published in 1606 though written much earlier, outlining for his auditors a map of *The Faerie Queene*'s master plan: the poem will "represent all the moral vertues, assigning to euery vertue, a Knight to be patron and defender of the same: in whose actions and feates of armes and chiualry, the operations of that vertue, whereof he is the protector, are to be expressed, and the vices & unruly appetites that oppose themselues against the same, to be beaten downe and ouercome."[40] And then, of course, there is the "Letter to Raleigh," in which Spenser is even more explicit (and elaborate) about his intentions, about the "generall end" of the poem and about the means he uses to get there.

As critics like Gordon Teskey and Jonathan Goldberg have helped us to see, however, there are many problems with using these statements of intention as keys to decoding or decrypting the poem as a whole.[41] For one thing, the "Letter to Raleigh" was not reprinted with the 1596 edition of the poem. Raleigh's disgrace at court in the intervening years between the publication of the two editions probably played a significant role in the letter's absence from the second edition, but a lot more than that may be at stake. Few readers of *The Faerie Queene* can fail to notice that the tone of the second set of three books constitutes a marked departure from the purposefulness of the first three books.[42]

The standard hypothesis is that Spenser became disillusioned with his project after presenting the poem at court following the publication of the first edition. Consider the first stanza of the Legend of Friendship:

> The rugged forhead that with graue foresight
> Welds kingdomes causes, and affairs of state,
> My looser rimes (I wote) doth sharply wite,
> For praising loue, as I haue done of late,
> And magnifying louers deare debate;
> By which fraile youth is oft to follie led,
> Through false allurement of that pleasing baite,
> That better were in vertues discipled,
> Then with vaine poems weeds to haue their fancies fed.
>
> (4.proem.1)

The "rugged forhead" is often identified, in annotated editions of the poem, as a sly allusion to Sir William Cecil, Lord Burghley.[43] When Spenser presented *The Faerie Queene* at court, did Burghley dismiss it as a "vaine" toy? Did Spenser take such criticism to heart, giving up, over the course of the 1596 edition, on his moral purpose? If so, is his giving up truly a sign of disenchantment and failure? Or is it, perhaps, a bolder response to Burghley's charges: *Yes, you're right—it's a vain poem, but that shouldn't matter*? These questions are not answerable without recourse to speculation about Spenser's intentions. Whatever the real case may be, the "Letter to Raleigh" was not reprinted when Spenser revised *The Faerie Queene* for the 1596 edition. This simple fact is sufficient to suggest that the letter's assertion of intention is itself no longer sufficient to account for the project and design of *The Faerie Queene*'s second installment.

Even if it had been included, the letter's internal ambiguities and ambivalences make it difficult for us to adopt its content as a programmatic statement of intention. To put the point bluntly: Spenser's intent may be explicit, but it is far from clear. In his chapter on *The Faerie Queene* in *The Seeds of Things*, Goldberg calls attention to the letter's rhetorical indeterminacies: the stuttering repetition of "gentle" in the phrase "to fashion a *gentle*man or noble person in vertuous and *gentle* discipline"; the opacity of the word "end" (to say nothing of the word "generall") in the phrase "the generall end . . . of all the booke"; and the possibility, as Goldberg puts it, that "the person being fashioned in this text may be the person being fashioned in this text, not its reader but the characters being read."[44] To this list of obscurities we could also add a pair of comments that critics like Teskey and Goldberg never mention, comments that run counter to, even as they run alongside, the whole notion of intention. At the outset of the letter, Spenser promises to "discouer vnto" Raleigh the poem's "general intention and meaning, which in the whole course thereof I haue fashioned, without expressing of any particular purposes or by-accidents therein occassioned" (714). Spenser returns to the notion of "accidents" at the end of the letter when, after outlining the main plots of each of the first three legends, he writes that "by occasion thereof, many other aduentures are intermedled, but rather as Accidents, then intendments" (718).

The *OED* defines the word "*accident*" (n., I.1.b) as "anything that happens without foresight or expectation; an unusual event, which proceeds from some unknown cause, or is an unusual effect of a known cause; a casualty, a contingency."[45] Casual rather than causal, untimely rather than opportune, an accident fractures the "foresight," the agency, by which self-government and state government operate effectively. It makes sense, then, that Burghley, that "rugged forhead that with graue *foresight* / Welds kingdomes *causes*," would be so annoyed by the 1590 *Faerie Queene*. And how much more irritated would he have been by the second installment? In the 1590 edition, the accidents tend to be kept to a minimum, redirected to the poem's purposeful telos. In the 1596 edition—and in particular in the Legend of Courtesy—the "intermedled accidents" usurp the poem's "intendments."

"Intermedled accidents" nicely designates the source of romance's pleasure. As Goldberg explains in his earlier study *Endlesse Worke*, the "incitement to pleasure" that the "Letter to Raleigh" "alludes to—the variety of stories, their endless interconnected play, the deferral of an explanation of a beginning—putting off the problem of connecting narrative and meaning, or of finding what is central and peripheral, the structural design that defers the beginning until the end . . . these pleasures assure a principle of frustration."[46] Notice how Goldberg's grammar performs the same "principle of frustration" that it identifies in *The Faerie Queene*. His sentence enacts at a grammatical level what the Legend of Courtesy enacts at a narrative level; like the subordinate clauses of Goldberg's sentence, the legend's virtually parenthetical subplots (of which the episode of Matilda and Sir Bruin is a prime example) take over the substance of the plot, in a digressive and interruptive form that we can recognize as *parabasis* thanks to our tour, in Chapter 3, through the work of Roger Ascham and Thomas Nashe. The parabases of romance are the very bases of romance—the roots of its delights as well as its dangers—and such pleasures appear to grow increasingly out of control for Spenser.

The degree to which these parabases pose a problem for Renaissance poetics can be measured by considering how Sir John Harington, in the defense of poetry printed with his 1591 translation of Ariosto's *Orlando furioso*, defends the poem against the charge that such disruptions make the poem defective. Just when the main terms of his defense have run their course, Harington addresses two more final "reproofs" against Ariosto:

> There follows only two reproofs, which I rather interpret two peculiar praises of this writer, above all that wrote before him in this kind. One, that he breaks off narrations very abruptly, so as indeed a loose unattentive reader will hardly carry away any part of the story. But this doubtless is a point of great art, to draw a man with a continual thirst to read out the whole work, and toward the end of the book to close up the diverse matters briefly and cleanly. If Sir Philip Sidney had counted this a fault, he would not have done so himself in his *Arcadia*. Another fault is that he speaketh so much in his own person by digression, which they say also is against the rules of poetry, because neither Homer nor Virgil did it. Methinks it is a sufficient defence to say, Ariosto doth it. Sure I am, it is both delightful and very profitable, and an excellent breathing-place for the reader. And even as if a man walked in a fair long alley, to have a seat or resting place here and there is easy and commodious, but if at the same seat were planted some excellent tree, that not only with the shade should keep us from the heat but with some pleasant and right wholesome fruit should allay our thirst and comfort our stomach, we would think it for the time a little paradise. So are Ariosto's morals and pretty digressions sprinkled through his long work, to the no less pleasure than profit of the reader.[47]

The moves of the defense are nothing short of clever. Harington simply revalorizes Ariosto's supposed narrative vices as narrative virtues. He turns the charge itself into a defense against the charge: the fact that *Ariosto* digresses seems to be "sufficient" justification for the fact that Ariosto *digresses*. And in addition to shifting the blame from the poet to the "loose unattentive reader," Harington also removes the taint of Italianate associations from Ariosto's parabases by locating the same kind of disruptive structures in Sidney's *Arcadia*.

As agile as Harington's logic is, his rhetoric betrays some unquestioned presuppositions. In the case of the first charge—the accusation of interruption—Harington implies that the dilated errancy of romance is fine as long as the poet "close[s] up the diverse matters briefly and cleanly." In the case of the second charge—the accusation of intrusion—Harington's elaboration of a pastoral conceit suggests that the *otium* of authorial pauses is a remedy; the pleasure provided by Ariosto's parabases is an alleviating kind of pleasure, thus rendering the way to profit easier to follow. Spenser's Legend of Courtesy gives the lie to both of these assumptions. In the first case, the ending of the legend is so drawn out and messy as to undermine any end(s)-oriented justification for errancy. In the second case, the legend characterizes as dangerous the kind of pastoral retreat on which Harington relies for his defense. The Legend of Courtesy suggests that if rest is a remedy, it is a remedy for a problem of which it is itself a cause. According to the legend's ambivalent poetics, the "shade" that keeps us from tedious heat can only ever be shady.[48] It is not that the Legend of Courtesy's "subject," to quote Patricia Parker, "seems to be *becoming* the ambivalences of romance itself";[49] it is, rather, that the intermeddled accidents of the legend's plot retrospectively establish the entire poem's subject as *always already having been* the ambivalences of romance. In the Legend of Courtesy, Spenser pushes to the extreme an interruptive impulse or drive—the very pleasure of romance—that the previous books try so hard to subdue.

To claim, however, that Spenser himself "pushes" this impulse is to ascribe to him a degree of agency that the "Letter to Raleigh," like the Legend of Courtesy, seems to want to deny: "by occasion thereof, many other aduentures *are intermedled*." The negation of authorial intention, agency, and authority has profound implications for the ending of the Legend of Courtesy. One might expect that the poem has reached its natural end when Calidore returns to his initial quest and successfully captures the Blatant Beast. But in one of the most astonishing and puzzling moments in all of early modern literature, Spenser confounds this expectation for ending by noting, with palpable disillusionment, that the Blatant Beast escapes Calidore's control. Still more, no subsequent knights are able to recapture the Beast, who now "raungeth through the world againe," hurling slanders at everyone regardless of "degree or state" (6.12.39–40). At this point *The Faerie Queene*, like a Möbius strip, twists upon itself in a recursive fashion, metatextually constituting itself as an object of the Beast's slanders:

> Ne spareth he most learned wits to rate,
> Ne spareth he the gentle Poems rime,
> But rends without regard of person or of time.
>
> Ne may this homely verse, of many meanest,
> Hope to escape his venemous despite,
> More then my former writs, all were they clearest,

From blamefull blot, and free from all that wite,
With which some wicked tongues did it backebite,
And bring into a mighty Peres displeasure,
That neuer so deserued to endite.
Therefore do you my rimes keep better measure,
And seeke to please, that now is counted wisemens threasure.

(6.12.40–41)

Thus, the poem ends with an invocation of pleasure as the only end that a poem is capable not just of successfully reaching but of aiming toward at all. In an essay on book 6 as a conclusion to *The Faerie Queene*, Maria R. Rohr Philmus argues that the closing lines of the legend "constitute an express rejection of the *utile* part of the aesthetic equation." However, such a rejection should not be read as what Philmus calls "a momentous *decision* on Spenser's part."[50] Closer to the mark is the following statement by Jeff Dolven: "What has happened to the poem at the end of Book VI is that it has capitulated to the enemies of romance by conforming to their critique, finally allowing itself to become the sort of idle, profitless toy that the schoolmasters deplored."[51] Given the pattern of passivity that pervades the legend, it is more accurate to say that the abandonment of a Horatian poetics is something that happens *to* Spenser and his poem, that the capitulation to the pleasure of the text is one of the many accidents by which the text loses control over itself and its aim to teach the ways of discipline.

The Poetry of Misconduct

In order to wrap up my discussion of the Legend of Courtesy, I would like to end not with the discussion of the ending that I just ended, but rather with a return to Calidore, who has been as absent from this chapter as he is from the Legend of Courtesy itself. Any discussion of Calidore must address the deficiency of his role in the poem as well as his retreat from service into the realm of pastoral and his pursuit of Pastorella. That truancy can easily be explained by calling attention to the primary ideological conflict that runs throughout the legend: a tension between a view of the court as a source of chivalry, courtesy, and virtue, on the one hand, and as a source of flattery, inconstancy, and what Calidore calls "gay shows" and "vaine shadowes," on the other (6.9.27). Spenser establishes this tension at the beginning of the poem through a play on the etymology of the word "courtesy." The proem ends with an invocation to Queen Elizabeth and a reference to the "Faire Lords and Ladies" who both "dwell" in and "adorne" Elizabeth's "Court, where courtesies excell" (6.proem.7), but this statement, which brings out the courtesy in the court by bringing out the "court" in *court*esy, is both repeated and qualified by the following line, at the very beginning of the first canto: "Of Court it seemes, men Courtesie doe call, / For that it there most vseth to abound" (6.1.1). The use of the word "seemes" introduces a tone of hesitancy with respect to the court. And this hesitancy ripples across the legend, so that Calidore's retreat from court to pastoral may be at least partially explained or excused.

What interests me about Calidore's truancy, however, isn't the question of whether or not it constitutes a moral lapse, an exemplum of misconduct that flies in the face of any ascetic virtue the poem wishes to impart, but rather the way in which his misconduct is tied up with the form of the poem itself. Indeed, it is difficult to attach the fault of errancy solely to the knight represented in the poem; the narration *of* the poem seems to be implicated as well. The first stanza of the legend admits the overwhelming attractions of the pleasure in error:

> The waies, through which my weary steps I guyde,
> In this delightfull land of Faery,
> Are so exceeding spacious and wyde,
> And sprinckled with such sweet variety,
> Of all that pleasant is to eare or eye,
> That I nigh rauisht with rare thoughts delight,
> My tedious trauell doe forget thereby;
> And when I gin to feele decay of might,
> It strength to me supplies, and chears my dulled spright.
>
> (6.proem.1)

Only at the end of the stanza, in the last two lines, does Spenser unequivocally characterize the pleasure in error as the source of much-needed reparative relief. It is thus a means to an end, a way of making Spenser's "tedious trauell" more bearable (the pun on travel/travail is as unmistakable as it is frequent in Spenser). Yet before the last two lines, that pleasure is cast in less comforting terms: the path of romance is "*exceeding* spacious and wyde," and its "sweet variety" leaves the narrator "rauisht." Moreover, the ambiguity of the phrase "My tedious trauell doe forget thereby" leaves it unclear whether the pleasure of the text leads Spenser to forget merely the *tediousness* of his "trauell" or leads him, like Calidore, to forget his "trauell" altogether.[52]

At the beginning of the legend's final canto, Spenser, using one of the most common emblems of, in, and for romance, retrospectively justifies both Calidore's delay and his own:

> Like as a ship, that through the Ocean wyde
> Directs her course vnto one certaine cost,
> Is met of many a counter winde and tyde,
> With which her winged speed is let and crost,
> And she her selfe in stormie surges tost;
> Yet making many a borde, and many a bay,
> Still winneth way, ne hath her compasse lost:
> Right so it fares with me in this long way,
> Whose course is often stayd, yet neuer is astray.
>
> For all that hetherto hath long delayd
> This gentle knight, from sewing his first quest,
> Though out of course, yet hath not bene mis-sayd,
> To shew the courtesie by him profest,
> Euen vnto the lowest and the least.
> But now I come into my course againe,
> To his atchieuement of the *Blatant beast*;
> Who all this while at will did range and raine,
> Whilst none was him to stop, nor none him to restraine.
>
> (6.8.1–2)

The defense may belatedly and retrospectively excuse both poet and character, but the very need for a defense fails to neutralize the suspicion that some kind of moral fault has been committed. Through the very act of justifying the actions of *both* the knight *and* the poet, the poem calls into question both their actions—and for the same reasons. Regardless of whether Calidore and/or Spenser are to be condemned and/or excused for traveling "out of course," these two stanzas establish the inextricability of their "stayd" courses.

What is at stake in thus aligning Spenser's poetics with Calidore's errancy? A great deal seems to be at issue, for critics have frequently recoiled from such an alignment. In his 1936 study *The Allegory of Love*, C. S. Lewis warns his readers that the "greatest mistake that can be made about [the Legend of Courtesy] is to suppose that Callidore's long delay among the shepherds is a pastoral truancy of Spenser's from his moral intention."[53] Hyperbolic though it may seem, Lewis's attempt to create a distance between Calidore and Spenser finds some support in the legend itself. At the beginning of canto 10, for instance, the narration creates that distance by censuring Calidore:

> Who now does follow the foule *Blatant Beast*,
> Whilest *Calidore* does follow that faire Mayd [i.e., Pastorella],
> Vnmindfull of his vow and high behest,
> Which by the Faery Queene was on him layd,
> That he should neuer leave, nor be delayd
> From chacing him, till he had it attchieued?
>
> (6.10.1)

But if Calidore is truly being censured here, then so should the poem. Read metatextually, the initial rhetorical question this stanza poses highlights the fact that *no one*, certainly neither Calidore nor Spenser, "follow[s] the foule *Blatant Beast*." Rather than making a beeline toward the telos of the main quest, both the knight *and* the poem display the interruptive tendency to pursue the intermeddled accidents that mark the journey's errant path. As William Nestrick writes, "Again and again, Spenser or one of his characters undrapes an intimate scene of restful delight. Such scenes exemplify the sweet variety that Spenser *and Calidore* find along their tedious way. Calidore does the same things that Spenser claims he himself is doing in this book."[54] The Legend of Courtesy thereby exemplifies Yeats's claim that Spenser was more interested in the journey than its end, and the tale less than the telling; Calidore functions as the figure within the poem that emblematizes this preference.

Given this structural redoubling whereby Calidore's truancy figures the poem's own errancy, it is difficult to read the Legend of Courtesy as a pedagogical exercise in discipline and courtesy—which is to say, as a conduct manual of the sort so popular in Renaissance culture. Nancy Armstrong and Leonard Tennenhouse have argued that "the literature of conduct and the conduct of the writing known as literature share a same history."[55] While literature and conduct literature may share, as Armstrong and Tennenhouse's chiasmus indicates, a same history—a history that stretches back to antiquity and forward to modernity, with important stops in the Renaissance along the way—the Legend of Courtesy ironically exposes the ways in which they may not share the same function or effects, despite what Spenser claims in the "Letter to Raleigh."[56] If *The Faerie Queene* as a whole sets out to work as a narrative of discipline, relying on the disciplinary force that *is* narrative to straighten out, in order to make use out of, the eruptions and interruptions of vain, errant, and ironic pleasure that constitute romance's hallmark, then the misconduct exemplified in and by Spenser's Legend of Courtesy provides a glimpse into how we might begin the impossible task of shuffling off this moral coil. Then again, the passivity inscribed throughout the legend denies any such agency, suggesting the ways in which romance, regardless of our intentions, might shuffle this moral coil off of us.

CHAPTER 5

Beyond Sublimation

But if something were to remain . . . once inscribed and interwoven, something that would not allow itself to be sublated [*relevé*] in the course of the philosophical presentation, would that something necessarily take the form of that which *falls away* [*la tombée*]? And what about such a fall? Couldn't it be read otherwise than as the excrement of philosophical essentiality—not in order to sublate it back into the latter, of course, but in order to learn to take it differently into account?

—JACQUES DERRIDA, *Dissemination*

In his 1762 *Letters on Chivalry and Romance*, Bishop Richard Hurd counted John Milton as an English inheritor of the "Gothic Romance":

> The greatest geniuses of our own and foreign countries, such as Ariosto and Tasso in Italy, and Spenser and Milton in England, were seduced by these barbarities of their forefathers; were even charmed by the Gothic Romances. Was this caprice and absurdity in them? Or, may there not be something in the Gothic Romance peculiarly suited to the views of a genius, and to the ends of poetry? And may not the philosophic moderns have gone too far, in their perpetual ridicule and contempt of it?[1]

Hurd's placement of Milton within a genealogy of romance poets contradicts Milton's own statements against romance, in *Paradise Lost*, in favor of the sublime religious content that more "justly gives heroic name/To person or to poem."[2] But the problem is in fact even more intricate than this simple contradiction suggests. Notice how romance exerts a textual effect in Hurd's discussion: he uses a vocabulary found *in* romance ("seduced," "charmed") to depict the influence *of* romance on poets such as

Milton and his predecessors in the heroic tradition. Milton is seduced by romance just as the heroes and heroines within romance are seduced by enchanters ranging from Homer's Circe to Milton's Satan.[3] By the logic of this analogy, Milton was led astray much as Eve was led astray, enchanted into using a form that his political, theological, and philosophical convictions—indeed, the very culture of his times—should have led him to forsake.

With these tensions in mind, we can begin to understand the vacillating rhetoric Milton uses throughout his career to characterize romance. In *Eikonoklastes*, for example, he takes aim at the "vain amatorious poem of Sir Philip Sidney's *Arcadia*" and more generally at what he pointedly calls the "polluted orts and refuse of *Arcadias* and romances."[4] Romance comes under attack here because of its association with the debased monarch: the context of the strike is Milton's condemnation of King Charles I, who appropriated the "ethnic" (that is, pagan) prayer of Pamela from book 3 of Sidney's romance.[5] Milton thus characterizes the *Arcadia* as "a book in that kind full of worth and wit, but among religious thoughts and duties not worthy to be named, nor to be read at any time without good caution, much less in time of trouble and affliction to be a Christian's prayer-book."[6] Just a few years earlier, though, in his *Apology for Smectymnuus*, Milton praised romance, recounting how his "younger feet wandered . . . among those lofty fables and romances, which recount in solemn cantos the deeds of knighthood founded by our victorious kings, and from hence had in renown over all Christendom" (851). Although such romances, he writes, may "to many others have been the fuel of wantonness and loose living," they provided for him instruction in the ways of chastity, that virtue so important to Milton throughout his career, that virtue which, as he characterizes it, "abhors the society of bordellos" (851). By the time of *Paradise Lost*, however, the "lofty fables and romances" become the "long and tedious havoc" of "fabled knights/In battles feigned" (9.30–31). Is Milton's relationship with romance so simply teleological, so easily cast in the form of a conversion narrative that displays a development from youthful indulgence to mature rejection? Or could it be that Milton, in the words of Steven Knapp, "is of Arthur's party without quite knowing it"?[7]

The problem of Milton's relationship to romance deserves unpacking because it constitutes an intriguing piece of, and thus provides an interesting way into, a much larger conflict that has divided the reception of the poet's work for the past several hundred years. Knapp's statement tropes on William Blake's well-known claim in *The Marriage of Heaven and Hell* that Milton "was a true Poet and of the Devil's party without knowing it."[8]

One of the many questions raised by this infamous assertion is how we should read Blake's "and," whether as additive (Milton was a true poet and *additionally* of the devil's party) or as causative (Milton was a true poet and *therefore* of the devil's party). In any case, Blake's radical appraisal clues us in to the perpetual tension between the pleasurable means and didactic ends of Milton's epic.[9] This is a tension that continues to structure the debates within Milton studies. "The argument over *Paradise Lost*," wrote Patricia Parker in 1979, "has most frequently been a conflict of historical views, between adherents of Blake's 'Of the Devil's Party without knowing it' and the attempt to reconstruct a more theological—or seventeenth-century—reading, behind, or beyond, the Romantic distortions."[10] The predominantly historicist climate of the several decades since Parker made this observation might lead us to believe that the second position—the "more theological" or seventeenth-century reading—has held sway.[11] In the interest of rescuing Milton's poetry from the charge of apolitical escapism (the failed revolutionary retreats into vain poetry), critics tend to align his poetic revolution with the politico-theological revolution in which he played such an important role. Such assumptions, for example, underwrite David Scott Kastan's claim that *Paradise Lost* is the "answer" to the question, "What is a Protestant and a republican epic?"[12]

But what if *Paradise Lost* were the question itself instead of the answer? To pose this question—that is, to pose the poem *as* a question—is to begin to sketch an oblique and counterintuitive portrait of Milton; it is to begin to reveal, in the words of Stephen Guy-Bray, "not the utterly self-assured poet who is still the prevalent image of Milton, but rather a more tentative poet, trying to work out the relation between his poetics and his religious duty."[13] Such a "tentative" poet is the version of Milton that I will explore in this chapter. Where much Milton criticism works under the assumption that Milton's poetry is coextensive with his theological and political commitments, my goal here is to hold open the gap between his poetics and those commitments for as long as possible in order to analyze elements of his poetry that get lost or rejected in the standard attempt to read Milton's texts as aimed toward redemption. In doing so, I would seem to join the rising chorus of recent Milton scholars, the self-styled "New Milton Critics," who have sought to denaturalize the conventional reading of Milton as a totalizing poet.[14] This attempt to track an uncertain version of the poet has been made most strongly in Peter C. Herman's *Destabilizing Milton*. Because Herman's study exemplifies the assumptions and claims of this recent wave of critics, I want to begin by briefly examining his argumentative maneuvers in order to register my distance from his claims and to position my own argument in the more general currents of Milton studies.

Falling and Failing

One of the most marked characteristics of the New Milton Criticism is its rehabilitation of William Empson's controversial book, *Milton's God.* Empson's claim that *Paradise Lost* "is not good in spite of but especially because of its moral confusions" is itself a rehabilitation of what he pointedly calls "the manly and appreciative attitude of Blake and Shelley," a rehabilitation, that is, of the Romantic reading of Milton that, at the time Empson was writing, "ha[d] been held in contempt since the last bold literary revolution, spearheaded by Mr T. S. Eliot."[15] The rebellious, or at least uncertain, Milton notoriously constructed first by the Romantics and then in the twentieth century by Empson would therefore stand against what Herman identifies as the three-pronged dominant paradigm of conventional Milton criticism: that "Milton is a poet of absolute, unqualified certainty"; that "*Paradise Lost* coheres"; and that the "critic's task is to make the poem cohere."[16]

While Empson represents a strong challenge to this paradigm, the paradigm itself, according to Herman, is embodied in and by the work of Stanley Fish—not only in Fish's classic study *Surprised by Sin*, but also in his more recent, boldly titled *How Milton Works*. Throughout his career, Fish presents a Milton "without either contradiction or tension," in his words, a Milton fixed on a single theological purpose: to achieve a union with deity.[17] Fish directs his argument against precisely the alternative line of criticism that begins with Blake and extends to Empson and more recent critics. Hence, he asserts that "conflict, ambivalence, and open-endedness—the watchwords of a criticism that would make Milton into the Romantic liberal some of his readers want him to be—are not constitutive features of the poetry but products of a systematic misreading of it, a misreading performed *in* the poetry by Comus and Satan, a misreading *of* the poetry as old as Blake and Shelley" and as new, he goes on to show, as a whole slew of contemporary Miltonists who "reinstate and reinvoke the dualism Milton so often rejects."[18] In declaring that Milton's poetry is coherent, certain, unified, total, and ultimately meaningful, Fish, for Herman, thereby reproduces the principal and prevailing claims of Milton scholarship. Following Empson, by contrast, Herman attempts to destabilize such coherency, revealing how *Paradise Lost* is structured by incertitude.

In claiming, however, that Fish never deviates from his totalizing interpretation of Milton, Herman sets up a totalizing interpretation of Fish. In other words, Herman does to Fish what he accuses Fish of doing to Milton.[19] Indeed, Fish doesn't so *simply* do to Milton what Herman says he does. In fact, throughout *How Milton Works* Fish acknowledges how Milton's single-minded project suffers from a precariousness that takes the form of a conflict between means and ends.[20] In a footnote to his discussion, Herman grants that "Fish gives a much more nuanced view" of Milton, later in *How Milton Works*, by pointing out patterns of indeterminacy. "Yet," Herman writes, "Fish contains these subversions, as it were, by concluding *How Milton Works* saying that 'everything that many readers find interesting in Milton's work—crises, conflicts, competing values, once-and-for-all dramatic moments—proceeds from error and is finally unreal.'"[21]

But *How Milton Works* doesn't actually conclude with this claim. Fish goes on to point out that, because it is the ground of history, error is the condition through which, in a postlapsarian universe, we *must* experience the world; "its attractions," he writes, "are therefore as 'natural' as they are fatal to entry into true life."[22] The necessary task of standing outside error and history, Fish acknowledges,

> is not a requirement that anyone can fulfill; but what one can do . . . is continue to be carried within the vehicles of time, plot, history, politics, projects, objects, discourses, but in a way that uses them—figuralizes them—rather than enjoys them for their own sake.
>
> This is what Milton does both *in* his poetry and prose and *with* his poetry and prose, which are themselves, after all, material forms of the kind that embody the ever-present danger of mistaking the historically real for the really real. The danger, Milton believes, must be engaged and even courted if it is to be (even temporarily) overcome; the forms that invite us to identify with their limitedness must be re-seen as signs of what they cannot contain. Nothing is to be rejected as a means; everything (except for the really real) is to be rejected as an end.[23]

What Fish presumably intends to say when he writes "This is what Milton does" is that Milton uses errant postlapsarian forms not for their own sake but as a means to more sublime ends. Yet it is curious that the immediate antecedent for Fish's "This" is "enjoys them for their own sake." Given his project, Fish hardly means to suggest that Milton's poetry and prose indulge in the pleasure in error for its own sake. Milton, especially Fish's Milton, is no Thomas Nashe. Nevertheless, the incertitude of Fish's own language—an incertitude that Herman's totalizing reading of Fish overlooks—performs the dangerous possibility of error that Milton, as Fish demonstrates, tries so hard to guard against. Fish *actually* concludes his study, despite what Herman claims and implies, with a bleak assertion of that danger's power: "Everything in the poetry provides the material and the occasion for going down another, disastrous, path. . . . The discipline is so severe that any one of us, including Milton and even the Son of God, is only half a beat away from relaxing it and so losing Paradise again."[24] Fish himself relaxes the discipline when, in half a beat, his ambiguous demonstrative pronoun allows for the Romantic counterinterpretation against which he positions his argument.

I've critiqued Herman's critique of Fish in order to show how, all appearances to the contrary, my own understanding of Milton's poetics of incertitude draws more of its inspiration from Fish's argument than from Herman's. I agree with Fish that Milton is a poet with totalizing intentions, but I wish to pry open, as wide as possible, the futilitarian gap between means and ends to which Fish's more nuanced conception of Milton points us. It is a matter of recognizing, then, not that Milton was of the devil's party without knowing it (the rebellious interpretation is no less a totalizing reading than the orthodox interpretation), but that his work is both formed and deformed around the possibility that he *may* be of the devil's party. The risk of falling, and thus failing, is inextricable from Milton's sublime intentions, not in spite of the fact but precisely because those intentions are so lofty and totalizing. Indeed, it would not be too tongue-in-cheek to claim that Milton's work is constantly haunted by the dangers of getting high, the risk that he himself "might err in things too high, / And no advantage gain," as Raphael warns Adam in *Paradise Lost* (8.121–22). This seems to have been a concern for Milton even from a young age. In "At a Vacation Exercise," for instance, he evokes his desire to be raised to sublime heights, "Such where the deep transported mind may soar / Above the wheeling poles, and at Heav'n's door / Look in, and see each blissful deity" (33–35), but he then chastises his Muse for such presumption: "But fie my wand'ring Muse, how thou dost stray!" (53). As this early poem makes clear, a union with deity may be an escape from vanity and error, but the vertical path required to achieve such a transcendent union may itself be a form of vanity and error, of "wand'ring" beyond bounds.

Milton's palpable fear of this potential risk—the possibility that his ambitious ends, however motivated by piety, will prove to have been vain in both senses of the word, making him into an example of prideful ambition and self-regard that will ultimately plunge him down into the abyss of pure futility—helps to account for the unique stylistic features of *Paradise Lost*. In his 1861 essay "On Translating Homer," Matthew Arnold characterized one key aspect of the poem's style—its utter fullness—in salient terms:

> Milton charges himself so full with thought, imagination, knowledge, that his style will hardly contain them. He is too full-stored to show us in much detail one conception, one piece of knowledge; he just shows it to us in a pregnant allusive way, and then presses on to another; and all this fulness, this pressure, this condensation, this self-constraint, enters into his movement, and makes it what it is—noble, but difficult and austere. . . . In reading Milton, you never lose the sense of laborious and condensed fullness.[25]

The qualities that Arnold describes here are perhaps best understood as constituting Milton's delaying tactics, his way of grappling with the sheer ambition of his project. At the level of its words (the puns, the neologisms), its lines (the caesuras and enjambments), its syntax (the amplifications and circumlocutions), its narrative structure (the delays, digressions, and flashbacks), and its wide range of reference (the "pregnant" allusiveness and display of erudition, the encyclopedic tour through countless genres and precursor texts), *Paradise Lost* displays a poetic fullness that, however much it is meant to service the divine fullness for which it aims, also works to defer its attainment of that aim.

Given the admittedly terrifying ambition required of any scholarly project that aims to understand not only the ambitious nature of Milton's own aims, but also his ambivalence about that ambition, it is difficult for commentators on *Paradise Lost* to avoid replicating the rhetorical and stylistic forms Milton employs. Accordingly, the path of my argument as it continues to unfold will be ineluctably wide-ranging and errant. Yet there is at least one key idea that will, I hope, unite in the end the various threads of the discussion that follows—namely, the precariousness of what I will call Milton's poetics of "*relève*ation." By this term I mean to evoke at once a range of notions, including elevation, revelation, relevance, relation, relief, and *la relève*. This last word, *la relève*, is Derrida's French translation for Hegel's *Aufhebung*—normally translated into English as "sublation" or "sublimation"—which designates, as the term is conventionally understood, the synthetic moment of the dialectic that at once raises, annuls, purifies, and recuperates negativity in the progressive movement of Spirit. I will track the interplay of all these tropes as they crisscross the discursive domains of Hegelian idealism, Christian theology, alchemy, (e)sc(h)atology, the aesthetics of sublimity, poststructuralist theory, and Milton's own body of work.[26]

However disparate these different contexts may appear to be, they all revolve, however obliquely, around a complicated desire for transcendence and can therefore help us critique the need for a dialectical deliverance from the possibility of vanity, error, and negativity. In the specific case of Milton, I argue throughout against this desire—against the temptation, that is, to resolve the tensions in Milton's poetry dialectically. I do so by attending to the "polluted orts and refuse," in Milton's own words, that inevitably remain or fall away after the purifying process denoted by the dialectic works its effects, not with the aim of sublating such remainders (to borrow from the epigraph to this chapter) but in order to take them differently into account. The remainder of this chapter is fashioned, then, according to a falling, as opposed to rising, pattern: I begin with the sublimity of Milton's lofty goals and I end in the bowels of Chaos and Hell, where, I suggest, we can find the grisliest analogies for the potential vanity and vain potential of poetic creation.

Vantage Points

At the beginning of his essay "The Principle of Reason," Derrida confesses to anxieties about his stated task, which is to examine, as he announces, the university's very reason for being, the view or prospect toward which higher education is or should be aimed. In this context, he compares himself to the prophet Elijah: "Was this inaugural lecture a well-chosen moment to ask whether the university has a reason for being? Wasn't I about to act with all the unseemliness of a stranger who in return for noble hospitality plays prophet of doom with his hosts, or at best eschatological harbinger, like Elijah denouncing the power of kings or announcing the end of the kingdom?"[27] If the reference to Elijah "denouncing the power of kings" reminds us of the resolutely antimonarchical Milton, that uncanny echo is compounded by Derrida's sheepishness about the quasi-prophetic nature of his project, which evokes the tentativeness that marks Milton's own role, as we will later see, as a *soi-disant* prophet.

Immediately after comparing himself to Elijah, Derrida makes a link between the subject of his discussion and the occasion of the essay, which was first delivered as a lecture at Cornell University. What he calls "the institutional scenography" of Cornell provides Derrida with another "cause for worry," he admits, insofar as he "find[s] [him]self involved already, quite imprudently, that is, blindly and without foresight, in an act of dramaturgy, writing out the play of that *view* in which Cornell, from its beginnings, has felt so much to be at stake."[28] Derrida is referring to the fact that Cornell's campus is located on top of a high hill overlooking the town of Ithaca, New York. He cites an account of the university's origins that points out that the plan of its founder, Ezra Cornell, to construct the university on this high ground "seems to have been shaped by the thematics of the Romantic sublime."[29] The sublimity of the university's site, however, is haunted by a death drive that gets manifested in the suicides for which the university is infamous—suicides accomplished by students who jump off the campus's bridges into the gorges that cut through the sublime heights of the hill on which the university is constructed: "Beneath the bridges linking the university to its surroundings, connecting its inside to its outside, lies the abyss."[30] Thus, the topic of Derrida's essay is entangled with the topos of its occasion—in his words, "the topolitics of the Cornellian point of view."[31]

Although "The Principle of Reason" is very much a cry of its modern, or post-Romantic, occasion, the motif on which it riffs—that of a high hill from which one may gain a clear vantage point, a sublime space or site of limpid vision and transparent truth—is part of a vast transhistorical construct in which Milton is implicated as well. In the rhetoric, logic, and history of Western metaphysics, such vantage points are often characterized not just as sites of revelation in themselves, but as spaces located quite pointedly above and beyond the labyrinth of error as well. In his essay "Of Truth," Sir Francis Bacon makes this distinction clear by quoting the opening lines of book 2 of Lucretius's *De rerum natura* (the italics designate Lucretius's words):

> The poet that beautified the sect [i.e., the Epicureans], that was otherwise inferior to the rest, saith yet excellently well: *It is a pleasure to stand upon the shore and to see ships tossed upon the sea; a pleasure to stand in the window of a castle and to see a battle and the adventures thereof below; but no pleasure is comparable to the standing upon the vantage-ground of truth* (a hill not to be commanded, where the air is always clear and serene), *and to see the errors and wanderings and mists and tempests in the vale below*; so always that this prospect be with pity, and not with swelling or pride.[32]

As throughout his work, Bacon here contrasts the high "vantage-ground of truth" with the vagaries so often associated, as we saw in Chapters 3 and 4, with romance; though Lucretius cannot have romance in mind, at least not in its early modern generic sense, what he calls the "errors and wanderings and mists and tempests in the vale below" cannot help but conjure associations with romance in this context.[33] In a quasi-Miltonic gesture, Bacon goes on to Christianize the Lucretian "vantage-ground" that is opposed to error: "Certainly it is heaven upon earth to have a man's mind move in charity, rest in providence, and turn upon the poles of truth."[34] In using this trope, Bacon is hardly alone among his contemporaries. According to John M. Steadman, seventeenth-century epistemology routinely drew distinctions between the hill and the labyrinth, preferring the swift ascent of the former, as opposed to the errancy of the latter, as the preferred emblem for the most direct path to truth.[35]

Given that the attainment of such a vantage point is one of the key aspirations of Milton's culture, an ambition long reinforced by both theology and philosophy, it is hardly surprising that the epic sweep of *Paradise Lost* culminates on literal moral high grounds. I refer to the hill in Eden to the top of which the archangel Michael leads Adam so that, following God's instructions, he may educate, and so redeem, the progenitor of all humankind after the tragedy of the Fall. By placing the poem's most explicit and detailed representation of instruction at the climax of its narrative, Milton makes clear the didactic ends of *Paradise Lost*. And by setting his scene of instruction on a hill, Milton further associates those ends with a symbolically loaded figure. What critics have long recognized as the uplifting sublimity of *Paradise Lost*—its tendency to raise itself, stylistically, thematically, and dialectically, to elevated heights—is a movement that can be said to reach its apogee on this hill.[36] In order to understand the tension between pleasure and instruction in the poem, it will therefore be necessary to examine carefully the pedagogy that takes place at this crucial vantage point. Yet it would also be prudent not to rush headlong into an analysis of Michael's instruction, at least not until we better understand what is at stake both in the trope of the vantage point and in the errancy against which that figure is so often defined. If for no other reason than the fact that Milton himself delays his poem's arrival at its moral high ground—that the ascent to the top of the hill takes place only after all the errant twists and turns and lengthy dilations of the pleasurable narrative movement that precedes it—our own journey to the top of that hill must be via expansive, crooked byways as well.

Throughout his career, Milton frequently deploys the trope of the high ground—from the "Hill of Heavn'ly Truth" in Sonnet 9, for example, to the title of his anticensorship tract, *Areopagitica*, which derives from the Areopagus ("Mars Hill"), the hill in Athens famous both as the site where Isocrates's seventh oration was delivered and as the site from which Saint

Paul evangelized the Athenians: "Then Paul stood in the midst of Mars' hill, and said, *Ye* men of Athens, I perceive that in all things ye are too superstitious" (Acts 17:22).[37] Elsewhere, as in *Of Education*, for instance, Milton employs the hill as an explicit figure for the modes of didacticism so characteristic of his writing. Solicited by the reformer Samuel Hartlib to supply his thoughts on the subject of pedagogy, Milton begins *Of Education* with a long diatribe against the Renaissance humanism in which he was trained and against which Hartlib aimed his reforms. The problems with humanistic education are captured in the vivid language Milton uses: it fills students' heads with "ragged notions and babblements," produces "souls so unprincipled in virtue and true generous breeding that flattery and court shifts and tyrannous aphorisms appear to them the highest points of wisdom," and leads those "of a more delicious and airy spirit" to "retire themselves, knowing no better, to the enjoyments of ease and luxury, living out their days in feast and jollity" (972–73). At this point Milton introduces an abrupt shift in the tract's content: "I shall detain you no longer in the demonstration of what we should not do, but straight conduct ye to a hillside, where I will point ye out the right path of a virtuous and noble education—laborious indeed at the first ascent, but else so smooth, so green, so full of goodly prospect and melodious sounds that the harp of Orpheus was not more charming" (973). Here Milton rhetorically presents himself as undertaking the same kinds of actions that Michael does in *Paradise Lost* to educate Adam.[38] This dialectical process—of demonstrating "what we should not do" as a means for pointing out "the right path"—is precisely the pedagogical process by which Michael performs his task. And just as Michael's instruction of Adam necessitates his leading him up a literal hill—literal, at least, within the world of the poem—so does Milton figure himself as leading his own readers to a high vantage point.

Some sense of the staying power and further significance of this figure can be taken from a comment that Stanley Fish makes in *How Milton Works* regarding Milton's *Lycidas*: that the tension "between the desire to lose oneself in a union with deity, and the desire either to defer the moment of union or to master it by intellectualizing it" is "a master theme" of *Lycidas* and thus "provides a vantage point from which we can make a kind of narrative sense of the poem's many and surprising twists and turns."[39] Fish's use of the phrase "narrative sense" is as telling as his use of the phrase "vantage point"; the latter functions for him much in the same way that the former does for Paul de Man—as a force of dialectical recuperation.[40] And if we take "twists and turns" to connote the forces encapsulated in the word "trope," then Fish's claim also resonates with de Man's observation that the process of narrative, insofar as it straightens out the displacements and deferrals of meaning perversely engendered by figural language, produces "the anamorphosis of the tropes, the transformations of the tropes, into the system of tropes, to which the corresponding experience is that of the self *standing above* its own experiences."[41] Whereas de Man, however, directs his critique *against* such a vantage point, Fish aims for nothing less: a locus of truth and sense-making that sublimates the errant "twists and turns" of Milton's notoriously difficult *Lycidas*.

The word "sublimates" is apposite here for a number of reasons: it intersects not only with the high grounds characteristic of aesthetic, theological, and philosophical sublimity, but also with the purifying processes that characterize both alchemy and dialectics. Hence, Lee Edelman reminds us that "the logic of sublimation—often associated, as Lacan points out, with forms of 'moral and spiritual elevation, that of the scale of values'—designates also a process for translating the impurities of ore into gold."[42] Interestingly enough, an early twentieth-century edition of *Lycidas* represents Milton's revisions of the poem in precisely these terms. Surveying the corrections that Milton made to the poem as it appears in the Trinity Manuscript, the editor, H. B. Cotterill, writes, "By some wondrous alchemy [Milton] transforms (sometimes by a single word) what seems of little value into pure gold"; Cotterill then goes on to cite comments made by Charles Lamb about encountering the poem in manuscript form: "I had thought of the *Lycidas*," writes Lamb, "as of a full-grown beauty—as springing up with all parts absolute—till in an evil hour I was shown the original copy of it in the Library of Trinity . . . How it staggered me to see the fine things in their ore! interlined! corrected! as if their words were mortal, alterable, displaceable at pleasure! as if inspiration were made up of parts, and these fluctuating, successive, indifferent!"[43] Upon close inspection, the signifier "ore" reveals itself, like a hypogram, all over Milton's oeuvre, from the famous opening lines of *Lycidas* itself ("Yet once m*ore*") to one of the most marked characteristics of Milton's style: what Herman calls the Miltonic "Or," that disjunctive conjunction that keeps the desire for dialectical resolution in the relentless grips of err*or* and ap*or*ia.[44] Much Milton criticism encapsulates and performs a desire for relief from the twists and turns of the Miltonic or(e), a desire, that is, for the quasi-alchemical sublimation or translation of or(e) into go(l)d.

The serene vantage point, then, is the desired locus of what I call "*relève*ation," where the word *relève*, as I pointed out earlier, is Derrida's translation of Hegel's *Aufhebung*. Because the sublime aspirations of Hegelian idealism, on the one hand, and Christian prophecy and eschatology, on the other, overlap in the form of such *relève*ation, it should come as no surprise that systematic readings of Milton tend to proceed according to a dialectical pattern. Such is the organizational structure, for instance, of Fish's *How Milton Works*: a movement from a paradigm to a counterparadigm to a paradigm reaffirmed. Michael Lieb's earlier study *The Dialectics of Creation* is arranged, not unexpectedly given its title, along similar lines.[45] Indeed, Lieb argues that dialectical patterns structure Milton's work throughout his career. With regard to Milton's prose, specifically *Areopagitica*, Lieb writes, "Dialectically, one might express Milton's attitude in this manner: one side of the argument confronts the opposing side, and these oppositions, in turn, manifest themselves in a higher union."[46] With regard to Milton's poetry, specifically *Paradise Lost*, Lieb writes, "Milton's 'great Idea' is not fulfilled through a straightforward presentation of answerable propositions and verifiable conclusions. On the contrary, the argument finds expression through a complex mode of indirection and nuance, in which each statement . . . has relevance for the whole."[47] The purpose of the Miltonic dialectics delineated by Lieb is by such "indirection[s]" to find directions out. This, as Fish also argues, is how Milton works.

But might not the specter of Milton's or(e) haunt even these axiomatic assertions about how Milton works? Milton's poetry may aim to ascend to a vantage point, and thereby attain and spread the good gift of *relève*ation, but are there no loose threads or remainders in his work that persist even as they are recuperated into a dialectical system by the force of *relève*ation? It is my contention that, yes, such remainders persist, which isn't to say that they necessarily or completely *re*sist Milton's desire for what Lieb calls "a higher union" (although I would add that they don't automatically reinforce this desire, either). Nor do I mean to argue that Milton's visions of grandeur are delusions of grandeur; they may, in fact, have been very real for him. But I do mean to ask whether Milton's poetry may be more skeptical, especially toward sublimity and sublimation, than we customarily give it credit for.

In his study *Sublimity and Skepticism in Montaigne and Milton*, David L. Sedley situates Montaigne and Milton, who are rarely conjoined, at a moment when the rise of both philosophical skepticism and the aesthetics of the sublime were coincident. Sedley asserts that "Milton forged sublimity . . . through his encounter with skepticism."[48] This comment, made in the introduction, may seem to recapitulate in different terms the all-too-conventional reading that Milton invokes the negativity and errancy of doubt as a mere means to grander ends. Yet Sedley's reading of *Paradise Lost* later in his study illustrates a more perverse argument. Demonstrating how Satan's fall ultimately supplies the full measure of true sublimity, Sedley nevertheless makes the claim that sublimity cannot completely escape or control the skepticism out of which it is created: "Because sublimity, as Satan accidentally demonstrates, does not confine doubt but turns it loose, the indeterminacy that characterizes skepticism also characterizes the parameters of the aesthetic category [i.e., the sublime] skepticism helps to create."[49] Sublimity, in other words, cannot completely exclude and thereby control skepticism because the latter is the former's own self-determining, but also self-undermining, limit.

Although Sedley doesn't cite Hegel here or elsewhere in his study, his reading of Satan nevertheless resonates with the philosopher's discussion of skepticism in *Phenomenology of Spirit*. Given that *Phenomenology of Spirit* recapitulates in putatively secular or philosophical terms so many of the theological issues with which Milton struggles in *Paradise Lost*, it is worth pausing on Hegel's arguments about skepticism. According to Hegel, the skeptical consciousness is divided against itself: on the one hand, Hegel writes, "it is itself determinateness as contrasted with the non-identical," but on the other hand, he adds, "it is just in this process that this consciousness, instead of being self-identical, is in fact nothing but a purely casual, confused medley, this dizziness of a perpetually self-engendered disorder."[50] Thus, the dialectics of skepticism is, for Hegel, an "*absolute dialectical unrest*," a negative dialectics.[51] The skeptical consciousness "passes back and forth from the one extreme of self-identical self-consciousness to the other extreme of the contingent consciousness that is both bewildered and bewildering."[52] The key point is that these oscillations between essentiality and contingency, self-identity and nonidentity, fail to culminate in a synthesis, a resolution that would manage, by manhandling negativity, to elevate consciousness into a state of positive *relève*ation, a vantage point from which one could sublate the "bewildered and bewildering" contingency and particularity of existence. In skepticism, consciousness "does not itself bring these two thoughts of itself together. At one time it recognizes that its freedom lies in rising above all the confusion and contingency of existence, and at another time equally admits to a relapse into occupying itself with what is unessential."[53] In skepticism, in other words, the essence of consciousness cannot escape its determination in and by the "unessential" contingency against which it identifies itself and above which it strives to rise.

The result of such division, as Jean Hyppolite explicates, is that skepticism "leads human consciousness to the double feeling of its nothingness and its grandeur."[54] Evoking the preacher of Ecclesiastes who proclaims that "all *is* vanity" (1:2), Hyppolite asserts that the contradiction that divides the skeptical consciousness from within can also be found in "the man who proclaims that all is vanity and that life is but the shadow of a day. In this very thought he rises above all vanity and poses authentic self-certainty in its sublime grandeur, but at the same time he himself appears as a contingency. By lowering himself he rises, but as soon as he rises and claims to reach that immutable certainty he descends anew. His immutable certainty is in contact with ephemeral life, and the eternity of his thought is a temporal thought of the eternal."[55] Hyppolite's reflections on "vanity" echo Milton's statement of his poetic intentions and vocation in *The Reason of Church Government*: taking Ariosto as his model, Milton strives "to fix all the industry and art [he] could unite to the adorning of [his] native tongue; not to make verbal curiosities the end, that were a toilsome vanity, but to be an interpreter and relater of the best and sagest things" (840). Here Milton explicitly states his self-certainty—his desire to "rise above all vanity," to use Hyppolite's words. But while Milton may be bent on being an "interpreter and relater"—which is to say, a sublater—the straight vertical trajectory of ascent is nevertheless bent by the ever-present threat of descent. The higher his aspirations, in other words, the more likely he is to fall—and the harder the fall will be.

I will have more to say later in this chapter about the forces of ascent and descent that, pulling in opposite directions, create strains in the poetic project of *Paradise Lost*. For now, however, with all of these twists and turns behind us (in both senses of the phrase), I would like finally to ascend the hill where Michael instructs Adam at the end of Milton's epic. "Ascend this Hill," Michael commands Adam (11.366–67); "it was a hill," Milton writes, "Of Paradise the highest, from whose top/The hemisphere of the earth in clearest ken/Stretched out to the amplest reach of prospect lay" (11.377–80). Michael's first action as divine instructor is to administer a remedy in order to remove the "film" that clouds Adam's vision after the Fall, a film "which that false fruit that promised clearer sight/Had bred" (11.413–14). Once he removes this film of error, Michael not only reveals to Adam a series of visions of the future course of human history, but also trains Adam in the proper ways of reading and interpreting these visions. The lesson ends in book 12 when Adam rehearses the morals that he has learned (12.553–73) and is able to leave Paradise, hand-in-hand with Eve, with a more contented mind.

Specifically, Michael uses a series of biblical tableaux as a way of training Adam to reject the Renaissance humanist forms that Milton disparages in *Of Education*. After Michael reveals the murder of Abel and then the rise of disease and death, for example, he displays a third vision: "A bevy of fair women, richly gay / In gems and wanton dress" (*PL*, 11.582–83). At first Adam is taken in by the ornamental signifying surface of these women, saying to Michael, "Much better seems this vision" (11.599), but Michael quickly corrects him in a lengthy sermon (11.603–27). In many ways, Michael's sermon can be read as a polemical jab against the extravagance of Renaissance *inventio* and *elocutio* ("studious they appear / Of arts that polish life, inventors rare" [11.609–10]). Moreover, the subsequent two visions deflate the inflated heroism typical of classical and Renaissance epic and romance as well as the kind of luxurious decadence ("pleasure, ease, and sloth, / Surfeit, and lust" [11.794–95]) that is, as Milton argues in *Of Education*, the inevitable result of an education in humanism.

With Michael's instruction, we thus seem to be fully in the realm of judicious Enlightenment reading. We also seem to be moving away from epic toward the novel, with its emphasis on the domestic and its attempt to represent, in a plain fashion, the plain virtues of middle-class men and women without the distortions of romance, error, pleasure, and rhetoric—all the by-products of Renaissance literary culture. As Nancy Armstrong and Leonard Tennenhouse write about this "scene of instruction," "The poetry of the fallen world is didactic poetry. . . . It identifies human deficiencies and establishes a standard for perfection. By bearing witness to human history, Adam acquires the knowledge of human progress required to produce such interpretations."[56] This claim encapsulates the standard reading of Michael's instruction reproduced by critics since Fish's *Surprised by Sin* called attention to the pedagogical techniques in and of *Paradise Lost*. Surveying the poem's tendency to mislead the reader linguistically and then to correct the interpretive errors it raises, Parker sums up Fish's position in telling terms: "Stanley Fish has *raised* this process of misprision and correction to *a dialectics of enlightenment*, a movement in which *the function of error is to educate*, or bring through."[57] Even where critics attempt to depart from Fish's argument about Milton's "dialectics of enlightenment," they still proceed from the assumption that Michael's pedagogy is successful, desirable, and ultimately redemptive.[58]

In its treatment of books 11 and 12, Milton criticism thus perpetuates rather than critiques the fantasy that those books generate: a Hegelian (which is also to say, a Judeo-Christian or more broadly idealist) fantasy that "gives us history," to borrow the words of Edelman, "as the continuous staging of our dream of eventual self-realization." This sort of fantasy works its effects, according to Edelman, "without letting us acknowledge that the future, to which it persistently appeals, marks the impossible place of an Imaginary past exempt from the deferrals intrinsic to the operation of the signifying chain and projected ahead as the site at which being and meaning are joined as One."[59] Michael's instruction installs this fantasy, this desire for a future return to an "Imaginary past" purged of error. Naturally enough, then, his instruction climaxes with the messianic hope that Christ will "bring back/Through the world's wilderness long wandered man/Safe to eternal Paradise of rest" (*PL*, 12.312–14). And just as this fantasy assuages Adam's perturbed postlapsarian conscience, so too does it assuage the conscience of critics who seek to justify the ways of *Milton* to man, those who wish to redeem *Paradise Lost* itself from any potential charge of incoherence, meaninglessness, or error. These critics continue to read books 11 and 12 as the vantage point from which such redemption is enacted to full effect.

Yet that hasn't always been the case. In "Transmuting the Lump," Fish narrates the critical history by which the final two books of *Paradise Lost* were, in fact, rescued from charges of incoherence, meaninglessness, and error.[60] Fish traces such charges about Michael's instruction back to Joseph Addison's 1712 comment that "if Milton's poem flags anywhere, it is in this Narration, where in some Places the Author has been so attentive to his Divinity, that he has Neglected his Poetry."[61] In the modern period that forms the focus of Fish's narrative, the flashpoint for such charges is C. S. Lewis's claim that books 11 and 12 present "an untransmuted lump of futurity," which, "coming in a position so momentous for the structural effect of the whole work, is inartistic."[62] Fish's essay details the trajectory by which Lewis's appraisal was dislodged over the course of several decades. With the rise of myth criticism, New Criticism, and typological interpretation, conditions come into play that allow critics to transmute the lump, such that, by 1972, Raymond Waddington's article on the controversy could begin: "Few of us today could risk echoing C. S. Lewis's condemnation of the concluding books of *Paradise Lost* as an 'untransmuted lump of futurity.'"[63]

The word "untransmuted" is particularly resonant here: like "sublimate," "transmute" is an alchemical term that designates the transformation of one substance into another, especially, according to the *OED*, "a baser metal into gold or silver" (1b). In using the phrase "untransmuted lump of futurity," Lewis implies that the final two books of *Paradise Lost*—the sublime vantage point toward which the poem's teleological narrative force drives—present a disordered and unsublimated series of visions, a prophetic vantage point that is less messianic than just plain messy. Where Addison claims that the success of the poem's didactic function subsumes the pleasure of its poetry in the final two books, Lewis suggests that the didactic function fails because it falls, because it cannot cohere or coalesce into the refined form of *relève*ation. Michael may lead Adam to a moral high ground, instruct him in the ways of right reading and right reason, and leave him with the sublime hope of "possess[ing] / A paradise within" (12.586–87). And yet, as Parker writes, such "a resolutely teleological reading of Milton's poem may be faithful, finally, to only one of its tendencies, and the experience of the poetry itself leads us back to . . . the question of how single-minded, or unidirectional, this process is."[64]

Along these lines, it is worth noting how the vantage point of Michael's education of Adam in *Paradise Lost* resembles that of Satan's seduction of Christ in *Paradise Regained*.[65] This is a comparison that *Paradise Lost* proleptically invites us to make when it describes the hill in Eden:

it was a hill
Of Paradise the highest, from whose top
The hemisphere of the earth in clearest ken
Stretched out to the amplest reach of prospect lay.
Not higher that hill nor wider looking round,
Whereon for different cause the Tempter set
Our second Adam in the wilderness,
To show him all Earth's kingdoms and their glory.
(*PL*, 11.377–84; my italics)

As is so often the case with Milton's grammar and syntax, the "that" in line 381 is ambiguous: it initially seems to refer to the hill that precedes it—the hill on which Michael educates Adam—but then refers to the hill that follows it—the hill on which Satan seduces Christ. It thus ironizes the distinction between the two hills that these lines attempt to make.

Moreover, the hill of instruction on which Milton's vision culminates also recalls the picture that Milton paints of the philosophizing devils in Hell in book 2 of *Paradise Lost*:

Others sat apart on a hill retired,
In thoughts more elevate, and reasoned high
Of providence, foreknowledge, will, and fate,
Fixed fate, free will, foreknowledge absolute,
And found no end, in wand'ring mazes lost.
(2.557–61)

Until the final line, this passage could just as easily describe Michael and Adam's activities in the final two books of the poem. The rhetorical proximity of these hills to that from which Michael instructs Adam suggests that no vantage point, except for God's "prospect high" (3.77), is finally exempt from the possibility of vanity and error.

Blindness and Insight

One shouldn't take too lightly the force of defensive efforts designed to counteract the terror that the risk of error produces—efforts that attempt to sublimate the temptation of error, to spin its negativity into something positive, to transmute or translate its dark, leaden ore into bright, shining gold. Such defensiveness, as the previous chapters demonstrated, constitutes the hallmark of late sixteenth-century poetic theory. But because so many Elizabethan writers, as we have seen, insistently revel in the pleasures of error and vanity, thus overwhelming and undermining their desire to profit from negativity, the defense mechanisms of Renaissance humanism were inevitably bound to fail—in theory, if not also in practice.

The opposite would seem to be the case with Milton. If the early modern period, as I established in Chapter 1, conceived of poetry as a *pharmakon*, both poison and remedy at once, then we might sketch the differences between Milton and his Elizabethan predecessors as follows: whereas Shakespeare, Sidney, Spenser, and especially Nashe are enchanted, despite themselves, by its poisonous Circean qualities, Milton seems (but only seems?) to celebrate its remedial benefits. This difference would help to explain the curative and purgative drugs that appear, like *deus ex machinas*, at the climaxes of Milton's most famous poetic explorations of the tensions between pleasure and virtue.[66] It also helps to explain the violent act of purgation by which Milton tries to abject the rhetoric and poetics of the Tudor-Stuart era: what in *Paradise Lost* he associates with the enchanting necromancy of Satan's rhetorical prowess and identifies with the epic and romance predecessors he tries to trump; what in *Of Education* he disparages as the idle, vain, and luxurious pleasures that result from an education in the humanist tradition; and what in *Eikonoklastes* he simply calls the "polluted orts and refuse of *Arcadias* and romances."

We have already seen how Milton's politics and theology raise the stakes of this historical difference, but it is also worth noting that Milton, in attempting to purge his writing of forms of error and vanity celebrated by the Renaissance, works in concert with revolutions in the philosophical arena as well. Renaissance courtiers, poets, and educators maximized the gap between signifier and signified—a disjunction that, from a Judeo-Christian viewpoint, is a direct consequence of the Fall—by indulging in, even as they were suspicious of, the pleasurable vanity of rhetoric, figure, and irony. By the time the Enlightenment revised Renaissance epistemology by valuing the ideology of realism, attempts to eliminate this linguistic error became more and more earnest. Written at the climax of a century that saw the publication of Bacon's *The Advancement of Learning* (1605), Descartes's *Discourse on Method* (1637), Hobbes's *Leviathan* (1651), Sprat's *History of the Royal Society* (1667), and Locke's *An Essay Concerning Human Understanding* (1690), *Paradise Lost* would appear to undertake the same project and, as Michael does to Adam, to usher its readers into an enlightened modernity.

Indeed, it is on this point that Milton joins company with philosophers whose epistemological systems he normally rejects. While scholars, for example, regularly pit Miltonic monism against Cartesian dualism,[67] even a cursory glance at Descartes's *Discourse on Method* reveals rhetorical affinities between his and Milton's goals of attaining the truth of spiritual redemption. Like Milton's, Descartes's method depends on an explicit rejection of poetry's pleasures, its "very ravishing delights and sensibilities," and, even more particularly, of the discursive materials of romance: what he calls "the extravagancies of the knightly heroes of romantic novels."[68] Once such "doubts and errors" are cleared away, the path to virtue—indeed, the path to heaven itself—should be easily traversable. But it is precisely here that Descartes stumbles upon an obstacle: "I respected our theology and hoped, as much as anyone else, to get to heaven. But once I learned, as something which is very certain, that the path to heaven is just as open to the most ignorant as to the most learned, and that the revealed truths which lead there are beyond our understanding, I did not dare subject them to the feebleness of my reasoning, and thought that one needed to have some extraordinary assistance from heaven and to be more than human in order to study them successfully."[69] This is also the problem that confronts Milton's writing in *Paradise Lost*. But because Milton composes an *epic*, there seems to be a ready-made solution to the problem: for "extraordinary assistance from heaven," Milton invokes the "aid" (1.13) of his heavenly Muse. By translating Milton from earth to heaven so that he may translate heaven to his readers on earth, Milton's Muse both guides and authorizes his "advent'rous song, / That with no middle flight intends to soar / Above th' Aonian mount" (*PL* 1.13–15).

A number of recent critics have offered counterintuitive readings of the proems to books 1, 3, 7, and 9, the passages in *Paradise Lost* where Milton invokes his Muse. While these critics proffer different treatments of these passages, they nevertheless call our attention to a tension within the poem:

namely, that Milton both must and must not present himself as a divinely inspired prophet.[70] Milton must declare himself "more than human," as Descartes phrases it, in order to access divine *relève*ation. But to do just that is to aspire beyond what is reasonably expected of the all-too-human Milton, perhaps even to reproduce what *Paradise Lost*, immediately after its opening invocation, identifies and vilifies as Satan's "ambitious aim" (1.41). How can we (or, for that matter, how can Milton) tell the difference between Milton's ambition and Satan's? They may have different aims—Satan wants to *equal* "the Most High" (1.40), whereas Milton more modestly wants to produce a theodicy that would "*justify* the ways of God" (1.26)—but the proximity of their ambition calls into question just how pure Milton's intent to "justify" God actually is. Given the ambivalence that Milton repeatedly displays toward his divine aid, the presence of the Muse aggravates rather than allays the poetic fears surrounding such questions. In this section, I want to focus first on specific instances in the poem where this tension erupts. In doing so, though, I would like to move beyond recent critics' treatment of this tension by viewing it not, with Stephen Fallon, as a "dialectic of assertion and anxiety," a "paradox [that] is resolvable . . . by our recognition of what Milton struggles to obscure,"[71] but rather as that which *exceeds* dialectical recuperation, a limit point that Milton struggles to obscure because it potentially obscures *him*, leaving him wandering in the shady dross of his poem's orts and refuse.

Let me begin, then, with the proem to book 3, Milton's invocation to "holy light" (*PL*, 3.1), which is structured rhetorically in the form of what we can identify, after Hegel, as a dialectical pattern. Having just descended from earth to Hell so that he can follow Satan's journey from Hell to earth, Milton asserts, as a *thesis*, his assurance that he now returns to the light that was absent during the "obscure sojourn" (3.15) of books 1 and 2: "thee I revisit safe, / And feel thy sov'reign vital lamp" (3.21–22). Immediately, though, Milton presents his blindness as the *antithesis*:

> but thou
> Revist'st not these eyes, that roll in vain
> To find thy piercing ray, and find no dawn;
> So thick a drop serene hath quenched his orbs,
> Or dim suffusion veiled.
>
> (3.22–26)

The inspiration of the poem therefore finds its limit in the obscurity through which Milton fails to see the world around him. He gives a catalogue of the pastoral imagery that now escapes him, lamenting that "cloud instead, and ever-during dark/Surrounds me" and that "Nature's works" are to him "expunged and razed" (3.40–49), recalling the fallen devils "blotted out and razed/ . . . from the Books of Life" (1.362–63).[72] With the inevitable dialectical sublation or *synthesis*, however, such darkness works to Milton's advantage:

So much the rather thou celestial light
Shine inward, and the mind through all her powers
Irradiate, there plant eyes, all mist from thence
Purge and disperse, that I may see and tell
Of things invisible to mortal sight.

(3.51–55)

Because Milton's goal, especially in this book as he turns to Heaven, is to "see and tell/Of things *invisible* to mortal sight," he requires not the mortal sight that has now escaped him but, rather, an "inward" vision. Thus, the negative limitation his inspiration encountered is sublimated in a dialectic of blindness and insight: external blindness is recuperated as *in*sight, as light "purge[s] and disperse[s]" the "dim suffusion" that "veil[s]" Milton's eyes much in the same way Michael clears Adam's foggy vision with euphrasy and rue.

Approached from a less resolute perspective, though, the invocation betrays the dialectical *relève*ation it sets up. In the midst of the proem, Milton compares himself to a series of blind ancient prophets, "equaled with me in fate/So were I equaled with them in renown": Thamyris, Maeonides (Homer), Tiresias, and Phineas. "With the exception of the blind poet Homer (Maeonides)," Reisner remarks, "the prophetic types of blind Thamyris, Tiresias, and Phineas are ambivalent, in that they all represent pagan prophets whose blindness was a form of punishment for presuming to peer into divine mysteries."[73] As a way of dialectically resolving this ambivalence, Reisner goes on to cite Milton's *Second Defence*, where Milton portrays the blindness of Tiresias and Phineas as, in Reisner's words, "a gift, not a curse."[74] Whatever Milton may say in the *Second Defence*, what the invocation to book 3 does is leave us nonetheless with the impression of what Fallon calls "an unspoken fear, that [Milton's] similarity to [these blind prophets] may lie in blindness as divine punishment."[75]

This "unspoken fear" may help to explain the disconcerting presence of the verb "may" at the climax of the invocation: "all mist from thence/Purge and disperse, that I *may* see and tell/Of things invisible to mortal sight." How are we to read this "may"? It seems to express permission, but there is also the lexical possibility that it expresses mere possibility. If it expresses permission, it may ironize the *presumption* of permission, especially when read alongside Milton's ambivalence toward his prophetic predecessors who were punished by the gods precisely for presuming such permission. If it expresses mere possibility, it would raise the concomitant possibility of *not* seeing and *not* telling of things invisible to mortal sight. In either case, the verb renders uncertain or ironic the seeming confidence of Milton's prophetic desires. It thus retrospectively sheds new light—or, more precisely, new darkness—on Milton's statement, in the proem to book 1, of the poem's aim, goal, and end: "That to the highth of this great argument/I *may* assert eternal providence,/And justify the ways of God to men" (1.24–26; my italics). The instability of this "may," which erupts, no less, at the rhetorical "highth" of Milton's "great argument," betrays a fundamental ironic uncertainty in the making of the poem.

The bleakness of such uncertainty, as well as its dire implications for Milton's own poetics, is expressed most dramatically in the proem to book 7, which reinforces how Milton's sublime ends are subject to potential errancy:

Up led by thee
Into the Heaven of Heavens I have presumed,
An earthly guest, and drawn empyreal air,
Thy temp'ring; with like safety guided down
Return me to my native element:
Lest from this flying steed unreined, (as once
Bellerophon, though from a lower clime)
Dismounted on the Aleian field I fall
Erroneous there to wander and forlorn.

(7.12–20)

Even though Milton seems to presume that he will not fall, "guided" as he is by his heavenly Muse, the specter of "erroneous . . . wander[ing]" nevertheless shadows his attempt to create a heavenly epic. In a postlapsarian world, *Paradise Lost* can only be suspended precariously between earth and heaven.

Editors and critics have routinely explicated how Milton's allusion here to Bellerophon—the classical mythological figure who attempted to ride Pegasus to heaven and ended up falling and wandering the Aleian field—functions as "a self-cautionary tale for the audacious poet."[76] But this passage also exhibits more implicit intertextual echoes that hearken back to the more recent past, specifically to the Elizabethan romance predecessors that Milton aims to forgo, trump, and discard in *Paradise Lost*. Both echoes are condensed in the word "unreined." In the first place, the word evokes a striking claim that Sidney, the author of those "polluted orts and refuse of *Arcadias* and romances," makes in his *Defence of Poesy*. The claim occurs at the precise moment that Sidney integrates the Horatian dictum into his tract. Characterizing what he calls "right poets," Sidney writes, "For these . . . be they which most properly do imitate to teach and delight, and to imitate borrow nothing of what is, hath been, or shall be; but range, only reined with learned discretion, into the divine consideration of what may be and should be."[77] The words "range" and "reined" designate opposing forces: the former pulls in the direction of aspiration, and perhaps even errancy and vanity, whereas the latter pulls in the direction of containment, rectification, and "discretion." Yet the line between them is difficult to draw, a difficulty redoubled by the alliteration and assonance that draws the two words together. Sidney therefore wields the same double-edged sword that Milton tries to balance. Even as Sidney attempts to avoid the charge, his phrasing raises the possibility of a ranging that becomes unreined, an impious, impertinent, imprudent, and improvident presumption ("Into the Heav'n of Heav'ns I have *presumed*," as Milton puts it in the invocation to book 7).

Milton's use of the trope of an "unreined" steed, especially when considered alongside the word "temp'ring" and the request to be "guided down," can also be read as a muted echo of book 2 of *The Faerie Queene*, the Legend of Temperance.[78] This echo would cast the narrator of *Paradise Lost* as the pedestrian knight Guyon: in the same way Guyon descends to the Cave of Mammon, so too is *Paradise Lost* at risk of falling were it not for the heavenly Muse, who functions much in the same way that Guyon's guide, the Palmer, does. In Spenser's poem, however, Guyon *does* lose his guide when he goes down to the cave of Mammon, where he almost dies. This is a fact that Milton curiously and infamously forgets when, in *Areopagitica*, he makes an explicit reference to the Legend of Temperance:

> Assuredly we bring not innocence into the world, we bring impurity much rather: that which purifies us is trial, and trial is by what is contrary. That virtue [i.e., chastity] therefore which is but a youngling in the contemplation of evil and knows not the utmost that vice promises to her followers, and rejects it, is but a blank virtue, not a pure; her whiteness is but an excremental whiteness; which was the reason why our sage and serious poet, Spenser, whom I dare be known to think a better teacher than Scotus or Aquinas, describing true temperance under the person of Guyon, brings him in *with his palmer* through the cave of Mammon and the bower of earthly bliss that he might see and

> know and yet abstain. . . . Therefore the knowledge and survey of vice is in this world so necessary to the constituting of human nature, and the scanning of error to the confirmation of truth.
>
> (939; my italics)

While the Palmer does travel with Guyon into the Bower of Bliss at the end of the Legend of Temperance, he does not, in fact, accompany the knight into Mammon's cave. Critics agree that Milton's error is no mere accident or oversight and that it must therefore serve some purpose, conscious or unconscious, rhetorical or otherwise.[79] One of the more recent entries into this conversation, by George F. Butler, rationalizes the error as follows: "Spenser's Guyon possibly displays greater strength and courage by confronting Mammon's temptations without the Palmer's help, and he comes across as a conventionally self-reliant hero. But for Milton, the presence of the Palmer affirms the propriety of Guyon's actions, since the Palmer is a moral guide."[80] Butler's "possibly" understates the case: Guyon *does* display "greater strength and courage by confronting Mammon's temptations without the Palmer's help"; why else would Spenser pointedly remind us of the fact that Guyon has "lost his trustie guyde" before entering Mammon's cave (*FQ*, 2.7.2.1)? By reestablishing the Palmer at Guyon's side, *Areopagitica* implies (perhaps inadvertently) that temperance alone is not enough to resist the temptations of evil.

Why might this be the case? To answer this question, it would be helpful to consider part of the passage in *Areopagitica* that precedes Milton's allusion to *The Faerie Queene*, for the terms in which that passage is couched bear affinity with *Paradise Lost*. "It was from out of the rind of one apple tasted," Milton writes, "that the knowledge of good and evil, as two twins cleaving together, leaped forth into the world. And perhaps that is the doom which Adam fell into of knowing good and evil, that is to say, of knowing good by evil" (*Areopagitica*, 728). If "that is to say" is a phrase that typically indicates paraphrase, what are we to make of the fact that Milton paraphrases "knowing good *and* evil" as "knowing good *by* evil"? Despite the fact that the rhetorical logic of paraphrase attempts to equate them here, these two phrases are not exactly the same. First, the text boldly announces that knowing good *and* knowing evil constitutes Adam's—and by extension all humanity's, including Milton's—doom. Then it leaps to the less troublesome assertion that this double knowledge means "knowing good *by* evil," which implies that evil is merely a dialectical means to the virtuous end of knowing good.[81] This paraphrase, however, does not erase the initial and inescapable statement Milton makes: that knowing good by (means of) evil *requires* the knowledge of evil as much as—indeed, *so that*—the knowledge of evil produces the knowledge of good. That is to say, the first bold assertion is that the knowledge of good and the knowledge of evil are required *together*; in his vivid breeding metaphor, Milton describes good and evil as "two twins cleaving together." Milton's paraphrase attempts to sublimate the boldness of this notion by reinscribing the relationship between good and evil in a dialectical ends-oriented economy, but the strain of that attempt is inscribed in the text as a rhetorical stutter.

At the end of *Paradise Lost*, Adam rejoices in Michael's vision of redemption by marveling, in an uncannily similar fashion, at how "all this good of evil shall produce/And evil turn to good" (11.470–71). Like Milton's "knowing good by evil," Adam's statement displays faith in the same recuperative and redemptive economy that Freud, according to Derrida, observed where the devil is concerned:

> We do not like to be reminded, Freud notes, of the undeniable existence of an evil which seems to contradict the sovereign goodness of God. But if this Devil . . . seems, then, in the eyes of Christians, . . . irreconcilable with God, we see now that it can also exculpate God. . . . In other words, the radical destruction can again be *reinvested* in another logic, in the inexhaustible *economistic* resource of an archive which capitalizes everything, even that which ruins it or radically contests its power: radical evil can be of service, infinite destruction can be reinvested in a theodicy, the devil can also serve to *justify*.[82]

"The devil can also serve to justify"—to justify, in other words, the ways of God to man. One could argue that Milton is "of" the devil's party, then, only on the condition that the devil's radical evil can be reinvested dialectically in order to serve the poet's ultimate positive aim to produce a theodicy. Lurking about this logic, though, like Satan insinuating himself in Eden, is the potential subversion and perversion of good ends that Satan articulates to Beelzebub in Hell:

> If then [God's] providence
> Out of our evil seek to bring forth good,
> Our labor must be to pervert that end,
> And out of good still to find means of evil
>
> (1.162–65)

If Milton feels compelled to place the Palmer at Guyon's side at all times, even in Mammon's hell-like cave (and not for nothing does Milton place Mammon in *Paradise Lost*'s own Hell), then perhaps that's because of the satanic potential for "pervert[ing]" the dialectic of good and evil, for "disturb[ing] / [God's] inmost counsels from their destined aim" (*PL*, 11.167–68). While Guyon alone *may* be able to ascertain good by means of evil, the very presence of the Palmer in Milton's odd revision suggests that he *may not* be able to. Milton invokes the Palmer for Guyon for the same intentions that he invokes the Muse for himself—namely, as a means of sublimating evil into good and thus elevating himself out of the (potential for) vanity that Satan both represents and performs. As we have seen, though, Milton himself is not exempt from the risk of vanity and error, a risk that casts a shadow on even the loftier aspects of his own "destined aim."

In the End: The Unsublime

Early in the *Confessions*, Saint Augustine laments the fact that "as a boy" he "gave pride of place" in his "affection" to "empty fables" like the *Aeneid* "rather than to more useful studies."[83] When the *Confessions* was printed in English in 1620, the Latin words translated here as "empty" and "useful" were translated instead as "vaine" and "profitable," the very terms that so many early modern writers use to characterize poetry's possible futility or utility.[84] It is worth pointing out, though, that the original Latin words are *inania* and *utilioribus*. Incidentally, *inania* is the same word that Virgil uses—in the *Aeneid*, no less—to characterize the domicile of Dis; it's also the same word used in the Vulgate translation of Genesis to describe chaos.[85] Augustine thus deploys a word *from* the *Aeneid* in order to disparage the *Aeneid*, but he specifically uses a word with loaded cosmological and theological connotations. Why would the vanity of poetry be associated with chaos? And how can Milton's depiction of Chaos in *Paradise Lost* help us understand the stakes of this association?

Asking these questions immediately thrusts us into chaotic territory in more ways than one. Milton's Chaos is like no other even as it resembles all others, drawing on Hesiod, Ovid, Lucretius, and the book of Genesis even as it departs from them. As a result, an often intense debate over the limits and ultimate significance of Milton's Chaos has emerged in the last couple of decades.[86] The debate centers on an apparent contradiction: Milton's monism seems to clash with the poem's representation of a more negative and unruly Chaos. In his *Of Christian Doctrine*, Milton argues for creation *de deo* instead of creation *ex nihilo*, claiming that the "original matter" used in Creation is coextensive with deity and, moreover, that "this original matter was not an evil thing, nor to be thought of as worthless: it was good, and it contained the seeds of all subsequent good" (1201). At times, *Paradise Lost* seems to support this view, never more so than when God asserts his infinitude:

> Boundless the deep, because I am who fill
> Infinitude, nor vacuous the space.
> Though I uncircumscribed myself retire,
> And put not forth my goodness
>
> (7.168–71)

The logic here is that God's spirit fills the "boundless . . . deep," but can "retire" his deity from certain regions of the universe. This logic confirms the statement that Raphael makes to Adam regarding original matter and God's singularity:

> O Adam, one Almighty is, from whom
> All things proceed, and up to him return,
> If not depraved from good, created all
> Such to perfection, one first matter all . . .
>
> (5.469–72)

However clearly this claim seems to support Milton's arguments in *Of Christian Doctrine* regarding creation *de deo*, the conditional phrase ("If not depraved from good") raises a, perhaps *the*, thorny complication: how can any matter be *possibly* "depraved from good" when all matter is *essentially* a part of God?

The debate over Chaos turns on this very question, resulting in what Regina Schwartz identifies as "a critical conspiracy to detoxify chaos."[87] The twists and turns of the debate are far too complicated to trace here. As a matter of fact, my initial claim is that such twists and turns are beside the point; despite the contentious differences that animate the conversation, all critics appear to participate unavoidably in a concerted effort to detoxify Chaos, to sublimate its negativity by resolving any contradiction such negativity may instigate in relation to Milton's monism and God's infinitude. Of all the critics who have entered the debate, none has tried so hard to counteract these processes of detoxification or purification as John Rogers. In this effort, he helpfully calls our attention to a potentially unsublatable moment in the poem's depiction of Creation:

> Thus God the heav'n created, thus the earth,
> Matter unformed and void: darkness profound
> Covered th' abyss: but on the wat'ry calm

His brooding wings the Spirit of God outspread,
And vital virtue infused, and vital warmth
Throughout the fluid mass, but downward purged
The black tartareous cold infernal dregs
Adverse to life.

(*PL*, 7.232–39)

"In one remarkable line," Rogers writes, "Milton appears to indicate that there remained a portion of the deep for which the process of spiritualization did not take: 'The black tartareous cold Infernal dregs' refuse assimilation into the vitalist world of Milton's poem."[88] Rogers's use of the verb "refuse" is doubly resonant here, for Milton seems precisely to depict the polluted orts and refuse, or waste, produced as a by-product of Creation. As Rogers explains, "The terms Milton employs for that which is excreted in the purgative step of this process—tartar and dregs—are the standard names in the period's natural philosophy for the inassimilable elements purged from the system in the process of digestion."[89] Rogers goes on to explain away these "inassimilable elements" by way of reference to Milton's political concerns, but overall his analysis prompts us to refuse to reuse dialectically what (the poem's account of) Creation scatologically expels as refuse.

Critics, to be sure, have frequently pointed out the persistent digestive and scatological tropes that permeate the poem's depictions of the universe's mechanics, and the "black tartareous cold infernal dregs" produced at Creation are certainly part of that alimental constitution.[90] Evocative of fecal matter, these dregs bring new meaning to the word "end-times": they bring out the scatology in Milton's eschatology, perversely revealing how the universe's salvational end or goal may be tainted by the shit that spits out of its rear end or hole.[91] Here we might think of Lacan, whose brief tour through Lutheran theology in Seminar 7 leads him into a consideration of "the essentially digestive and excremental schema forged by a thought that draws ultimate consequences from the form of exile in which man finds himself relative to any good in the world whatsoever."[92] According to Lacan, this schema forms the basis of Luther's conception of postlapsarian humans: Luther, he says, "renewed the very basis of Christian teaching when he sought to express our dereliction, our fall in a world where we let ourselves go. . . . Luther says literally, 'You are that waste matter which falls into the world from the devil's anus.'"[93] The dregs of *Paradise Lost* partake of a similar schema, but whereas Lacan and Luther, in quite different ways, view it as a by-product of the Fall, Milton's poem figures that schema as a by-product of Creation itself.

The dregs of Creation are also linked in subtle ways to other evil and pointedly unsublime figurations of matter in the poem. I am thinking particularly of the "asphaltic slime" (*PL*, 10.298) that, in Teskey's vivid words, "bubbles up in the lowest, nastiest part of chaos."[94] In an illuminating discussion, Teskey makes a number of points about this slime: it was said to be the binding agent for the bricks of the Tower of Babel and the walls of Babylon, and it was thought to boil up from hell at three sites of radical evil along the Fertile Crescent: Babylon, Egypt, and Sodom. Teskey even raises the interesting, albeit ultimately unprovable, hypothesis that this queer slime or tar is the referent for the black tartareous dregs of the Creation narrative. He sums up the negative implications of this substance as follows: "Although all matter in Milton's cosmos is supposed to have its origin ultimately in God and to return to God at the end of time, recuperated entirely, this one substance appears to stand outside the system, as a heterological, virulent remainder of the kind Georges Bataille theorized, something incapable of assimilation to the world."[95]

Teskey's reference to Bataille is made merely en passant, but I wish to pick up the thread that he drops. One reason is that Bataille is one of the most perverse readers of Hegel and one of the more forceful critics of dialectical thinking and can therefore provide us with a model for how to consider Milton from a more oblique, undialectical position.[96] As Teskey's comment suggests, Bataille's enterprise draws a distinction between the *homogeneous* and the *heterogeneous*. The homogeneous, for Bataille, "signifies the commensurability of elements . . . [and] the consciousness of the possible identity of delineable persons and situations"; its basis is production and utility, and thus in order to maintain itself it must exclude every "useless element." The heterogeneous, on the other hand, signifies "elements that are impossible to assimilate," like the tar Teskey analyzes, insofar as they are the result of "*unproductive* expenditure" and must, therefore, be expelled as refuse.[97] Whereas the homogeneous, then, signifies the coherence and stability—in Hegelian terms, the essentiality or self-identity—of any system, the heterogeneous is that which undermines and supports homogeneity, indeed supports it by being sacrificed because it undermines it.

Although this pattern has long been familiar from the work of Derrida, who is, like so many of his generation, heavily indebted to Bataille, what is striking about Bataille's *particular* theoretical schema, especially in relation to *Paradise Lost*, is that he locates both the sacred and the profane within the realm of the heterogeneous.[98] Bataille argues that "religions bring about a separation within the sacred domain, dividing it into a superior world (celestial and divine) and an inferior world (demoniacal, a world of decomposition)." Although he immediately suggests that "such a division necessarily leads to a progressive homogeneity of the entire superior domain"—that such a division, in other words, can be dialectically reinscribed within a homogeneous system—he nevertheless claims that homogeneity "automatically limits itself by producing of its own accord its own waste products, thus liberating in a disordered way the heterogeneous excremental element."[99] Redirecting this claim toward *Paradise Lost*, we might say that Milton's monistic intentions have an unintended and potentially uncontrollable dualistic effect: in order to subsume the heterogeneous under the logic of the homogeneous, he must liberate and inscribe within his poem the very heterogeneity to be subsumed.

In early modern theology, philosophy, and mathematics, the potential heresy of this sort of heterogeneity was condensed in the knotty ontological and epistemological status of "zero." As J. Hillis Miller explains, "What struck conservative Renaissance thinkers as blasphemous about the use of zero in computation was that it reintroduced a void that God with his creative fiat had replaced once and for all with a full creation, a plentiude. Only the devil is void, empty, a nothing dwelling in Hell. Hell is a nothing place, a place of infinite, non-determinate, unsublatable negation."[100] Although Milton nowhere writes directly about zero, his argument for creation *de deo* rather than creation *ex nihilo* suggests that the "blasphemous" significance of zero—the zero as void, nothing, negation—was at the front of his mind, even if only as an object of abjection.

It was also in the forefront in the work of one of Milton's contemporaries: Blaise Pascal. In "Pascal's Allegory of Persuasion," de Man demonstrates how the homogeneous coherence of Pascal's systematic geometry is "entirely dependent on the introduction of an element—the zero and its equivalences in time and motion—that is itself entirely heterogeneous with regard to the system and is nowhere part of it. The continuous universe . . . is interrupted, disrupted *at all points* by a principle of radical heterogeneity [i.e., the zero] without which it cannot come into being."[101] The mathematical and geometrical accuracy of such claims is less relevant for our purposes than the rhetorical strategies by which de Man makes his case for the simultaneously foundational and disruptive status of the zero. As de Man's use of the language of heterogeneity implies, his reading of Pascal helps us refocus onto seventeenth-century epistemology and theology the general psychosocial dynamics that Bataille theorizes. Following every step along the errant path of de Man's heady, complicated argument is beyond the scope of this chapter, but it is surely significant that de Man's reading considers whether any elements of Pascal's text disrupt the all-powerful force of the

Pascalian dialectic in the same way the heterogeneous zero disrupts the principles of totality, infinity, and homogeneity. Critiquing the Pascalian dialectic, it turns out, is as formidable a task as critiquing the Miltonic dialectic. As de Man confesses, in terms that could just as well be applied to Milton, "Negation, in a mind as resilient as Pascal's, is always susceptible of being reinscribed in a system of intelligibility."[102] Despite the ease with which one could, and should, recuperate such negation dialectically, de Man persists in his search for nonrecoverable, inassimilable negativity, a search that leads him to compare the disruptions of Pascal's system to the language of irony in ways that recall his lecture "The Concept of Irony." Irony, one might recall, is disruptive for de Man because its permanent negativity "undoes the reflexive and the dialectical model, both of which are . . . the basis of any narration."[103]

In Chapter 3, I turned to de Man's theory of irony in order to approach the pleasure of poetry's potential vanity. Let me take it up here, once more, in order to return to the specific question with which this section began: what is the relationship between poetry and chaos? As chance would have it, de Man's reading of Friedrich Schlegel in "The Concept of Irony" ends on this very question. "This is the original of all poetry," writes Schlegel, "to suspend the notions and the laws of rational thought and to replace us within a beautiful confusion in the original chaos of human nature."[104] However, as his recourse to the phrase "beautiful confusion" reveals, Schlegel—like Pascal, Milton, and even, at points, Bataille—must think this chaos dialectically: "Is not this entire infinite world built out of nonunderstanding, out of chaos, by means of understanding?"[105] "That sounds very nice," de Man acerbically replies, "but you should remember that the chaos is error, madness, and stupidity, in all its forms . . . Any attempt to construct—that is, to narrate—on no matter how advanced a level, is suspended, interrupted, disrupted, by a passage like this."[106]

Milton studies is one, though certainly not the only, contemporary intellectual arena where the desire to smooth out such chaotic suspensions, interruptions, and disruptions is felt most strongly. Such desire makes eminent sense. In light of the benefits gained from viewing (Milton's) poetry as an agent of *relève*ation, the costs of bringing out the chaos of irony and the irony of chaos are bound to be too high. As de Man writes elsewhere, again in strikingly Miltonic terms, "irony is instantaneous like an 'explosion' *and the fall is sudden*."[107] But what if the costs of maintaining the fantasy of *relève*ation—the fantasy of what Edelman, in a different context, calls "reproductive futurism"—are even higher? More specifically, what if this fantasy depends on a constitutive misreading of poetry?

In Edelman's work, the by-product of such a fantasy is the *sinthomo*-sexual, the figure who, unlike Raphael or Michael, "won't offer a blessed thing by way of salvation, won't promise any transcendence or grant us a vision of something to come."[108] This is the perfect place to recall that one of Edelman's chief examples of *sinthomo*sexuality, the devilish villain Leonard (Martin Landau) in Alfred Hitchcock's *North by Northwest* (1959), is nearly responsible for causing a character allegorically named Eve (played by the even-more-allegorically named Eva Marie-Saint) to fall from the sublime heights of Mount Rushmore (Rush*more*), the vantage point on which the film climaxes, into the abyss below until Leonard is shot and falls off the mount, purged from the narrative like Satan being expelled out of Heaven following his rebellion, and Eve is subsequently rescued, virtually miraculously, by the film's main character—her lover and, by the end of the film, husband, who is also appropriately named, given the fact that he occupies the moral high ground by film's end, Roger Thorn*hill* (Cary Grant). The compassion that Hitchcock's Thornhill, like Milton's Adam, comes to learn and embody is read by Edelman in terms of de Man's theory of irony: "In that case this version of compassionate love, intended to buck up the order of desire whose form is reproductive futurism, would allegorize, to the profit of dialectic, the expense of the unrecuperable irony that compassion necessarily abjects in whomever it reads as *sinthomo*sexual."[109]

In *Paradise Lost*, Milton gives his readers a compelling portrait of the *sinthomo*sexual par excellence: Satan. What if poetry, though, far from merely *representing* paradigmatic *sinthomo*sexuals like Satan, is itself *sinthomo*sexual in (dis)orientation? What if the "unrecuperable irony" of poetry, in other words, functions as an impediment to, rather than a vehicle for, the progressive work of redemption and salvation? According to Edelman, "the *sinthomo*sexual erupts from within [the Symbolic order] as the obstacle to such a fantasy of eventual totalization, and, therefore, as an obstacle to fantasy as such."[110] And just as the *sinthomo*sexual "erupts" from within this fantasy, so too does irony "erupt," as Fallon writes, through the "surface" of Milton's poetry in the form of "unintended and displaced self-representations, allowing us to view a Milton normally hidden from us and . . . from Milton himself."[111]

As it happens, the kind of "eruption" of which both Edelman and Fallon figuratively speak is literalized in *Paradise Lost* itself, where the unsublime, heterogeneous landscape of Hell boils and bubbles with volcanoes:

> There stood a hill not far whose grisly top
> Belched fire and rolling smoke; the rest entire

Shone with a glossy scurf, undoubted sign
That in his womb was hid metallic ore,
The work of sulphur.

(1.670–74)

"The terrestrial globe," writes Bataille, "is covered with volcanoes, which serve as its anus."[112] As we have seen, divine creation, not unlike Milton's poetry, works by sublimating or "turn[ing] / Metals of drossiest ore to perfect gold" (5.442), but this process produces black tartareous waste, polluted orts and refuse. Criticism will continue, no doubt, to try to dispose of, or cover over, or dialectically recycle the negativity this waste figures in order to build literary monuments on moral high grounds. Yet from a more skeptical perspective, the unsublimity of Chaos and Hell suggests that such vantage points may not be stable hills so much as unstable, unsublatable volcanoes from within which irony spurts forth its dross, a "metallic ore" that allegorizes the very stuff of the Miltonic or(e). The real task, then, is to theorize a critical space wherein that or(e) is taken differently into account, viewed not simply as abjected refuse but as a source of queer pleasure and as the undesired end, in every sense of the word "end," of the salvational, redemptive, and generative desires we foist onto poetry. "After the volcano, the 'abyss,'" writes Derrida. "The blind men that we are, *almost all of us*, live in this language, above an abyss. . . . But the seers, the lucid ones, fall into it—this is what we must understand."[113]

CODA

Less Matter, More Art

At this point we may ask: what is the purpose of all this?
Has this analysis taught us anything about the stories in question?
But that would be a bad question.

—TZVETAN TODOROV, "Structural Analysis of Narrative"

In *Paradise Lost*, after being created out of Adam's rib, Eve lays herself down on a "green bank," and in a "clear/Smooth lake, that . . . seemed another sky,"[1] she gazes at her reflection, in a pointed re-inflection of the Narcissus myth. Retrospectively reflecting and speculating on the significance of this mirror stage, Eve relates what could have happened but didn't: "there I had fixed/Mine eyes till now, and pined with vain desire,/Had not a voice thus warned me" (4.465–67). That voice, the voice of God, leads Eve away from the lake—away from Narcissus's fate, in fact—toward Adam and toward her redeemed and redeeming future as the "Mother of human race" (4.475). Explicating this scene in "The Mirror and the Tank," Lee Edelman writes, "Where Narcissus, in the Ovidian narrative from which Milton draws in this . . . scene, pays for his specular fixation by 'dying at life's prime,' Eve escapes such a fate through the external mediation of the divine voice, a third term whose linguistic intervention both lays down and *is* the Law."[2] And because that intervention "both lays down and *is* the Law," the narrative path toward which it directs Eve is inevitable. As Eve says, "What could I do,/But follow straight, invisibly thus led?" (4.475–76).

Insofar as the force of that Law exerts itself on us, too, we have no choice but to read Eve's question as a rhetorical one, as a statement that there is no other choice than the duty to "follow straight." But what if we were to indulge in the irony of poetic language, even for just a moment, and take Eve's question literally, not just rhetorically? What if we were to assume, in other words, that Eve is *actually asking* what other courses, and dis-courses, are available beyond the overdetermined teleological and allegorical narrative path that Milton, inspired by God, lays out for her? Read in such a way, her question raises the contingent possibility that she *could* have stayed or strayed by the lake and thus "pined with vain desire." If she had gone the way of Narcissus, though, the logic of hedonophobia would require us to read her fate, like the Fall itself, as "tragic" (9.6). Her inevitable death would be seen, then, as too high a price to pay for a moment's pleasure. Nevertheless, the irony that erupts at this moment also opens up a space of pleasure into which literary theory, I argue, can and should insinuate itself. What can we do but follow "straight"? As we've seen throughout this book, pleasure must always ultimately lose out in any dialectical contest with virtue. Early modern writers repeatedly come to imagine, however fleetingly, what would happen if pleasure were to win such a contest. Like us, their contemporary partners in humanism, they recoil in horror from that possibility. How can we learn to read and write from a position where the possibility of a pleasure unreconciled to virtue becomes an occasion for pleasure rather than horror?

Considering that this book as a whole questions the very logic of ends, I am tempted to end the book on this question. Judith Roof, among others, argues that "our comfort in the end is produced by a cause/effect logic where the end promises an ultimate result." "The payoff of the end, then," she goes on, "would seem to be some kind of transcendence over life's inevitable mysteries."[3] Teleology, Madhavi Menon similarly remarks, "shuns both instability and inconsequence."[4] Like those facile "learning outcomes" that the corporatized university demands be included on instructors' syllabi, the all-but-universal desire for the satisfaction of an ending—the gratification of a narrative that vigilantly ensures, from the beginning and even more so in the end, the necessity, transparency, utility, and payoff of its creative and/or critical energies and investments—leaves little room for the futilitarian pleasures of contingency, surprise, errancy, inconsequence, and mystery. To end with this question, then, would be to recapture those pleasures by withstanding the compulsion to complete, withholding an account of the study's potential results or payoffs, and leaving any such conclusion in the indefinite state of a (con)summation always devoutly to be wished.

More specifically, I am tempted to end with this particular question because it remains unclear to me whether we could ever revalorize—never mind put into practice—a pleasure unreconciled to virtue. The query Eve asks in *Paradise Lost*—"What could I do, / But follow straight?"—can be taken, as I pointed out, either rhetorically or literally. As a rhetorical question, which is how Milton *must* intend it, its implicit answer is "nothing"; as a literal question, it invites an exploration of possible answers other than "nothing," suggesting that there are, or may be, still unimagined alternatives to the teleological demand to "follow straight." In this spirit, I would intend my own question to be taken as both a rhetorical and a literal question. While the question's rhetorical meaning would bespeak this study's pessimism regarding the possibility of indulging in futilitarian pleasures with impunity, its status as a literal question would express the hopeful other half of this project's half-hearted investigation of pleasure—leaving open, and so inviting others to explore, the possibilities that this book has appeared so often (I am well aware) to have precluded.

An attempt to answer this question, then, would inevitably lead us back to square one, right back into the trap of subordinating to the logic of utility the unpredictable excess of pleasure that this book has tried to make and inhabit. Yet this book hasn't exactly been interested in embracing the sheer futility of pointless pleasures, either. "To question certainty," Barbara Johnson writes, "is not the same as to affirm uncertainty."[5] Similarly, questioning utility need not entail any unqualified affirmation of futility. The current crisis in higher education leads me to believe that it is not entirely unreasonable to expect from this study some sort of payoff—a useful program, if not a strategic battle plan, for moving forward. In this context, and in this coda, I feel more than ever the urgent need to forsake the mirror for the tank. Over the course of working on this project, I have been both intrigued and unnerved by the fact that those who have encouraged me to be less cautious and ambivalent in my embrace of futilitarianism have tended to be tenured senior scholars. Ecstatically abandoning oneself, or at least one's work, to the pleasures of contingency and the contingencies of pleasure is perhaps a luxury reserved and realizable only for those whose firmly secured status in the profession does not rank them, as it were, among the untenured or among the growing numbers of what we have come to call, all too aptly, "contingent faculty." The answer, then, cannot *simply* be a restatement of the question any more than the answer can *simply* be an invitation to reject the duty to be useful.

I am thus caught, in the end, in a double bind—faced, like Hercules at the crossroads, with two equally unattractive, and possibly irreconcilable, options. If I embrace the luxury of futility by declining to answer the question, I run the risk of frustrating my readers and of opening myself (even further than I already have) to the charge of self-indulgence, of being content to watch the humanities burn from whatever self-enclosed Epicurean garden I have tried to cultivate. If I embrace the demand for utility by answering the question and outlining what I hope to be the useful and profitable dividends for those who have invested the time and effort to read this book, I court the risk of invalidating the preceding critique of utility. Yet if this seemingly infelicitous impasse is to be more than a source of mere malaise, then we may take some comfort in knowing that it is yet another iteration of the conflict with which so many early modern writers, especially those working in the mode of romance, struggled. As Patricia Parker puts it, with regard to Spenser, "The controlled 'error' which is the project of *The Faerie Queene* is flanked by two problems, wandering lost with no hope of arrival and a concern for the end which diminishes the delights to be found along the way."[6] The task for writers like Spenser and Milton, as for us, is to steer clear of the Scylla of teleological ends without being swallowed whole by the Charybdian abyss of absolute futility. Neither option on its own is as compelling as the suspension or balance between them, at least to my mind (yes, I'm a Libra).[7]

In light of all of this, let me re-pose the question on the table, this time inflecting it with a little more urgency: how *can* we learn to read and write from a position where the possibility of a pleasure unreconciled to virtue becomes an occasion for pleasure rather than horror? Wagering that it is possible both to answer this question and to acknowledge that such an answer repeats the demand for utility that the book interrogates—that it is possible, in other words, to have one's utility (or futility) and eat it too—I want to suggest that one answer to this question is the one in which I have already been, all along, engaged. Although we cannot *entirely* shirk the demand for utility, the implicit metacritical argument of this book has been that we can nevertheless reconceive scholarly and critical writing to make *more* room for the idle, pointless, and playful pleasures that early modern writers, not unlike their postmodern heirs, half-heartedly embrace.

In attempting to enact, and not simply to discuss, those pleasures, I have of course taken a cue from what Leah Marcus calls "the playful, performative criticism that often accompanies" queer theory, a mode of scholarship that, as Marcus remarks, has "barely penetrated the field" of early modern studies.[8] In order to flesh out how such criticism performs the critiques that it offers, and to confront the limits that any such performance often runs up against, let me first juxtapose two passages, each from a recent monograph in early modern studies that has profoundly influenced my own project. The first is from Will Stockton's *Playing Dirty: Sexuality and Waste in Early Modern Comedy*:

> The chapters in this book are additionally playful in the sense of being analytically promiscuous. . . . Such "lack of focus" may frustrate some readers, but I did not conceive this book in monogamous fidelity to a single big idea. Rather, I conceived it while flirting with ideas that were sometimes interconnected—ideas that only came together as a monograph because I allowed myself to entertain the implications of the queer critique of teleology and chronology for the standard scholarly monograph that usually presents arguments more historically and theoretically bounded, more narrowly focused and cumulative. This book is accordingly full of promiscuous shifts in attention.[9]

Instead of shaping his arguments to the form that monographs are supposed to take—"bounded," "focused," and "cumulative," its threads tied together through a teleological and unified narrative in which, as in Hegel's characterization of the dialectical progress of Spirit, "the length of [the] path has to be endured because, for one thing, each moment is necessary"[10]—Stockton offers a "playful" mode full of potentially disorienting and frustrating "shifts in attention." Moreover, his use of an erotic vocabulary to describe his stylistic and methodological choices—his book is "promiscuous" rather than "monogamous"—can hardly be considered gratuitous or merely ornamental. As many queer theorists have shown, and as I hope this book has continued to show, non-normative narrative is so often implicated in—if not in essence then at least by frequent association with—non-normative sexuality.

Like Stockton's *Playing Dirty*, Judith Haber's *Desire and Dramatic Form in Early Modern England* is invested in exploring modes of promiscuous and pointless play in early modern literature, at the level of that literature's form as well as its content. And like Stockton, Haber recognizes that the content of her own study can, and perhaps should, affect the form and style with which that content is conveyed. Even still, she pulls back from fully mimicking the nonteleological play she discusses, in terms that are revealing: "The criticisms of narrative that underlie my argument necessarily pose a problem in the structuring of my own story. I have tried to give them their due by avoiding an overly constricting master narrative, while I also attempt to avoid the imitative fallacy (and to respect institutional strictures) by charting clear connections among the texts I examine—and between them and other contemporary texts—and by considering how they respond to the constraints of their time."[11] Not nearly as well known as the intentional and affective fallacies, what Haber calls the "imitative fallacy" is the assumption, also critiqued by the New Critics, that the form of a text should imitate its content; railing against difficult modernist poetry, many New Critics deplored the idea that a poem about boredom should itself be boring, or that a poem about the fragmentation of life in modernity should take the form of fragments.[12] Although the New Critics were writing specifically against the imitative fallacy in poetry, it is easy to see why such imitative tendencies in criticism would be considered even more fallacious. Because critical writing so often effaces its status *as* writing in the name of scholarly decorum and objectivity, literary studies has become habituated and committed to the watertight distinction between literature and criticism.

For those who study early modern literature, however, the New Critical critique of the imitative fallacy can be considered its own kind of fallacy. Surely the notion that imitative writing is fallacious would be foreign to a culture so committed to self-reflexive imitation as the Renaissance. Hence, Spenser constructs a meandering poem about meandering knights, Nashe writes a treatise *on* dreams that mirrors the associative structure *of* dreams, Milton composes a dilated epic about the dilation of postlapsarian time, and so forth. Trained from grammar school onward in the art of imitation, early modern writers approached the texts, especially the ancient texts, they read with the question, "What do I make of this?"—not (or not only) in the sense of "How do I understand this?" but in the sense of "What do I create out of this?" or even, "What do I steal from this?" Thus, Sean Keilen proposes that "one way to understand the literature of the English Renaissance is to imitate it—a hypothesis, even, that we ought to aspire in our literary history and criticism to the poetic license that Renaissance writers took with their ancient sources."[13] However much we might recoil from the notion that "poetic license" is something to which literary criticism ought to aspire, that aspiration may ultimately be less fallacious or anachronistic than treating Renaissance literature with the Enlightenment assumptions of objectivity, transparency, and linearity that historicist and materialist critics so often bring to it.

Even beyond the field of early modern studies, it seems to me that the distinction between literature and criticism deserves to be challenged—especially now more than ever. One can assume that, over time, scholarly criticism purged itself of literariness in order to establish its utility and value in the modern academy, in relation to "harder" disciplines in the social sciences and physical sciences. The ironic, counterproductive side effect of this process, however, has been that criticism has relegated itself to an abject or secondary position in relation to the literature it treats.[14] In the current crisis in liberal arts education, few people dispute the value of literature itself; what *is* devalued is the study or criticism of literature, and it will still be devalued as long as we continue to view criticism as something other than or less than art. There needs no Oscar Wilde come from the grave to argue yet once more for the critic as artist, but perhaps literary scholars do need to be reminded that the difference between literature and criticism may be, as Paul de Man once put it, "delusive."[15] "No wonder there are no poems to the Muse of Criticism," Geoffrey Hartman writes. "Does she exist? What pleasures her, or what pleasure is in her?"[16] O for a Muse of Criticism that would ascend the brightest heaven of invention!

Thankfully, there are signs that this situation may be changing, and I hope that my own efforts here will contribute to such a change. In addition to the experiments with critical style in which queer theorists have engaged (not to say indulged), recent work by Michel Chaouli, Andrew Miller, and Eric Hayot, among others, has reopened the question of the literariness of criticism.[17] Miller, for example, distinguishes between two modes of critical writing: conclusive criticism and implicative criticism. The former "aims . . . to establish facts, convey information, or make judgments"; assertive conclusions are its goal, and therefore it invites no "continuation from its readers." Implicative criticism, by contrast, "does not have ending as an end, is not justified by its conclusions, by any facts established, information conveyed or judgments made; instead it is successful to the extent that it implicates, it enfolds its readers."[18] Miller is honest enough to admit that there are risks to a more implicative, less conclusive criticism: "allusions can go unnoticed and can appear obscurantist (can be obscurantist); underexplanation can be ungenerous or a cover for complacency; ellipses can be coy." But he is also bold enough to acknowledge that "there are also risks to thinking that maximum explicitness and clarity are ideal," inviting us to entertain the possibility that "lucidity is not the sole or perhaps the highest aim of critical prose. There are other virtues—say, amplitude of implication or range of resonance. And those virtues may require that you leave your stones unturned."[19] Leaving one's stones unturned entails failing to produce what D. A. Miller calls criticism that is "too readable to need to be read further," a phrase that perfectly encapsulates the dead ends, so to speak, of conclusive criticism.[20]

As these characterizations suggest, the pleasures of implicative criticism are not unlike the pleasures of literary writing. The question remains why critics tend to be more willing to associate those pleasures with literature than with criticism, and thus to permit them more free rein in the former than in the latter. According to Hayot, "Minimally it's weird for a profession to have one theory of language for its object and another for its products. Why shouldn't the open productivity of the literary—its astonishing dynamic and reproductive capacities in the realms of imagination, feeling, thought, and aesthetics—be thought of as a feature of scholarship itself?"[21] Hayot's essay itself enacts the "open productivity of the literary" in its form, relaying its argument in a quasi-Joycean array of different styles and modes, including snippets of staged schizophrenic dialogue with himself:

> "What if literary criticism were one of the major nonfictional genres of the twentieth century? What if we were to write a history of that genre, not as a story of schools of thought succeeding one another (New Criticism to New Historicism) but as a history of experiments in structure, rhetoric, and style?"
>
> "The only thing that's interesting about that is how completely obvious it would be if you said it about some other genre of writing."[22]

Such stylistic choices are bound to frustrate those who demand transparency and maximum utility from (critical) writing, but at least they have the virtue of attempting to prove in practice the point Hayot tries to convey: that "communication, argument, and feeling can happen well in modes other than the declamatory or the plain."[23] Indeed, the other welcome strand of Hayot's argument—despite its reliance on the language of "productivity" and "reproductiv[ity]" to characterize the dynamism of the literary—is its scrupulous attention to the fact that the injunction to plain style is often posed against a self-indulgence more or less tacitly associated, as it was in the Renaissance (though not only in the Renaissance), with the feminine, the foreign, the queer, and the disabled. It is no mere coincidence, then, that queer theorists, as Chaouli recognizes, are among those who have been most invested in "attuning readers to style and changing the tone of criticism."[24]

Let me re-pose, then, for one final time, the question this coda aims to answer: how can we learn to read and write from a position where the possibility of a pleasure unreconciled to virtue becomes a source of pleasure rather than horror? We can begin by blurring, even if only provisionally, the distinction between literature and criticism; by questioning the institutional structures that such a barrier serves; by attempting to reconceive literary criticism as an art or form of literature in its own right; by entertaining the possibility that the pleasure of criticism, not unlike the pleasure of literature, may exceed or even thwart whatever goals of utility it aims to reach and secure; by embracing the charge of self-indulgence so often levied against queer writers. With the caveat that, as early modern writers learned all too well, there are no guarantees when it comes to pleasure, and that any end must therefore be contingent, we may conclude that injecting a little more pleasure and a little less utility, a little more art and a little less matter, into critical writing might be one way, however counterintuitive, of making that writing matter again.

ACKNOWLEDGMENTS

I feel tremendously lucky to have the opportunity to convey my gratitude to the mentors, colleagues, students, editors, friends, and family members who have contributed to this book—whether directly or indirectly, wittingly or unwittingly. Some of those contributions came in long before I started working on this project; others came in long before I ever even knew I wanted to enter this profession. In any case, they were all integral and are all cherished.

At the same time, the act of writing these words has been marred by the common and inevitable, though no less demoralizing, realization that whatever I print here can only be scandalously insufficient; the thanks I owe to those who have helped me along the way can only be expressed properly in a document that would surely amount to hundreds and hundreds of pages. With the full acknowledgment, then, that they deserve much fuller acknowledgments, I'd like to list the names of my accomplices, guides, and inspirations. At the very least, it's wonderful to see so many people from so many different stages and arenas of my life and career gathered together in this form: Nancy Armstrong, Sarah Balkin, Dave Ben-Merre, Daniel Block, Eugenie Brinkema, Jeff Covington, Denise Davis, Lee Edelman, Carla Freccero, Lowell Gallagher, Kelly Sheahen Gerner, Khristina Gonzalez, Sin Guanci, Katie, Will, and Quentin Holmes, Jacques Khalip, Wendy Lee, Joan Pong Linton, Michelle Malonzo, Madhavi Menon, Steve Mentz, Jeff Neilson, David Orvis, Sarah Osment, Richard Rambuss, Ravit Reichman, Debapriya Sarkar, Jennifer Schnepf, Jonathan Schroeder, Julia Shaw, Robert Sheahen, Hannah Sikorski, Ray Sultan, Leonard Tennenhouse, Stephanie Tilden, Amy Vegari, Jacqueline Wernimont, and Jay Zysk.

Arthur Little, Coppélia Kahn, Jean Feerick, and Ellen Rooney constitute a dazzling group of mentors whose guidance has sustained me, and whose own work has energized me, for quite some time. Arthur launched me on this path in the first place, and the awe-inspiring force of his reading, writing, teaching, and thinking continues to propel me. Coppélia, Jean, and Ellen were instrumental in helping me form this project from the beginning and throughout, but their generous contributions to my development as a scholar and teacher began well before that, and in the years since I finished graduate school I have been the grateful beneficiary of their ongoing care and company. I also want to acknowledge here one of the best glitterary critics I know, Stephen Guy-Bray, who deserves special recognition for, among many other things, teaching me so much of what I know about futilitarianism and poemitude in the Renaissance and beyond.

This book owes its current form and ultimate completion to the considerable and considerate support provided by my colleagues at Fordham, particularly Mary Bly, John Bugg, Ed Cahill, Mark Caldwell, Heather Dubrow, Ben Dunning, Carl Fischer, Moshe Gold, Glenn Hendler, Melanie Holm, Lea Puljcan Juric, Eve Keller, Julie Kim, Rebecca Sanchez, Jordan Stein, Dennis Tyler, and Keri Walsh. It truly is the most encouraging and delightful community I can imagine working with. Andrew Albin—*amicus certus in re incerta*—generously read the entire manuscript; his insightful suggestions helped me find the concord of this discord, one of many reasons I am fortunate to be able to count him as a friend.

Hospitable audiences at Fordham, Brown, the Institute for Comparative Literature and Society at Columbia, and various meetings of the Shakespeare Association of America over the years helped me to see more clearly the contours of this project. I'd also like to thank my undergraduate and graduate students at Fordham for allowing me to experiment with my ideas and, more important, for helping to transform those ideas through their boundless curiosity.

At Fordham University Press, Thomas Lay has been an ideal editor: inviting, encouraging, responsive, discerning, and savvy. His unwavering support in making this, my first book, possible means a lot to me. I am thankful as well for the assistance of Eric Newman, Katie Sweeney, and other members of the Press staff, especially the copyeditors and designers, for their work—seemingly effortless and miraculous, from my point of view—in creating a book, an object in the world, out of a series of Word documents.

I also would like to express thanks to my family: to all of my aunts, uncles, and cousins, for perpetually rejuvenating my spirits; to my sister and brother, for their constant support; to my father, for teaching me the pleasures of wordplay; to my mother, for teaching me the pleasures of popular culture; to my grandmother, for teaching me the pleasures of storytelling; and to my godfather, my Uncle Tim, who reminded me, at just the right moment, of the importance of valuing pleasure over profit.

So much of this book was hammered out, over the course of many years, in countless conversations—over the phone, on the road, at the gym, across the table, under library and coffee-shop roofs, by e-mail or by text, during seminar, workshop, and writing group meetings, in Providence, Boston, New York City, and Ithaca—with my brilliant, hilarious, and kindhearted friend Chris Holmes. I dedicate this book to him with all the admiration and appreciation I can muster, in meager exchange for all of the feedback and good cheer he has supplied in abundance.

Portions of Chapters 1 and 3 originally appeared in "Nashe's Vain Vein: Poetic Pleasure and the Limits of Utility," in *The Age of Thomas Nashe: Text, Bodies, and Trespasses of Authorship in Early Modern England*, ed. Stephen Guy-Bray, Joan Pong Linton, and Steve Mentz (Burlington, Vt.: Ashgate, 2013), 153–68. Reprinted by permission of the publishers.

An early and shorter version of Chapter 2 was originally published as "Bonfire of the Vanities: Pleasure, Theory, Shakespeare," in *differences: A Journal of Feminist Cultural Studies* 24, no. 1 (2013): 139–70. Copyright 2013, Duke University Press. Reprinted by permission of the publisher.

An early and shorter version of Chapter 4 was published as "Spenser's Unhappy Ends: The Legend of Courtesy and the Pleasure of the Text," in *ELH* 79, no. 4 (2012): 797–822. Copyright © 2012 The Johns Hopkins University Press. Reprinted with permission by Johns Hopkins University Press.

NOTES

FUTILITARIANISM: AN INTRODUCTION

1. Susan Sontag, *"Against Interpretation" and Other Essays* (1966; repr., New York: Picador, 2001), 5.

2. Consider the following far-from-exhaustive list of books, all published within the last decade and a half: Catherine Belsey, *A Future for Criticism* (Malden, Mass.: Blackwell, 2011); Rita Felski, *Uses of Literature* (Oxford: Blackwell, 2008); Marjorie Garber, *A Manifesto for Literary Studies* (Seattle: University of Washington Press, 2003); Garber, *The Use and Abuse of Literature* (New York: Pantheon, 2011); Gregory Jusdanis, *Fiction Agonistes: In Defense of Literature* (Stanford, Calif.: Stanford University Press, 2010); Caroline Levine, *Provoking Democracy: Why We Need the Arts* (Malden, Mass.: Blackwell, 2007); Martha C. Nussbaum, *Not for Profit: Why Democracy Needs the Humanities* (Princeton, N.J.: Princeton University Press, 2010); Mark William Roche, *Why Literature Matters in the 21st Century* (New Haven, Conn.: Yale University Press, 2004); and Daniel Schwarz, *In Defense of Reading: Teaching Literature in the Twenty-First Century* (Malden, Mass.: Wiley-Blackwell, 2008).

3. Jusdanis, *Fiction Agonistes*, 1.

4. Ibid., 8.

5. See Frank Bruni, "College, Poetry and Purpose," *New York Times*, Feb. 18, 2015, http://www.nytimes.com/2015/02/18/opinion/frank-bruni-college-poetry-and-purpose.html.

6. Frank Bruni, "From 'Hamlet' to Hillary," *New York Times*, May 2, 2015, http://www.nytimes.com/2015/05/03/opinion/sunday/frank-bruni-from-hamlet-to-hillary.html.

7. This ends-oriented perspective can be seen, for example, in Martha Nussbaum's *Not for Profit: Why Democracy Needs the Humanities*. Although Nussbaum argues against measuring the humanities and the arts in terms of their profitability in the global economy, her defense measures them in relation to less literal kinds of profitability: "the ability to think critically; the ability to transcend local loyalties and to approach world problems as a 'citizen of the world'; and, finally, the ability to imagine sympathetically the predicament

of another person" (7). Thus, Nussbaum shares with her opponents the notion that the value of literature and the arts depends on the redemptive ends they lead to, even if what they lead to is, for Nussbaum, more qualitatively than quantitatively, more figuratively than literally, profitable.

8. Throughout this study, I use the word "poetry" more or less in the capacious early modern sense of the term, as denoting fictional or imaginative literature in general. The term applies not only to the forms of verse writing we moderns call "poetry," but also to plays and works of prose fiction. Thus, when discussing early modern texts and contexts, I tend to use "poetry"; when discussing modern texts and contexts, I tend to use "literature."

9. Unless otherwise noted, all quotations from Shakespeare's plays in this book will be taken from *The Norton Shakespeare, Based on the Oxford Edition*, gen. ed. Stephen Greenblatt (New York: Norton, 1997), and will be parenthetically cited in the text by act, scene, and line numbers.

10. It might be worth commenting further here on my selection of particular authors, and particular texts, for the archive this book analyzes. One of the readers of the manuscript for Fordham University Press noted the absence of a chapter on Sidney, especially his *Defence of Poesy*. It would be inaccurate to say that Sidney is entirely absent from the book, since I draw on and offer local analyses of his writings in nearly every chapter. Nevertheless, I have deliberately selected writers who come from backgrounds more modest than the aristocratic Sidney. Because the threat of failure was more pressing for them, for various reasons, writers such as Shakespeare, Ascham, Nashe, Spenser, and Milton articulate the stakes and dangers of poetic pleasure in heightened, urgent ways that Sidney, given his privileged background, never does. I would feel quite satisfied if this book were to prompt other critics to test out the contours and limits of its argument about the pleasures of futility in relation to other demographics of early modern writers—including wealthier, more privileged writers (Sidney, Sir Walter Raleigh, Sir Francis Bacon), writers of popular prose fiction (John Lyly, Robert Greene, Thomas Lodge), women writers (Isabella Whitney, Aemilia Lanyer, Margaret Cavendish, Katherine Philips), professional playwrights (Christopher Marlowe, Ben Jonson, Thomas Middleton, John Fletcher, Francis Beaumont), and so forth.

Moreover, because my project is largely interested in exploring pleasure at the level of form, style, and textuality, I have devoted my attention to texts that do not always *explicitly* take up the question of pleasure, particularly unproductive sexual pleasures. A more thematically oriented argument might have pursued readings of Shakespeare's *Antony and Cleopatra* instead of *Richard II*, Nashe's erotic poem "The Choice of Valentines" instead of *The Unfortunate Traveller*, book 2 of Spenser's *The Faerie Queene* instead of book 6, and

Milton's *A Maske at Ludlow Castle* instead of *Paradise Lost*. In declining to address these more obvious representations of pleasure, I have taken a cue from Roland Barthes: "The text of pleasure is not necessarily the text that recounts pleasures; the text of bliss is never the text that recounts the kind of bliss afforded literally by an ejaculation. The pleasure of representation is not attached to its object." Roland Barthes, *The Pleasure of the Text*, trans. Richard Miller (New York: Hill and Wang, 1975), 55. For a reading of Renaissance poetry and drama that is similarly inspired by Barthes, and that has deeply inspired my study in turn, see Stephen Guy-Bray, *Against Reproduction: Where Renaissance Texts Come From* (Toronto: University of Toronto Press, 2009).

11. See, for example, Robert Matz, *Defending Literature in Early Modern England: Renaissance Literary Theory in Social Context* (Cambridge: Cambridge University Press, 2000); David Glimp, *Increase and Multiply: Governing Cultural Reproduction in Early Modern England* (Minneapolis: University of Minnesota Press, 2003); Laurie Ellinghausen, *Labor and Writing in Early Modern England, 1567–1667* (Aldershot, U.K.: Ashgate, 2008); and David Baker, *On Demand: Writing for the Market in Early Modern England* (Stanford, Calif.: Stanford University Press, 2010).

12. See Cynthia Marshall, *The Shattering of the Self: Violence, Subjectivity, and Early Modern Texts* (Baltimore: The Johns Hopkins University Press, 2002); Gail Kern Paster, Katherine Rowe, and Mary Floyd-Wilson, eds., *Reading the Early Modern Passions: Essays in the Culture History of Emotion* (Philadelphia: University of Pennsylvania Press, 2004); Tanya Pollard, *Drugs and Theater in Early Modern England* (Oxford: Oxford University Press, 2005); Katherine Craik, *Reading Sensations in Early Modern England* (New York: Palgrave Macmillan, 2007); Elizabeth Spiller, *Reading and the History of Race in the Renaissance* (Cambridge: Cambridge University Press, 2011); and Katherine Craik and Tanya Pollard, eds., *Shakespearean Sensations: Experiencing Literature in Early Modern England* (Cambridge: Cambridge University Press, 2013).

13. I hasten to add that such tendencies are not confined to historicist criticism; they also suffuse even those critical views that are positioned, to some extent, against historicism. Since the turn of the millennium, a good deal has been written about the "new formalism," a tag that designates a movement of critics who wish to bring considerations of literary form back into conversation. In the realm of early modern studies, new formalist critics question the historicist tendency to dissolve poetry into the vaguely general categories of "writing," "letters," or "discourse." "For at least some Renaissance thinkers and writers," Stephen Cohen writes, "an understanding of the formal features of literature that distinguished it from other discourses did not inhibit but on the contrary enabled an understanding of its social efficacy." Stephen Cohen, "Between Form and Culture: New Historicism and

the Promise of a Historical Formalism," in *Renaissance Literature and Its Formal Engagements*, ed. Mark David Rasmussen (New York: Palgrave, 2002), 31. But what if, from the point of view of early modern literary culture, the distinctive features of poetry *did* inhibit an understanding of its social efficacy, not to mention its social efficacy altogether? The claim Cohen makes here is beneficial to the extent that it reveals the need to read poems as poems and not, for example, as conduct books or medical manuals. But it still presupposes, and so leaves unquestioned, the "social efficacy" of poetry.

14. Examples of presentist critiques of historicism include Terence Hawkes, *Shakespeare in the Present* (London: Routledge, 2002); Ewan Fernie, "Shakespeare and the Prospect of Presentism," *Shakespeare Survey* 58 (2005): 169–84; Hugh Grady and Terence Hawkes, eds., *Presentist Shakespeares* (Abingdon, U.K.: Routledge, 2007); Evelyn Gajowski, ed., *Presentism, Gender, and Sexuality in Shakespeare* (New York: Palgrave, 2009); and Cary DiPietro and Hugh Grady, eds., *Shakespeare and the Urgency of Now: Criticism and Theory in the 21st Century* (London: Palgrave, 2013).

Queer critiques of historicism can be found in Arthur L. Little Jr., *Shakespeare Jungle Fever: National-Imperial Re-Visions of Race, Rape, and Sacrifice* (Stanford, Calif.: Stanford University Press, 2000); Carla Freccero, *Queer/Early/Modern* (Durham, N.C.: Duke University Press, 2006); Jonathan Goldberg and Madhavi Menon, "Queering History," *PMLA* 120, no. 5 (2005): 1608–17; Madhavi Menon, *Unhistorical Shakespeare: Queer Theory in Shakespearean Literature and Film* (New York: Palgrave, 2008); and Will Stockton, *Playing Dirty: Sexuality and Waste in Early Modern Comedy* (Minneapolis: University of Minnesota Press, 2011). Carolyn Dinshaw's *Getting Medieval: Sexualities and Communities, Pre- and Postmodern* (Durham, N.C.: Duke University Press, 1999), has also been an important influence on my writing here. Such approaches, however, have hardly been welcomed with open arms; see especially Valerie Traub's critique in "The New Unhistoricism in Queer Studies," *PMLA* 128, no. 1 (2013): 21–39.

15. Even scholars who have attempted to draw connections between the current state of the humanities and early modern humanism tend to do so merely as a framing gesture, relegating such connections to prefaces and afterwords while devoting the body of their monographs to the task of historicizing the differences between the two periods. See, for example, Rebecca Bushnell, *A Culture of Teaching: Early Modern Humanism in Theory and Practice* (Ithaca, N.Y.: Cornell University Press, 1996), 1–9, and Matz, *Defending Literature*, 15–17 and 128–36. Consider, for instance, the following claim Matz makes: "Contemporary historicist criticism has found in the sixteenth century's anxious defense of literature's place an echo of its own concerns, and has responded by adopting rather than historicizing that defense" (17). In

response, I would argue that historicizing that defense, as Matz goes on to do, is yet another way of adopting it; my intention, then, is to theorize, rather than historicize, the "echo" Matz both invokes and shies away from.

16. On this development, see the opening to Eugenie Brinkema's *The Forms of the Affects* (Durham, N.C.: Duke University Press, 2014), where she diagnoses "a larger reawakening of interest in problematics of embodiment and materiality in the wake of twentieth-century Western theory that, for many, was all semiotics and no sense, all structure and no stuff" (1).

17. Jonathan Goldberg, *Shakespeare's Hand* (Minneapolis: University of Minnesota Press, 2003), viii.

18. See Terence Cave, *The Cornucopian Text: Problems of Writing in the French Renaissance* (Oxford: Clarendon, 1979); Patricia Parker, *Inescapable Romance: Studies in the Poetics of a Mode* (Princeton, N.J.: Princeton University Press, 1979); Jonathan Goldberg, *Endlesse Worke: Spenser and the Structures of Discourse* (Baltimore: The Johns Hopkins University Press, 1981); Thomas M. Greene, *The Light in Troy: Imitation and Discovery in Renaissance Poetry* (New Haven, Conn.: Yale University Press, 1982); and Jonathan Crewe, *Unredeemed Rhetoric: Thomas Nashe and the Scandal of Authorship* (Baltimore: The Johns Hopkins University Press, 1982). For a more recent essay that reads early modern literature in this spirit, see Stephen Guy-Bray, "Middleton's Language Machine," in *The Oxford Handbook of Thomas Middleton*, ed. Gary Taylor and Trish Thomas Henley (Oxford: Oxford University Press, 2012), 346–59.

19. Representative here is David Scott Kastan's claim that "it is only by attending to the actual conditions of playwrighting in early modern England that the historical Shakespeare can be *saved* either from the mystifications of idealist criticism or from the no less mystifying moves of poststructural theory, where instead of disappearing into the putative unity and self-sufficiency of form he would disappear into the assumed priority of the linguistic order itself." David Scott Kastan, *Shakespeare after Theory* (New York: Routledge, 1999), 38; my italics.

20. Paul de Man, *Critical Writings, 1953–1978*, ed. Lindsay Waters (Minneapolis: University of Minnesota Press, 1989), 220. Despite the blatant and too often stressed differences between de Man's deconstructive version of close reading and that of the New Critics under whom he studied, they concur (at the very least) when it comes to the limitations of paraphrase. See Cleanth Brooks, "The Heresy of Paraphrase," in *The Well-Wrought Urn: Studies in the Structure of Poetry* (New York: Harvest, 1947), 192–214. For a more recent critique, see Ellen Rooney, "Form and Contentment," in *Reading for Form*, ed. Susan J. Wolfson and Marshall Brown (Seattle: University of Washington Press, 2006), 25–48. Rooney argues that "the generalization of

reading-as-paraphrase . . . robs cultural *and* literary studies of the power to make any essential contribution to critical work already moving confidently ahead in history, sociology, anthropology, and communications. These are all disciplines that have long since mastered the art of reading-as-summary, reading sans form; cultural studies and literary studies must offer them something more" (34).

21. Elizabeth Freeman, *Time Binds: Queer Temporalities, Queer Histories* (Durham, N.C.: Duke University Press, 2010), xvi–xvii. On the potential queerness of lingering, see also Cary Howie, "Stay," in *Shakesqueer: A Queer Companion to the Complete Works of Shakespeare*, ed. Madhavi Menon (Durham, N.C.: Duke University Press, 2011), 146–51.

22. Barbara Johnson, *The Wake of Deconstruction* (Cambridge, Mass.: Blackwell, 1994), 31. In some recent work on Alfred Hitchcock, D. A. Miller, a perennial devotee of the art and craft of close reading, pushes its counterproductive tendencies to the extreme by both theorizing and practicing a method he calls "Too Close Reading." See his "Hitchcock's Hidden Pictures," *Critical Inquiry* 37, no. 1 (2010): 106–30; and "Hitchcock's Understyle: A Too-Close View of *Rope*," *Representations* 121 (2013): 1–30. For commentary on this approach, see Frances Ferguson, "Now It's Personal: D. A. Miller and Too-Close Reading," *Critical Inquiry* 41, no. 3 (2015): 521–40.

23. Friedrich Nietzsche, *Daybreak: Thoughts on the Prejudices of Morality*, ed. Maudemarie Clark and Brian Leiter, trans. R. J. Hollingdale (Cambridge: Cambridge University Press, 1997), 5.

24. Leo Bersani, *The Culture of Redemption* (Cambridge, Mass.: Harvard University Press, 1990), 1.

25. See Lee Edelman, *No Future: Queer Theory and the Death Drive* (Durham, N.C.: Duke University Press, 2004).

26. See Eve Kosofsky Sedgwick, "Paranoid Reading and Reparative Reading, or, You're So Paranoid You Probably Think This Essay Is about You," in *Touching Feeling: Affect, Pedagogy, Performativity* (Durham, N.C.: Duke University Press, 2003), 125–51; Michael Snediker, *Queer Optimism: Lyric Personhood and Other Felicitous Persuasions* (Minneapolis: University of Minnesota Press, 2009); José Esteban Muñoz, *Cruising Utopia: The Then and There of Queer Futurity* (New York: New York University Press, 2009); and Christopher Castiglia and Christopher Reed, *If Memory Serves: Gay Men, AIDS, and the Promise of the Queer Past* (Minneapolis: University of Minnesota Press, 2012). An early distillation of this debate can be found in Robert L. Cesario et al., "The Antisocial Thesis in Queer Theory," *PMLA* 121.3 (2006): 819–26. See also Heather Love, *Feeling Backward: Loss and the Politics of Queer History* (Cambridge, Mass.: Harvard University Press, 2007); Sara Ahmed, *The Promise of Happiness* (Durham, N.C.: Duke University Press,

2010); Lauren Berlant, *Cruel Optimism* (Durham, N.C.: Duke University Press, 2011); and Lauren Berlant and Lee Edelman, *Sex, or the Unbearable* (Durham, N.C.: Duke University Press, 2014).

27. Muñoz, *Cruising Utopia*, 1.

28. James M. Bromley, *Intimacy and Sexuality in the Age of Shakespeare* (Cambridge: Cambridge University Press, 2011), 27. See also Menon, *Unhistorical Shakespeare*; Guy-Bray, *Against Reproduction*; and Judith Haber, *Desire and Dramatic Form in Early Modern England* (Cambridge: Cambridge University Press, 2009).

29. See Richard Strier, *The Unrepentant Renaissance: From Petrarch to Shakespeare to Milton* (Chicago: University of Chicago Press, 2011).

30. Leo Bersani and Ulysse Dutoit, *Forms of Being: Cinema, Aesthetics, Subjectivity* (London: British Film Institute, 2004), 126.

31. Dinshaw, *Getting Medieval*, 2–3.

1. PLEASURE WITHOUT PROFIT

1. Edmund Spenser, *The Faerie Queene*, 2nd ed., ed. A. C. Hamilton (Harlow, U.K.: Pearson Longman, 2007), book 2, canto 2, stanzas 44–45. All subsequent quotations of *The Faerie Queene* are taken from this edition and will be cited in the text. Citations of the poem itself will refer to book, canto, and stanza numbers; citations of Spenser's "Letter to Raleigh" will refer to page number.

2. John Milton, *The Complete Poetry and Essential Prose of John Milton*, ed. William Kerrigan, John Rumrich, and Stephen M. Fallon (New York: Modern Library, 2007), 939.

3. Stanley Fish, *Surprised by Sin: The Reader in "Paradise Lost"* (New York: St. Martin's, 1967), and *How Milton Works* (Cambridge, Mass.: Belknap Press of Harvard University Press, 2001). For an extension of such arguments to Spenser's work, see Maureen Quilligan, *Milton's Spenser: The Politics of Reading* (Ithaca, N.Y.: Cornell University Press, 1983).

4. The question of futility in early modern literature has been opened up in part by Kathryn Schwarz's "Queer Futility: Or, *The Life and Death of King John*," in *Shakesqueer: A Queer Companion to the Complete Works of Shakespeare*, ed. Madhavi Menon (Durham, N.C.: Duke University Press, 2011), 163–70. Much of my effort here can be read as an attempt to explore beyond *King John* (and beyond the early modern period) the issues raised by Schwarz in her illuminating discussion of the play.

5. Jeff Dolven, "When to Stop Reading *The Faerie Queene*," in *Never Again Would Birds' Songs Be the Same: Essays on Early Modern and Modern Poetry in Honor of John Hollander*, ed. Jennifer Lewin (New Haven, Conn.: Beinecke Library, 2002), 54.

6. See Xenophon, *Memorabilia*, trans. Amy L. Bonnette (Ithaca, N.Y.: Cornell University Press, 1994), 2.1.21–34. The most comprehensive treatment of this allegory's influence on the Renaissance can be found in Erwin Panofsky, *Hercules am Scheideweg* (Leipzig: B. G. Teubner, 1930).

7. Edmund Spenser, *The Shorter Poems*, ed. Richard A. McCabe (New York: Penguin, 1999), 131.

8. "In the theater the professional dramatist was visible, if at all, only as an actor. And when, on rare occasions, his work got into print, it was likely to be anonymous. In neither their acted nor their printed form were his plays exercises in self-presentation. . . . A professional, like Heywood in his *Apology for Actors*, or an amateur, like Sidney in his *Defence of Poesy*, could, in good humanist fashion, make a far higher claim for drama or poetry, but he rarely presented himself or his own work . . . in such lofty terms." Richard Helgerson, *Self-Crowned Laureates: Spenser, Jonson, Milton, and the Literary System* (Berkeley: University of California Press, 1983), 35–36, 38.

9. Ibid., 55.

10. Horace, "The Art of Poetry," in *Ancient Literary Criticism: The Principal Texts in New Translations*, ed. D. A. Russell and M. Winterbottom (Oxford: Oxford University Press, 2003), 288.

11. On this point, see Madeleine Doran, *Endeavors of Art: Studies of Form in Elizabethan Drama* (Madison: University of Wisconsin Press, 1954), 85–86; cited in Matz, *Defending Literature in Early Modern England: Renaissance Literary Theory in Social Context* (Cambridge: Cambridge University Press, 2000), 1.

12. This figure of speech hardly originates with Mary Poppins. In his *Discourses on the Heroic Poem* (1594), Torquato Tasso follows Lucretius (*De rerum natura*, 1.936–50) and other ancient writers when he asserts that poetic pleasure "should be like the honey smeared on a cup when one gives medicine to a child," an appraisal that Sir John Harington endorses in the "Apology" for poetry printed with his 1591 translation of Ludovico Ariosto's *Orlando furioso*. See Tasso, *Discourses on the Heroic Poem*, trans. Mariella Cavalchini and Irene Samuel (Oxford, U.K.: Clarendon, 1973), 11; and Sir John Harington, "An Apology for Ariosto: Poetry, Epic, Morality (1591)," in *English Renaissance Literary Criticism*, ed. Brian Vickers (Oxford: Clarendon, 1999), 306–7.

13. In this way, textual pleasure might be compared to the concept of tone, as theorized by Sianne Ngai, who writes, "tone is never entirely reducible to a reader's emotional response to a text or reducible to the text's internal representations of feeling (though it can amplify or be amplified by both)." Sianne Ngai, *Ugly Feelings* (Cambridge, Mass.: Harvard University Press, 2005), 29–30.

14. Victoria Kahn, "The Passions and the Interests in Early Modern Europe: The Case of Guarini's *Il Pastor fido*," in *Reading the Early Modern Passions: Essays in the Cultural History of Emotion*, ed. Gail Kern Paster, Katherine Rowe, and Mary Floyd-Wilson (Philadelphia: University of Pennsylvania Press, 2004), 221. See also Patricia Parker, *Inescapable Romance: Studies in the Poetics of a Mode* (Princeton, N.J.: Princeton University Press, 1979); Daniel Javitch, *Proclaiming a Classic: The Canonization of "Orlando Furioso"* (Princeton, N.J.: Princeton University Press, 1991); and David Quint, *Epic and Empire: Politics and Generic Form from Virgil to Milton* (Princeton, N.J.: Princeton University Press, 1993).

15. George Puttenham, *The Art of English Poesy: A Critical Edition*, ed. Frank Whigham and Wayne A. Rebhorn (Ithaca, N.Y.: Cornell University Press, 2007), 243.

16. Ibid., 259.

17. Ibid., 340; my italics.

18. Jacques Lacan, "The Instance of the Letter in the Unconscious or Reason since Freud," in *Écrits: The First Complete Edition in English*, trans. Bruce Fink (New York: Norton, 2006), 412–41, esp. 423–24: "Of course, as it is said, the letter kills while the spirit gives life. I don't disagree, . . . but I also ask how the spirit could live without the letter. The spirit's pretensions would nevertheless remain indisputable if the letter hadn't proven that it produces all its truth effects in man without the spirit having to intervene at all." Without citing Lacan, Stanley Fish importantly explores these contradictions in his arguments about Milton (whom I discuss in Chapter 5): "It is the letter . . . from which Milton, following the example of Christ, wishes to drive us, yet it is only by means of the letter—of those material forms instinct with spirit but all too capable of being detached from spirit and made into idols—that living and writing can proceed" (*How Milton Works*, 139).

19. Roland Barthes, *The Pleasure of the Text*, trans. Richard Miller (New York: Hill and Wang, 1975), 7. My citations here of Continental theorists like Lacan and Barthes should not be taken as gratuitous, anachronistic, or irrelevant to the study of early modern writers, given that Anglo-American writers, in the Renaissance no less than now, so often project the playful insistence of the letter *onto* the Continent; hence Puttenham, in his discussion of anagrammatic games, goes out of his way to point out, almost predictably, that such ostentatiously vain wordplay is "so well allowed of in France and Italy" (*Art of English Poesy*, 197).

20. Geoffrey Hartman, *Scars of the Spirit: The Struggle against Inauthenticity* (New York: Palgrave Macmillan, 2002), 117.

21. I am deeply grateful to my colleagues Andrew Albin and Julie Kim for posing perceptive questions that led me to these crucial considerations.

22. Sir Philip Sidney, *An Apology for Poetry; or, The Defence of Poesy*, ed. Geoffrey Shepherd, rev. R. W. Maslen (Manchester: Manchester University Press, 2002), 95.

23. Ibid., 95.

24. Stephen Gosson, *"The Schoole of Abuse" (1579) and "A Short Apologie of 'The School of Abuse'" (1579)*, ed. Edward Arber (London: A. Murray and Son, 1869), 20.

25. Jacques Derrida, *Dissemination*, trans. Barbara Johnson (Chicago: University of Chicago Press, 1981), 61–171. On literary writing as a drug, see Avital Ronell, *Crack Wars: Literature, Addiction, Mania* (1992; repr., Urbana: University of Illinois Press, 2004), esp. 78: "The horizon of drugs is the same as that of literature: they share the same line, depending on similar technologies and sometimes suffering analogous crackdowns before the law. They shoot up fictions, disjuncting a whole regime of consciousness. Someone once said that literature, as a modern phenomenon dating from the sixteenth or seventeenth century, was contemporaneous with European drug addiction." On Renaissance drama more particularly, see Tanya Pollard, *Drugs and Theater in Early Modern England* (Oxford: Oxford University Press, 2005).

26. Oscar Wilde, *The Picture of Dorian Gray*, ed. Robert Mighall (London: Penguin, 2000), 75.

27. Karl Marx, *Grundrisse: Foundations of the Critique of Political Economy*, trans. Martin Nicolaus (1973; repr., London: Penguin, 1993), 111.

28. Stephen Greenblatt, *Learning to Curse: Essays in Early Modern Culture* (1990; repr. New York: Routledge Classics, 2007), 15.

29. Barthes, *The Pleasure of the Text*, 4. On this quote, and on the difficulties of translating *jouissance* more generally, from a feminist angle, see Jane Gallop, "Beyond the *Jouissance* Principle," *Representations* 7 (1984): 110–15.

30. Fredric Jameson, "Pleasure: A Political Issue" (1983), in *The Ideologies of Theory: Essays, 1971–1986*, vol. 2, *Syntax of History* (Minneapolis: University of Minnesota Press, 1988), esp. 71.

31. Michel Foucault, *The Use of Pleasure*, vol. 2 of *The History of Sexuality*, trans. Robert Hurley (1985; repr., New York: Vintage, 1990), 7.

32. Tim Dean, "The Biopolitics of Pleasure," *South Atlantic Quarterly* 111, no. 3 (2012): 482, 485. Dean continues: "The various hermeneutics of suspicion I've been sketching, in their feminist, Marxist, and psychoanalytic guises, are not wrong to question dominant forms of pleasure; but they have made it harder for us to embrace, much less intensify, the pleasures we have, especially when those pleasures are palpably imbricated with power relations."

33. Barthes, *The Pleasure of the Text*, 57.

34. Joseph Litvak, *The Un-Americans: Jews, the Blacklist, and Stoolpigeon Culture* (Durham, N.C.: Duke University Press, 2009), 45.

35. David Halperin, *How to Be Gay* (Cambridge, Mass.: Belknap Press of Harvard University Press, 2012), 236.

36. Jameson, "Pleasure," 65.

37. "I am suddenly struck by the fact that no one has mentioned these archetypal (male) quest-figures lately, or any of their accompanying cortege from the portrait gallery of bourgeois individualism, such as the Adventurer. Is it possible that they have disappeared altogether from consumer society, and that their former passions have been reduced or expanded, either into psychopathology—as in the former 'gluttony'—or into the badge and sign of microgroup behavior—as in gay promiscuity?" (ibid., 62).

38. In surveying the legacy of Kant and the gender and sexual discrimination involved in rejections of aestheticism and formalism, Heather Dubrow captures this point: "Is it not possible . . . that formalism's association with the fluid sexualities of Bloomsbury and other writers associated with art for art's sake further encouraged the rejection of it in some quarters? Real men don't eat villanelles." Heather Dubrow, "Guess Who's Coming to Dinner?: Reinterpreting Formalism and the Country House Poem," in *Reading for Form*, ed. Susan J. Wolfson and Marshall Brown (Seattle: University of Washington Press, 2006), 86.

39. Cf. Halperin: "If gay male aestheticism gives rise to an identification with the upper classes, that is because gay male culture values *pleasure* over *utility*. It takes as objects of aesthetic delectation what others have created for mere use. . . . Gay aestheticism annexes these by-products of other people's serious, single-minded striving to its own ironic, disaffiliated quest for pleasure" (*How to Be Gay*, 238–39).

40. Ibid., 277–78. Recent research has shown that even economic capital isn't so easy to come by for gay men, who suffer from wage discrimination relative to their heterosexual male peers in a way that lesbians, relative to their heterosexual female peers, tend not to—which is not, of course, to deny the still-persistent and deplorable income disparity to which women of any sexual orientation are subjected. See Bruce Elmslie and Edinaldo Tebaldi, "Sexual Orientation and Labor Market Discrimination," *Journal of Labor Research* 28 (2007): 436–53. Such findings can help cast suspicion on the marketing and advertising industry's ongoing account, so to speak, of a largely untapped, upwardly mobile "gay market" with expensive tastes and a seemingly inexhaustible spending power. The facile association of gay men with elitist aestheticism and consumerism—an association produced by Marxist intellectuals no less than the capitalist machine against which Marxists define their project—obscures the social, economic, racial, and political inequalities

that continue to shape and misshape the place of sexual minorities in the sociocultural arena.

41. Stephen Guy-Bray, *Against Reproduction: Where Renaissance Texts Come From* (Toronto: University of Toronto Press, 2009), 15.

42. In addition to Guy-Bray's *Against Reproduction*, see Jeffrey Masten, *Textual Intercourse: Collaboration, Authorship, and Sexualities in Renaissance Drama* (Cambridge: Cambridge University Press, 1997); Graham L. Hammill, *Sexuality and Form: Caravaggio, Marlowe, and Bacon* (Chicago: University of Chicago Press, 2000); Daniel Juan Gil, *Before Intimacy: Asocial Sexuality in Early Modern England* (Minneapolis: University of Minnesota Press, 2006); Madhavi Menon, *Unhistorical Shakespeare: Queer Theory in Shakespearean Literature and Film* (New York: Palgrave, 2008); Judith Haber, *Desire and Dramatic Form in Early Modern England* (Cambridge: Cambridge University Press, 2009); Will Stockton, *Playing Dirty: Sexuality and Waste in Early Modern Comedy* (Minneapolis: University of Minnesota Press, 2011); James M. Bromley, *Intimacy and Sexuality in the Age of Shakespeare* (Cambridge: Cambridge University Press, 2011); and Joseph Campana, *The Pain of Reformation: Spenser, Vulnerability, and the Ethics of Masculinity* (New York: Fordham University Press, 2012).

43. See Donald Morton, "Changing the Terms: (Virtual) Desire and (Actual) Reality," in *The Material Queer: A Lesbigay Cultural Studies Reader*, ed. Donald Morton (Boulder, Colo.: Westview, 1996), 1–33. For commentary on Morton in particular, and on criticisms of ludic queer theory in general, see Carla Freccero, *Queer/Early/Modern* (Durham, N.C.: Duke University Press, 2006), 13–20; as well as Elizabeth Freeman, *Time Binds: Queer Temporalities, Queer Histories* (Durham, N.C.: Duke University Press, 2010), 9.

44. As Joseph Litvak notes, "anti-intellectual and antigay ideologies are often 'naive' enough to collaborate, sensing between *jouissance esthétique* and *jouissance érotique* so close an affinity that sexual gayness and intellectual happiness can seem wonderfully to indict each other, even or especially once pathologized as the mores that are really less." Joseph Litvak, *Strange Gourmets: Sophistication, Theory, and the Novel* (Durham, N.C.: Duke University Press, 1997), 147.

45. Jacques Derrida, "'This Strange Institution Called Literature': An Interview with Jacques Derrida," in *Acts of Literature*, ed. Derek Attridge (New York: Routledge, 1992), 56.

46. Ibid., 57.

47. Ibid., 56.

48. Barbara Johnson, "Art for Something's Sake," *Journal of Aesthetic Education* 36, no. 3 (2002): 28–29.

49. Barbara Johnson, *Mother Tongues: Sexuality, Trials, Motherhood, Translation* (Cambridge, Mass.: Harvard University Press, 2003), 131.

50. See Max Weber, *"The Protestant Ethic and the 'Spirit' of Capitalism" and Other Writings*, ed. and trans. Peter Baehr and Gordon C. Wells (New York: Penguin, 2002). See also Victor Turner, *From Ritual to Theatre: The Human Seriousness of Play* (New York: PAJ Publications, 1982), 37–39; and Stephen Innes, *Creating the Commonwealth: The Economic Culture of Puritan New England* (New York: Norton, 1995), 107–59. For an investigation of the complex role that aesthetic pleasure played in the literary and political culture of the early United States, see Edward Cahill, *Liberty of the Imagination: Aesthetic Theory, Literary Form, and Politics in the Early United States* (Philadelphia: University of Pennsylvania Press, 2012), esp. 37–41 and 64–98. Although the literature I discuss predates the late-eighteenth-century aesthetic philosophy so central, as Cahill demonstrates, to early American writers, the degree to which Protestantism influences attitudes toward pleasure provides an important point of comparison between the milieu of Renaissance England and the milieu of colonial/revolutionary America.

51. All quotations of Andrew Marvell's "A Dialogue, between the Resolved Soul and Created Pleasure" are taken from Elizabeth Story Donno, ed., *Andrew Marvell: The Complete Poems* (1972; repr., London: Penguin, 2005), and will be cited in the text by line number.

52. Frank Kermode, *Shakespeare, Spenser, Donne: Renaissance Essays* (1971; repr., Abingdon, U.K.: Routledge, 2005), 84–87.

53. Jacques Lacan, *The Ethics of Psychoanalysis, 1959–1960: The Seminar of Jacques Lacan, Seminar VII*, ed. Jacques-Alain Miller, trans. Dennis Porter (New York: Norton, 1997), 185.

54. Theodor Adorno, *Negative Dialectics*, trans. E. B. Ashton (New York: Seabury Press, 1973), xix.

55. *Sublation*, along with *sublimation*, is the conventional English translation of Hegel's *Aufhebung*, which literally evokes "up-lifting" and thus also suggests the elevated heights of the sublime. As Clayton Crockett writes, "In the history of philosophy, one can trace a trajectory from the Kantian (dynamical) sublime to Hegelian sublation (*Aufhebung*) to Freudian sublimation." Clayton Crockett, *Interstices of the Sublime: Theology and Psychoanalytic Theory* (New York: Fordham University Press, 2007), 59. The conjunction of these various terms and meanings will be central to my reading of Milton in Chapter 5, but it also remains implicit throughout the book.

56. Timothy Bewes, *Reification; or, The Anxiety of Late Capitalism* (London: Verso, 2002), 35.

57. Ibid., 44.

58. The bibliography here is vast. For a start, see Adorno, *Negative Dialectics*, esp. 300–60; Georges Bataille, "Hegel, Death and Sacrifice," trans. Jonathan Strauss, *Yale French Studies* 78 (1990): 9–28; Jacques Derrida, "From Restricted to General Economy: A Hegelianism without Reserve," in *Writing and Difference*, trans. Alan Bass (Chicago: University of Chicago Press, 1978),

251–77; Jean-Luc Nancy, *Hegel: The Restlessness of the Negative*, trans. Jason Smith and Steven Miller (Minneapolis: University of Minnesota Press, 2002); and Lee Edelman, *No Future: Queer Theory and the Death Drive* (Durham, N.C.: Duke University Press, 2004). French thinkers such as Bataille, Derrida, and Nancy owe their readings of Hegel to Alexandre Kojève's influential lectures on *Phenomenology of Spirit*; see Kojève, *Introduction to the Reading of Hegel*, ed. Allan Bloom, trans. James H. Nichols Jr. (Ithaca, N.Y.: Cornell University Press, 1980). Another important influence on Derrida in particular is Jean Hyppolite's *Genesis and Structure of Hegel's "Phenomenology of Spirit,"* trans. Samuel Cherniak and John Heckman (Chicago: Northwestern University Press, 1974). On the place of Hegel in modern French thought, see Judith Butler, *Subjects of Desire: Hegelian Reflections in Twentieth-Century France* (New York: Columbia University Press, 1987).

59. Derrida, "From Restricted to General Economy," 259–60, 273.

60. Jonathan Gil Harris, *Untimely Matter in the Time of Shakespeare* (Philadelphia: University of Pennsylvania Press, 2009), 92–93.

61. Jacques Derrida, *Archive Fever: A Freudian Impression*, trans. Eric Prenowitz (Chicago: University of Chicago Press, 1995), 74.

62. Lee Edelman, "Against Survival: Queerness in a Time That's Out of Joint," *Shakespeare Quarterly* 62, no. 2 (2011): 161.

63. Ibid., 162.

64. Ibid., 163.

65. David L. Orvis, "'Thy glorious household-stuffe': Doctrinal (Re) Inscription in George Herbert's Church Furnishing Poems," in *The Sacred and Profane in English Renaissance Literature*, ed. Mary A. Papazian (Newark: University of Delaware Press, 2008), 285–320.

66. See Richard Rambuss, *Closet Devotions* (Durham, N.C.: Duke University Press, 1998), esp. 35–37; Michael C. Schoenfeldt, *Bodies and Selves in Early Modern England: Physiology and Inwardness in Spenser, Shakespeare, Herbert, and Milton* (Cambridge: Cambridge University Press, 1999), 96–130; and Harris, *Untimely Matter*, 32–65.

67. George Herbert, *The Complete English Poems*, ed. John Tobin (1991; repr., New York: Penguin, 2004), 6, lines 1–6.

68. Ryan Netzley, *Reading, Desire, and the Eucharist in Early Modern Religious Poetry* (Toronto: University of Toronto Press, 2011), 46.

69. Ibid., 47.

70. Stephen Greenblatt, *Marvelous Possessions: The Wonder of the New World* (Chicago: University of Chicago Press, 1991), 1. Greenblatt is citing Walter Benjamin, "The Storyteller: Reflections on the Works of Nikolai Leskov," in *Illuminations*, ed. Hannah Arendt, trans. Harry Zohn (New York: Schocken, 1968), 86.

71. Matz, *Defending Literature*, 17.

2. BONFIRE OF THE VANITIES

1. Philip Schaff, *History of the Christian Church*, vol. 5, part 2 (New York: Charles Scribner's Sons, 1910), 699. Two compelling recent biographies of Savonarola are Desmond Seward's *The Burning of the Vanities: Savonarola and the Borgia Pope* (Stroud, U.K.: Sutton, 2006), and Lauro Martines's *Fire in the City: Savonarola and the Struggle for Renaissance Florence* (New York: Oxford University Press, 2006).

2. See Mario DiGangi, *The Homoerotics of Early Modern Drama* (Cambridge: Cambridge University Press, 1997); 117–19; and Madhavi Menon, "*Richard II* and the Taint of Metonymy," *ELH* 70, no. 3 (2003): 653–75.

3. Laura Frost, *The Problem with Pleasure: Modernism and Its Discontents* (New York: Columbia University Press, 2013), 12. Frost's examination of modernist writers' ambivalence toward pleasure aligns with my attempt to explore similar questions in the work of early modern writers.

4. Katherine Philips, *Poems* (London, 1664), sig. K4r–K4v.

5. J. Hillis Miller, "Presidential Address, 1986: The Triumph of Theory, the Resistance to Reading, and the Question of the Material Base," *PMLA* 102, no. 2 (1987): 284.

6. Ibid., 284.

7. On deconstructive theory, see also Jonathan Loesberg, *Aestheticism and Deconstruction: Pater, Derrida, and de Man* (Princeton, N.J.: Princeton University Press, 1991).

8. In thinking about these questions, I've been inspired by a number of comments regarding the politics of attacks against deconstruction. The first is Ellen Rooney's assertion, in *Seductive Reasoning: Pluralism as the Problematic of Contemporary Theory* (Ithaca, N.Y.: Cornell University Press, 1989), that attacks made from self-proclaimed "pluralist" camps "may in fact have less to do with the play of the signifier than with the problem of sexual (or racial or class) difference" (38). Derrida himself has referred to one (anonymous) professor who claimed that deconstruction, as Derrida paraphrases, "was mostly supported, within the university, by homosexuals and feminists—a fact which seemed very significant to [this professor], and doubtless a sign of asexuality." Jacques Derrida, *Eyes of the University: Right to Philosophy* 2, trans. Jan Plug et al. (Stanford, Calif.: Stanford University Press, 2004], 132. In light of J. Hillis Miller's statements against the sterility of deconstruction, these comments by Rooney and Derrida are doubly intriguing in their implications: the politics they expose seems to mark not only *attacks* against theory's narcissistic navel-gazing but also *defenses* of theory's value.

9. Frank Lentricchia, *Criticism and Social Change* (Chicago: University of Chicago Press, 1983), 51.

10. David Scott Kastan, *Shakespeare after Theory* (New York: Routledge, 1999), 17. Madhavi Menon offers a trenchant critique of this quote

in particular, in *Unhistorical Shakespeare: Queer Theory in Shakespearean Literature and Film* (New York: Palgrave, 2008), 2; see 52–55 for her more general critique of Kastan's book.

11. Karl Marx and Friedrich Engels, *The German Ideology (Selections)*, ed. C. J. Arthur (New York: International Publishers 2001), 47.

12. Paul de Man, *The Resistance to Theory* (Minneapolis: University of Minnesota Press, 1986), 11.

13. Ibid., 121. Given de Man's project in his late essays, one can guess the direction in which his reading of Marx might have taken him: toward what he calls, in his essay "Kant's Materialism," "a materialism much more radical than what can be conveyed by such terms as 'realism' or 'empiricism.'" *Aesthetic Ideology*, ed. Andrzej Warminski (Minneapolis: University of Minnesota Press, 1996), 121.

14. Roger Kimball, *Tenured Radicals: How Politics Has Corrupted Our Higher Education*, rev. ed. (Chicago: Elephant Paperbacks, 1998), ix.

15. For a reading of Lentricchia's critique of de Man in the context of a discussion of Shakespeare's *Othello*, see Stephen Bretzius, *Shakespeare in Theory: The Postmodern Academy and the Early Modern Theater* (Ann Arbor: University of Michigan Press, 1997), 75–92. Rooney also discusses Lentricchia's view of de Man in *Seductive Reasoning*, 172–73.

16. Barbara Johnson, "Art for Something's Sake," *Journal of Aesthetic Education* 36, no. 3 (2002), 28.

17. Victor Davis Hanson, John Heath, and Bruce S. Thornton, *Bonfire of the Humanities: Rescuing the Classics in an Impoverished Age* (Wilmington, Del.: ISI Books, 2001); subsequent citations will appear in the text.

18. Lee Edelman, *Homographesis: Essays in Gay Literary and Cultural Theory* (New York: Routledge, 1994), 116.

19. Marjorie Garber, *Shakespeare After All* (New York: Pantheon, 2004), 239.

20. William Shakespeare, *Richard II*, Arden Shakespeare, 3rd ser., ed. Charles R. Forker (London: Arden Shakespeare, 2002), 2.1.66. All subsequent quotations from *Richard II* are taken from this edition and will be cited in the text by act, scene, and line number. Quotations from Forker's introduction to the edition will be cited by page number.

21. As Jean Feerick explains, "In emphasizing the unstable and variable properties of bloodlines, the language of degeneracy pointed to the fault lines that hovered beneath the ideal language of blood as securing an intergenerational continuity of identity." Jean Feerick, *Strangers in Blood: Relocating Race in the Renaissance* (Toronto: University of Toronto Press, 2010), 16.

22. Leonard Tennenhouse, *Power on Display: The Politics of Shakespeare's Genres* (New York: Methuen, 1986), 76.

23. As Judith Brown writes, Richard's is "a reign more thoroughly, openly, and delightedly sensual than it is cautious, abstemious, or juridical." Judith Brown, "Pretty Richard (in Three Parts)," in *Shakesqueer: A Queer Companion to the Complete Works of Shakespeare*, ed. Madhavi Menon (Durham, N.C.: Duke University Press, 2011), 287.

24. Jean E. Howard and Phyllis Rackin, *Engendering a Nation: A Feminist Account of Shakespeare's English Histories* (London: Routledge, 1997), 142, 143, 146, 148.

25. This point is confirmed by the monologue Richard delivers in one of Shakespeare's source texts, *The Mirror for Magistrates* (1559), in which the king admits that he "ruled all by lust" and refers to his "lecherous minde that must/To Venus pleasures always be in awe"; Richard's farming of his realm is merely an action designed for "mayntenaunce" of his erotic hedonism. See Lily B. Campbell, ed., *The Mirror for Magistrates* (New York: Barnes and Noble, 1873), 113.

26. Lee Edelman, *No Future: Queer Theory and the Death Drive* (Durham, N.C.: Duke University Press, 2004), 113.

27. Ibid., 35, 38.

28. Ibid., 113–14, 73, 35.

29. Ibid., 114.

30. Ibid., 72–73.

31. Ibid., 165–66n10. See also Edelman's "Against Survival: Queerness in a Time That's Out of Joint," *Shakespeare Quarterly* 62, no. 2 (2011), where he extends the arguments of *No Future* in part through a reading of Shakespeare's *Hamlet.*

32. Coppélia Kahn, *Man's Estate: Masculine Identity in Shakespeare* (Berkeley: University of California Press, 1981), 66–67.

33. All quotations from the *Metamorphoses* are taken from John Frederick Nims, ed., *Ovid's Metamorphoses: The Arthur Golding Translation, 1567* (Philadelphia: Paul Dry, 2000); hereafter cited in the text by book and line numbers.

34. As Stephen Guy-Bray notes, "the difference in the story between the man and the man he loves is that the latter is not only not another man but in fact not a man at all: Narcissus desires a representation of a beautiful man." Guy-Bray, "No Present," in *Sex, Gender, and Time in Fiction and Culture*, ed. Ben Davies and Jana Funke (New York: Palgrave Macmillan, 2011), 45.

35. Barbara Johnson, *Persons and Things* (Cambridge, Mass.: Harvard University Press, 2007), 49.

36. Kathryn Schwarz, *Tough Love: Amazon Encounters in the English Renaissance* (Durham, N.C.: Duke University Press, 2000), 25.

37. Joseph Litvak, *Strange Gourmets: Sophistication, Theory, and the Novel* (Durham, N.C.: Duke University Press, 1997, 73.

38. Brown, "Pretty Richard," 288.

39. Only in the last few decades have critics been willing to bring out the sodomitical implications of Richard's relationship with his favorites. In addition to the important work of DiGangi, *Homoerotics*, and Menon, "*Richard II*," see Paul Gaudet, "The 'Parasitical' Counselors in Shakespeare's *Richard II*: A Problem in Dramatic Interpretation," *Shakespeare Quarterly* 33, no. 2 (1982): 147. DiGangi and Menon, it should be noted, are more hospitable to the possibility of a sodomitic interpretation than Gaudet is.

40. After Gaunt dies, Richard seizes his estate, Bolingbroke's rightful inheritance, to fund his wars in Ireland: "Towards our assistance we do seize to us / The plate, coin, revenues and moveables / Whereof our uncle Gaunt did stand possessed" (2.1.160–62). This seizure prompts York to censure Richard for "tak[ing] from Time / His charters and his customary rights" (195–96), and also prompts Bolingbroke to return from banishment.

41. The contemporary resonance of this trope can be gauged by recalling the following comment that the homophobic televangelist Pat Robertson made at the height of the AIDS crisis: "AIDS is God's way of weeding his garden." Qtd. in Eve Kosofsky Sedgwick, *Epistemology of the Closet* (1990; repr., Berkeley: University of California Press, 2008), 129. Here I'm reminded of Arthur L. Little Jr.'s comment, in *Shakespeare Jungle Fever: National-Imperial Re-Visions of Race, Rape, and Sacrifice* (Stanford, Calif.: Stanford University Press, 2000), that "culture names itself through . . . the moment it obliterates, the histories it erases, the institutional hands it does not admit or does not know it owns, the bodies it pretends not to see or doesn't" (9).

42. At the end of the play, Richard ironically and ingeniously turns the same garden of signifiers against *Bolingbroke's* supporters. Just prior to being separated from Isabel, Richard warns Northumberland that the newly crowned King Henry "shall think that thou, which knowst the way / To *plant* unrightful kings, *wilt* know again / . . . / To *pluck* him headlong from the usurped throne," an accusation to which Richard adds: "Doubly divorced! Bad men, you violate / A twofold marriage, 'twixt my crown and me / And then betwixt me and my married wife" (5.1.62–73; my italics).

43. Menon, "*Richard II*," 666.

44. Karen Edwards, "Caterpillar," *Milton Quarterly* 39, no. 4 (2005): 251. This association of caterpillars with papistry helps to explain why Richard's indulgent court is said to be under the reprehensible influence of Italy; hence, York refers to "fashions in proud Italy, / Whose manners still our tardy-apish nation / Limps after in base imitation" (2.1.21–23). In the following chapter, I will explore, through an analysis of the texts of Roger Ascham and Thomas Nashe, the ways in which antipoetic and antiromance attitudes overlap with

anti-Italian sentiment. As Steve Mentz notes, such sentiment can be read in conjunction with the Francophobia that animates attacks against deconstruction. Mentz, *Romance for Sale in Early Modern England: The Rise of Prose Fiction* (Aldershot, U.K.: Ashgate, 2006), 130n16. Indeed, York sounds like Anglo-American scholars who accuse deconstructive critics of aping "fashionable" Continental theories.

45. Edelman, *No Future*, 164n10.

46. Stephen Gosson, *"The Schoole of Abuse" (1579) and "A Short Apologie of 'The School of Abuse'" (1579)*, ed. Edward Arber (London: A. Murray and Son, 1869), 20.

47. D. A. Miller, *Jane Austen; or, The Secret of Style* (Princeton, N.J.: Princeton University Press, 2003), 8.

48. Donovan Sherman, "'What more remains?': Messianic Performance in *Richard II*," *Shakespeare Quarterly* 65, no. 1 (2014): 26.

49. Ibid., 48.

50. Tennenhouse, *Power on Display*, 81.

51. Menon, "*Richard II*," 669.

52. On the homoeroticism that pervades the plays' representations of Hal, see Jonathan Goldberg, *Sodometries: Renaissance Texts, Modern Sexualities* (1992; repr., New York: Fordham University Press, 2010), 145–75; Richard Corum, "Henry's Desires," in *Premodern Sexualities*, ed. Louise Fradenburg and Carla Freccero (New York: Routledge, 1996), 71–97; and Vin Nardizzi, "Grafted to Falstaff and Compounded with Catherine: Mingling Hal in the Second Tetralogy," in *Queer Renaissance Historiography: Backward Gaze*, ed. Vin Nardizzi, Stephen Guy-Bray, and Will Stockton (Farnham, U.K.: Ashgate, 2009), 149–69.

53. Goldberg, *Sodometries*, 160.

54. Throughout the course of working on this project I have encountered, again and again, the figure of the bee, even in the unlikeliest and most disparate of contexts. In his essay "The Principle of Reason," which critiques an ends-oriented conception of the university, Derrida cites Aristotle, Marx, and Schelling "on the philosophical *topos* of the bee, the sense and senses of the bee, and the bee's reason for being" (*Eyes of the University*, 131). In *Against Reproduction: Where Renaissance Texts Come From* (Toronto: University of Toronto Press, 2009), Stephen Guy-Bray consistently returns to the image of the bee's asexual reproduction, as presented in Virgil's *Georgics*, as a counter-model to the heteronormative reproductive metaphor by which early modern writers determined the creation and value of poetry. Ross Chambers, in his study of digression and errancy in modern literature, *Loiterature* (Lincoln: University of Nebraska Press, 1999), 26ff., does a brilliant riff on the idiom of a "beeline"—a straight, uninterrupted path transgressed by errancy. In *The*

Schoole of Abuse, Gosson writes: "*Aristotle* thinketh that in greate windes, the Bees carry little stones in their mouthes to peyse their bodyes, least they be carryed away, or kepte from their Hiues, vnto which they desire to returne with the fruites of their labour" (43). In *Persons and Things*, Johnson cites Lacan on the difference between human language and bee language: bees lack the capacity that humans have to tell lies (58). I'm still not quite sure what to make of this uncanny return or repetition except to say that it has produced the feeling of being caught in a labyrinth and also that the bee, as a contradictory figure of both industrious utility and poisonous disruption, is a nice figure for poetry as the Renaissance theorized and practiced it.

55. Joseph Litvak, *The Un-Americans: Jews, the Blacklist, and Stoolpigeon Culture* (Durham, N.C.: Duke University Press, 2009), 17.

56. Barbara Johnson, *A World of Difference* (Baltimore: Johns Hopkins University Press, 1987), 17.

3. ART FOR NOTHING'S SAKE

1. Juan Luis Vives, *The Education of a Christian Woman: A Sixteenth-Century Manual*, ed. and trans. Charles Fantazzi (Chicago: University of Chicago Press, 2000), 75.

2. Patricia Parker, *Inescapable Romance: Studies in the Poetics of a Mode* (Princeton, N.J.: Princeton University Press, 1979), 19.

3. On the place of romance in the context of the Reformation, see Tiffany J. Werth, *The Fabulous Dark Cloister: Romance in England after the Reformation* (Baltimore: Johns Hopkins University Press, 2011); and Dennis Austin Britton, *Becoming Christian: Race, Reformation, and Early Modern English Romance* (New York: Fordham University Press, 2014).

4. Victoria Kahn, for example, argues in *Wayward Contracts: The Crisis of Political Obligation in England, 1640–1674* (Princeton, N.J.: Princeton University Press, 2004), that seventeenth-century romance "was particularly well suited to staging the problematic coexistence of coercion and consent, passion and interest, in contemporary theories of the contract" (195). Amelia Zurcher Sandy echoes Kahn's statement when she writes in *Seventeenth-Century English Romance: Allegory, Ethics, and Politics* (New York: Palgrave, 2007), 7, that romance's problematizing or ironizing of divine providence makes it "uniquely suited" for addressing questions of political ideology. Benedict S. Robinson declares in *Islam and Early Modern English Literature: The Politics of Romance from Spenser to Milton* (New York: Palgrave Macmillan, 2007), that "the genre of romance enabled new ways of thinking about identity and difference" as early modern England engaged in cross-cultural encounters, and that romance is therefore "affectively and ideologically productive" (3, 16). And Brian C. Lockey demonstrates how romance—"a form

condemned for frivolity"—was nevertheless "able to accommodate the ethical and political issues of transnational justice and the laws of war." Brian C. Lockey, *Law and Empire in English Renaissance Literature* (Cambridge: Cambridge University Press, 2006), 7.

A notable exception to this trend can be found in Jeff Dolven, *Scenes of Instruction in Renaissance Romance* (Chicago: University of Chicago Press, 2007), which explores the ambivalence that English Renaissance romance writers displayed toward their injunction to instruct; my readings of Ascham, Nashe, and Spenser in this chapter and the next expand on Dolven's work by considering such ambivalence from the other side of the Horatian dictum, the side of pleasure, which Dolven, at the very beginning of his study, locates outside his argument's explicit ambit: "It is the central commonplace of Renaissance literary theory that the purpose of poetry is to please and instruct. Criticism's stewardship of poetic pleasure is not my subject here, at least not directly; what I am concerned with is teaching, toward which our attitude is often confused" (1).

5. Robinson, *Islam and Early Modern*, 18.

6. C. S. Lewis, *English Literature in the Sixteenth Century* (Oxford: Clarendon, 1954), 416.

7. Jonathan Crewe's *Unredeemed Rhetoric: Thomas Nashe and the Scandal of Authorship* (Baltimore: Johns Hopkins University Press, 1982), is still perhaps the best example of this approach, particularly in its Derridean or deconstructive strand, but see also Ann Rosalind Jones, "Inside the Outsider: Nashe's *Unfortunate Traveller* and Bakhtin's Polyphonic Novel," *ELH* 50, no. 1 (1983): 61–81, and Lorna Hutson, *Thomas Nashe in Context* (Oxford: Clarendon, 1989), both of whom read Nashe in Bakhtinian terms.

8. Steve Mentz, *Romance for Sale in Early Modern England: The Rise of Prose Fiction* (Aldershot, U.K.: Ashgate, 2006), 185. See also Georgia Brown, *Redefining Elizabethan Literature* (Cambridge: Cambridge University Press, 2004); Ellinghausen, *Labor and Writing in Early Modern England, 1567–1667* (Aldershot, U.K.: Ashgate, 2008); and David Baker, *On Demand: Writing for the Market in Early Modern England* (Stanford, Calif.: Stanford University Press, 2010).

9. Hutson, *Thomas Nashe in Context*, 5. Rehearsals of this gesture range from Raymond Stephanson's suggestion that "a plunge into the very heart of the ambiguities and distortions [of Nashe's *The Unfortunate Traveller*] will uncover important clues which redeem the work as a serious and perhaps consistent expression of some 'view of life,'" to Wendy Hyman's argument that the unruliness of Nashe's writing constitutes "a deliberate form of 'travel' and transgression . . . and intentional subversion." Raymond Stephanson, "The Epistemological Challenge of Nashe's *The Unfortunate Traveller*," *SEL:*

Studies in English Literature, 1500–1900 23, no. 1 (1983): 22; and Wendy Hyman, "Authorial Self-Consciousness in Nashe's *The Vnfortunate Traveller*," *SEL: Studies in English Literature, 1500–1900* 45, no. 1 (2005): 24–25.

10. Crewe's *Unredeemed Rhetoric*, as its title indicates, offers in part a rare departure from the recuperative tendencies in Nashe studies, in ways that deeply inform my reading in this chapter. At various points in his groundbreaking study, Crewe is attentive to the limits and costs of Nashe's indulgence in the play of "pure" rhetoric, pointing out that such play "does not necessarily imply any emancipation or freedom of self-fashioning" (39). Yet Crewe's attentiveness to the negativity of Nashe's work is consistently tempered, qualified, or in some places undercut by his parallel argument that Nashe displays "a certain capacity to defer resolution, to *capitalize* on an indeterminate situation, and to play out contradictions" (34; my italics). For Crewe, that ability to "capitalize" on, to profit from, the negativity of pure rhetoric reaches its apotheosis in *Lenten Stuffe*, Nashe's final completed work. According to Crewe, *Lenten Stuffe* "achieves a saving grace absent in many of Nashe's earlier performances" (92); it gives us "a Nashe rarefied and consciously controlled, displaying the self-possession that makes [it] eminently successful as a performance" (93).

11. A useful outline of the perpetually precarious nature of Nashe's career can be found in Jones, "Inside the Outsider," 62–63. Within the overarching argument of Jones's essay, however, that summary functions primarily as mere background—indeed, almost as an afterthought—that never directly informs her readings of, and subsequent arguments about, Nashe.

12. Quoted in Lawrence V. Ryan, *Roger Ascham* (Stanford, Calif.: Stanford University Press, 1963), 1.

13. Witness Nashe's comments on Ascham in his *Lenten Stuffe*: "Well, he was her Maiesties Schoolemaster, and a *S. Iohns* man in Cambridge, in which house once I tooke vp my inne for seuen yere together lacking a quarter, and yet love it still, for its and euer was the sweetest nurse of knowledge in all that Vniversity. Therefore I will keepe faire quarter with him." In Ronald McKerrow, ed., *The Works of Thomas Nashe*, 6 vols. (London: A. H. Bullen, 1904–10; repr., Oxford: Basil Blackwell, 1958), 3:181. All quotations from Nashe's texts are taken from this edition and will be cited in the text by volume and page number. On Nashe's intellectual relationship with Ascham, see Marshall McLuhan, *The Classical Trivium: The Place of Thomas Nashe in the Learning of His Time* (Corte Madera, Calif.: Ginko, 2005), 213–17.

14. See Roger Ascham, *The Scholemaster*, ed. Lawrence V. Ryan (Ithaca, N.Y.: Cornell University Press for Folger Shakespeare Library, 1967), 5–9. Subsequent citations are to this edition and will appear in the text.

15. Joel Fineman, "The History of the Anecdote: Fiction and Fiction," in *The New Historicism*, ed. H. Aram Veeser (New York: Routledge, 1989), 61.

See also Jane Gallop, *Anecdotal Theory* (Durham, N.C.: Duke University Press, 2002).

16. For paraphrases of Ascham's evident hostility toward romance, see Robert Adams, "Bold Bawdry and Open Manslaughter: The English New Humanist Attack on Medieval Romance," *Huntington Library Quarterly* 23, no. 1 (1959): 33–48; Carol Kaske, "How Spenser Really Used Stephen Hawes in the Legend of Holiness," in *Unfolded Tales: Essays on Renaissance Romance*, ed. George M. Logan and Gordon Teskey (Ithaca, N.Y.: Cornell University Press, 1989), 119–21; Richard Helgerson, *Forms of Nationhood: The Elizabethan Writing of England* (Chicago: University of Chicago Press, 1992), 42; R. W. Maslen, *Elizabethan Fictions: Espionage, Counter-Espionage, and the Duplicity of Fiction in Early Elizabethan Prose Narratives* (Oxford: Clarendon, 1997), 2–7, 40–52; Alex Davis, *Chivalry and Romance in the English Renaissance* (Woodbridge, U.K.: D. S Brewer, 2003), 7; and Joshua Phillips, "Chronicles of Wasted Time: Anthony Munday, Tudor Romance, and Literary Labor," *ELH* 73 (2006): 788.

17. Melanie Ord, *Travel and Experience in Early Modern English Literature* (New York: Palgrave Macmillan, 2008), 206.

18. On the ends-oriented nature of Ascham's conceptions of reading, see Alan Stewart, *Close Readers: Humanism and Sodomy in Early Modern England* (Princeton, N.J.: Princeton University Press, 1997), 148–50.

19. Davis, *Chivalry and Romance*, 7. See also Arthur B. Ferguson, *The Indian Summer of English Chivalry: Studies in the Decline and Transformation of Chivalric Idealism* (Durham, N.C.: Duke University Press, 1960).

20. Davis does acknowledge that "ascriptions of a taste for chivalric literature were in fact far more complex than a formulaic opposition between humanism and chivalry might suggest" (*Chivalry and Romance*, 9). In the case of *The Scholemaster*, however, he declines the opportunity to analyze the text and thereby joins company with the scholars whom he criticizes for engaging merely in the "selective quotation of detractors such as Ascham" (24).

21. Shannon Miller, *Invested with Meaning: The Raleigh Circle in the New World* (Philadelphia: University of Pennsylvania Press, 1998), 27.

22. Ibid., 28.

23. Robert Matz, *Defending Literature in Early Modern England: Renaissance Literary Theory in Social Context* (Cambridge: Cambridge University Press, 2000), 17–18.

24. See Virginia Krause, *Idle Pursuits: Literature and Oisiveté in the French Renaissance* (Newark: University of Delaware Press, 2003).

25. Max Weber, *"The Protestant Ethic and the 'Spirit' of Capitalism" and Other Writings*, ed. and trans. Peter Baehr and Gordon C. Wells (New York: Penguin, 2002), 106.

26. Dolven, *Scenes of Instruction*, 68.

27. Edmund Spenser, *The Faerie Queene*, 2nd ed., ed. A. C. Hamilton (Harlow, U.K.: Pearson Longman, 2007), book 2, canto 2, stanza 6. All subsequent quotations of *The Faerie Queene* are taken from this edition and will be cited in the text. Citations of the poem itself will refer to book, canto, and stanza numbers.

28. Ryan J. Stark, "Protestant Theology and Apocalyptic Rhetoric in Roger Ascham's *The Scholemaster*," *Journal of the History of Ideas* 69, no. 4 (2008): 520.

29. Davis, *Chivalry and Romance*, 15.

30. Roland Barthes, *The Pleasure of the Text*, trans. Richard Miller (New York: Hill and Wang, 1975), 18. I quote the original French from *Le plaisir du texte* (Paris: Éditions du Seuil, 1973), 32–33.

31. D. A. Miller addresses this kind of temptation in an essay on the ironies, errors, and failures of Alfred Hitchcock's *Rope*. "If one looks for perfection in *Rope*," he writes, "the film will seem chock-full of errors, but no sooner does one attend to irony than—presto!—the errors all seem to have vanished in a knowing wink." D. A. Miller, "Hitchcock's Understyle: A Too-Close View of *Rope*," *Representations* 121 (2013): 21. In an implicitly de Manian move, Miller provides reasons for "doubting" the film's "dialectical reunification by irony"; he examines the "unpredictable, unrecognized, and unavoidable flaws" that Hitchcock can neither predict nor control (23), in ways analogous to the readings of Ascham and Nashe this chapter unfolds.

32. Anne Cotterill, *Digressive Voices in Early Modern English Literature* (Oxford: Oxford University Press, 2004), 1.

33. Ibid., 30.

34. Ibid., 44; my italics.

35. Fredric Jameson, *Postmodernism; or, The Cultural Logic of Late Capitalism* (Durham, N.C.: Duke University Press, 1991), 254.

36. Paul de Man, *Aesthetic Ideology*, ed. Andrzej Warminski (Minneapolis: University of Minnesota Press, 1996), 168.

37. For a reading of this passage along these lines, see Madhavi Menon, "Introduction: Queer Shakes," in *Shakesqueer: A Queer Companion to the Complete Works of Shakespeare* (Durham, N.C.: Duke University Press, 2011), 8–9.

38. De Man, *Aesthetic Ideology*, 169.

39. Ibid., 169–70.

40. Ibid., 181.

41. Crewe, *Unredeemed Rhetoric*, 23.

42. For a reading of the gendered poetics and politics of *The Anatomie of Absurditie*, see Maria Teresa Micaela Prendergast, *Renaissance Fantasies: The Gendering of Aesthetics in Early Modern Fiction* (Kent, Ohio: Kent State University Press, 1999), 26–34.

43. Joshua Phillips, for example, writes that "Ascham's anger [toward romances] finds voice, as well, in the work of Thomas Nashe," and then goes on to quote the passage from *The Anatomie of Absurditie*. Joshua Phillips, *English Fictions of Communal Identity, 1485–1603* (Farnham, U.K.: Ashgate, 2010), 39. See also Roger Dalrymple, *Language and Piety in Middle English Romance* (Cambridge: D. S. Brewer, 2000), 144.

44. George Puttenham, *The Art of English Poesy: A Critical Edition*, ed. Frank Whigham and Wayne A. Rebhorn (Ithaca, N.Y.: Cornell University Press, 2007), 340.

45. Crewe, *Unredeemed Rhetoric*, 20. "Euphuistic" style refers to the highly mannered fashion of writing—of which alliteration was a key feature—that Lyly's 1578 prose romance *Euphues: The Anatomy of Wit* sparked among Elizabethan writers. Nashe's indebtedness to this style in his early work has been frequently noted, although Steve Mentz has established Nashe's attempt to distance himself from this vogue (*Romance for Sale*, 211).

46. Pertinent in this context, then, would be Krause's observation that early modern European humanists "increasingly likened romance to babble—volumes without end" (*Idle Pursuits*, 137).

47. Barthes, *Pleasure of the Text*, 4; *Le plaisir du texte*, 10.

48. Barthes, *Pleasure of the Text*, 7.

49. Confirming these claims beyond any doubt I may have had, a reader of an earlier version of this argument commented on my own writing: "I could have done without *your* alliteration." That is exactly the point. Alliteration, like paronomasia, may not always be useless, but it is important to recognize that it is often *thought* to be something futile and excessive—indeed, futile because excessive. It is a linguistic feature one could, and probably should, "do without." Is it needless to say at this point that I have indulged in alliterative play, here and throughout, as a way of theorizing through performance the tension between pleasure and utility that this book is about?

50. Hutson, *Thomas Nashe in Context*, 120. (*The Anatomie of Abuses* is the title of Phillip Stubbes's 1583 antitheatrical tract, whereas the title of Nashe's text is *The Anatomie of Absurditie*.)

51. Here I am alluding to the sentence that precedes Lewis's famous pronouncement of Nashe having "nothing to say": "Paradoxically, though Nashe's pamphlets are commercial literature, they come very close to being, in another sense, 'pure' literature: literature which is, as nearly as possible, without a subject" (Lewis, *English Literature*, 416). Commenting on this passage, David Landreth notes that "Lewis is recognizing that what's at stake in Nashe's prose is not so much 'Nothing' as the approach to nothing—the asymptotic relation of prose to nothing as it 'come[s] very close,' 'as nearly as possible.'" David Landreth, "Wit without Money in Nashe," in *The Age of*

Thomas Nashe: Text, Bodies, and Trespasses of Authorship in Early Modern England, ed. Stephen Guy-Bray, Joan Pong Linton, and Steve Mentz (Burlington, Vt.: Ashgate, 2013), 140.

52. Crewe, *Unredeemed Rhetoric*, 17.

53. Ibid., 8.

54. Katherine Duncan-Jones, "Nashe and Sidney: The Tournament Scene in *The Unfortunate Traveller*," *Modern Language Review* 63 (1968): 3–7.

55. On the connection between Nashe's ostrich and Shakespeare's ostriches, see C. G. Harlow, "Shakespeare, Nashe, and the Ostrich Crux in *I Henry IV*," *Shakespeare Quarterly* 17, no. 2 (1966): 171–74.

56. Dolven, *Scenes of Instruction*, 169.

57. On this aspect of *Orlando furioso*, to which many critics of Ariosto were allergic, see Daniel Javitch, *Proclaiming a Classic: The Canonization of "Orlando Furioso"* (Princeton, N.J.: Princeton University Press, 1991), 86–105.

58. Puttenham, *Art of English Poesy*, 318.

59. De Man, *Aesthetic Ideology*, 178.

60. Ibid., 181. For a reading of early modern literature (specifically Thomas Middleton's *The Wisdom of Solomon Paraphrased*) that uses the trope of the "machine" to characterize the rhetorical operations of the text (though by way of Heidegger rather than de Man), see Stephen Guy-Bray, "Middleton's Language Machine," in *The Oxford Handbook of Thomas Middleton*, ed. Gary Taylor and Trish Thomas Henley (Oxford: Oxford University Press, 2012).

61. Jonathan Sawday, *Engines of the Imagination: Renaissance Culture and the Rise of the Machine* (New York: Routledge, 2007), 190.

62. "Nature," Sidney writes in *An Apology for Poetry; or, The Defence of Poesy*, ed. Geoffrey Shepherd, rev. R. W. Maslen (Manchester, U.K.: Manchester University Press, 2002), "never set forth the earth in so rich tapestry as divers poets have done; neither with pleasant rivers, fruitful trees, sweet-smelling flowers, nor whatsoever else may make the too much loved earth more lovely. Her world is brazen, the poets only deliver a golden" (85).

63. Julian Yates, *Error, Misuse, Failure: Object Lessons from the English Renaissance* (Minneapolis: University of Minnesota Press, 2003), 128–29.

64. Mentz, *Romance for Sale*, 197. Aside from these parallels, Spenser's influence on *The Unfortunate Traveller*, and on Nashe's work more generally, constitutes a conspicuous lacuna in Nashe criticism.

65. Alexander Leggatt, "Artistic Coherence in *The Unfortunate Traveller*," *Studies in English Literature, 1500–1900* 14, no. 1 (1974): 32.

66. In addition to Leggatt (ibid.), see Stephen S. Hilliard, *The Singularity of Thomas Nashe* (Lincoln: University of Nebraska Press, 1986): "The banqueting house is put in perspective by the plague and civic disorder outside

its walls. . . . The plague and the breakdown of order that it causes are the norms of human experience; the banqueting house is an artificial glimpse of a better life" (126).

67. Jessica Wolfe, *Humanism, Machinery, and Renaissance Literature* (Cambridge: Cambridge University Press, 2004), 57.

68. Leggatt, "Artistic Coherence," 33.

69. For an analysis of Nashe's *Lenten Stuffe* that explores a similarly ironic blurring between blame and praise, see Jennifer Andersen, "Blame-in-Praise Irony in *Lenten Stuffe*," in Guy-Bray, Linton, and Mentz, *Age of Thomas Nashe*, 45–62.

70. As Nashe's contemporary biographer, Charles Nicholl, writes, Nashe's "praise of the Catholic emphasis on 'good workes' sounds suspiciously sincere." Charles Nicholl, *A Cup of News: The Life of Thomas Nashe* (London: Routledge and Kegan Paul, 1984), 159.

71. As if we missed the point implied by the last perversion in this list, Jack tells us, at the conclusion of the narrative, how he "hasted so fast out of the *Sodom* of *Italy*" (2:327). For a reading of sodomy and anality in *The Unfortunate Traveller*, see Will Stockton, *Playing Dirty: Sexuality and Waste in Early Modern Comedy* (Minneapolis: University of Minnesota Press, 2011), 67–96.

72. As Hyman, "Authorial Self-Consciousness," puts it, the earl "seems to exist primarily to be flouted, as his wan didacticism is annulled by the whole of Nashe's scintillating travelogue" (35).

73. See Richard Helgerson, *The Elizabethan Prodigals* (Berkeley: University of California Press, 1976).

74. Abrupt endings are a signature of Nashe's style, though in other texts he more explicitly announces that abruptness, as in *Pierce Penniless* ("And so I breake off this endlesse argument of speech abruptlie" [1:245]) and *The Terrors of the Night* ("Thus I shut vp my Treatise abruptly" [1:386]).

75. Hutson, *Thomas Nashe in Context*, 72.

76. D. A. Miller, *8 1/2*, BFI Film Classics (Houndmills, U.K.: Palgrave Macmillan, 2008), 91. Incidentally, the "nothing to say" with which C. S. Lewis charged Nashe is central to Fellini's film, and to Miller's analysis of it, as well. The film's protagonist, the director Guido Anselmi (Marcello Mastroianni), admits about the content and significance of the movie he is making, "I have really nothing to say . . . but I want to say it anyway." Miller identifies Guido's comment as "the most important statement in *8 1/2*; the entire film may be understood as a gradual unpacking of the ambiguities and paradoxes condensed in it" (32). For an exploration of the "nothing to s[illegible] in the work of Barthes (cf. my epigraph to this chapter), see also M[illegible] short essay "Foutre! Bougre! Ecriture!," *Yale Journal of Critici*[illegible] (2001): 503–11.

77. Georgia Brown, *Redefining Elizabethan Literature*, 6; my italics.

78. Ibid., 59; my italics.

79. Ibid., 22.

80. Ibid., 59n15.

81. Hutson, *Thomas Nashe in Context*, 120.

82. Nicholl provides a detailed account of this issue in his *Cup of News*, 112–21. In *Lenten Stuffe*, Nashe refers back to the trouble his allegory caused when he rails against lawyers who "haue fisht out such a deepe politique state meaning as if I had al the secrets of court or commonwealth at my fingers endes. Talke I of a beare, O, it is such a man that emblazons him in his armes, or of a woolfe, a fox, or a camelion, any lording whom they do not affect it is meant by" (3:214).

83. I quote the English translation from Ovid, *The Poems of Exile*, trans. Peter Green (New York: Penguin, 1994), 88.

84. At the end of his erotic poem *The Choice of Valentines*, Nashe excuses the bawdiness of his verse on the basis that "Ouids wanton Muse did not offend"—a line we must take as ironic, perhaps even prophetic, given that Ovid's wanton Muse *did* offend—and in the next line refers to Ovid as "the fountaine whence my streames doe flowe" (3:415). After Nashe fled London in the wake of the *Isle of Dogs* scandal, one of his contemporaries, Francis Meres, comforted the outlaw in his *Palladis tamia* by contrasting Nashe's exile with Ovid's, though the fact that Nashe's precarious situation leads Meres to think of Ovid in the first place qualifies any absolute contrast between the two: "Yet God forbid that so braue a witte should so basely perish, thine are but paper dogges, neither is thy banishment like *Ouids*, eternally to conuerse with the barbarous *Getes*. Therefore comfort thy selfe sweete *Tom.* with *Ciceros* glorious return to Rome, & with the counsel *Aeneas* giues to his seabeaten soldiors." Quoted in Daniel D. Moss, *The Ovidian Vogue: Literary Fashion and Imitative Practice in Late Elizabethan England* (Toronto: University of Toronto Press, 2014), 21. On Ovid's influence on Nashe, see also Anthony Ossa-Richardson, "Ovid and the 'Free Play with Signs' in Thomas Nashe's *The Unfortunate Traveller*," *Modern Language Review* 101, no. 4 (2006): 945–56, and Georgia Brown, "Sex and the City: Nashe, Ovid, and the Problems of Urbanity," in Guy-Bray, Linton, and Mentz, *Age of Thomas Nashe*, 11–26.

4. Spenser's Unhappy Ends

1. William Butler Yeats, *The Cutting of an Agate* (New York: Macmillan, 1912), 213–14.

2. Jane Grogan, *Exemplary Spenser: Visual and Poetic Pedagogy in "The* [illegible]*e Queene"* (Surrey, U.K.: Ashgate, 2009), 15.

[illegible] Edmund Spenser, "Letter to Raleigh," in *The Faerie Queene*, 2nd ed., [illegible]amilton (Harlow, U.K.: Pearson Longman, 2007), 714. All subsequent quotations of *The Faerie Queene* are taken from this edition and will be cited in the text. Citations of the poem itself will refer to book, canto, and stanza numbers; citations of Spenser's "Letter to Raleigh" will refer to page number.

4. Stephen Greenblatt, *Renaissance Self-Fashioning: From More to Shakespeare* (1980; repr., Chicago: University of Chicago Press, 2005), 175.

5. Ibid., 176–77.

6. See especially Michael C. Schoenfeldt, *Bodies and Selves in Early Modern England: Physiology and Inwardness in Spenser, Shakespeare, Herbert, and Milton* (Cambridge: Cambridge University Press, 1999), 52–71; Robert Matz, *Defending Literature in Early Modern England: Renaissance Literary Theory in Social Context* (Cambridge: Cambridge University Press, 2000), 94–95, 121; Paul Cefalu, *Moral Identity in Early Modern English Literature* (Cambridge: Cambridge University Press, 2004), 190–91; Jonathan Goldberg, *The Seeds of Things: Theorizing Sexuality and Materiality in Renaissance Representations* (New York: Fordham University Press, 2009), 63–121; and Joseph Campana, *The Pain of Reformation: Spenser, Vulnerability, and the Ethics of Masculinity* (New York: Fordham University Press, 2012), 139–40.

7. Campana, *Pain of Reformation*, 130.

8. Ibid., 159.

9. Goldberg, *Seeds of Things*, 67.

10. Patricia Parker, *Inescapable Romance: Studies in the Poetics of a Mode* (Princeton, N.J.: Princeton University Press, 1979).

11. *Roland Barthes*, trans. Richard Howard (New York: Farrar, Straus and Giroux, 1977), 63–64. Here it is worth pointing out that Barthes's first name is shared by one of the most paradigmatic heroes of romance in the Western tradition: Roland/Orlando. And as long as hashish is on the table, consider the following quotation from Avital Ronell's *Crack Wars: Literature, Addiction, Mania* (1992; repr., Urbana: University of Illinois Press, 2004): "Drugs are linked to a mode of departing, to desocialization—much like the activity of writing, to the extent that it exists without the assurance of arriving anywhere. Considered non-productive and somehow irresponsible, a compulsive player of destruction, Being-on-drugs resists the production of value which, on another, more Bataillean register, indicates that it disrupts the production of meaning" (105–6).

12. Sigmund Freud, *Three Essays on the Theory of Sexuality*, trans. James Strachey (New York: Basic, 2002), 16.

13. In this connection, let me cite the following comments made by Northrop Frye in *The Secular Scripture: A Study of the Structure of Romance* (Cambridge, Mass.: Harvard University Press, 1976): "The central element of romance is a love story, and the exciting adventures are normally a foreplay

leading up to a sexual union. Hence romance appears to be designed mainly to encourage irregular or excessive sexual activity. This may be masturbation, which is the usual model in the minds of those who speak with contempt of 'escape' reading, or it may be a form of voyeurism" (24).

14. Grogan, *Exemplary Spenser*, 157.

15. See Jeff Dolven, *Scenes of Instruction in Renaissance Romance* (Chicago: University of Chicago Press, 2007).

16. See, e.g., Patricia Fumerton, "Introduction: A New New Historicism," in *Renaissance Culture and the Everyday*, ed. Patricia Fumerton and Simon Hunt (Philadelphia: University of Pennsylvania Press, 1999), esp. 3–4.

17. In addition to *Secular Scripture*, see Northrop Frye, *Anatomy of Criticism: Four Essays* (Princeton, N.J.: Princeton University Press, 1957), esp. 186–206.

18. For a discussion of Heliodorus's influence on Elizabethan prose fiction, see Steve Mentz, *Romance for Sale in Early Modern England: The Rise of Prose Fiction* (Aldershot, U.K.: Ashgate, 2006).

19. Frye, *Secular Scripture*, 4.

20. Mentz, *Romance for Sale*, 43; see also Frank Kermode, *The Sense of an Ending: Studies in the Theory of Fiction* (London: Oxford University Press, 1966), 6.

21. Jonathan Goldberg, *Endlesse Worke: Spenser and the Structures of Discourse* (Baltimore: Johns Hopkins University Press, 1981), 26. See also Parker, *Inescapable Romance.*

22. Humphrey Tonkin, *Spenser's Courteous Pastoral: Book Six of "The Faerie Queene"* (Oxford: Clarendon, 1972), 69.

23. Lee Edelman, *No Future: Queer Theory and the Death Drive* (Durham, N.C.: Duke University Press, 2004), 149.

24. Leonard Tennenhouse, *Power on Display: The Politics of Shakespeare's Genres* (New York: Methuen, 1986), 175.

25. Lee Edelman, "Ever After: History, Negativity, and the Social," *South Atlantic Quarterly* 106 (2007): 470.

26. See Mentz, *Romance for Sale*, esp. 51–53.

27. Parker, *Inescapable Romance*, 109.

28. Cf. Chaucer's Merchant's Tale: "she hadde / Mo goode thewes than her vices badde" (ll. 1541–42), in Geoffrey Chaucer, *The Canterbury Tales: Complete*, ed. Larry D. Benson (Boston: Houghton Mifflin, 2000).

29. Tonkin, *Spenser's Courteous Pastoral*, 65.

30. Brian C. Lockey, *Law and Empire in English Renaissance Literature* (Cambridge: Cambridge University Press, 2006), 136.

31. Ibid., 137. Lockey is not the first critic to point out the Bruin / Fitz-Ursula connection; see also Robert E. Stillman, "Spenserian Autonomy and

the Trial of New Historicism: Book Six of *The Faerie Queene*," *ELR* 22, no. 3 (1992): 306–7; and, much earlier, Arnold Williams, *Flower on a Lowly Stalk: The Sixth Book of "The Faerie Queene"* (East Lansing: Michigan State University Press, 1967), 71.

32. Clare Regan Kinney, *Strategies of Poetic Narrative: Chaucer, Spenser, Milton, Eliot* (Cambridge: Cambridge University Press, 1992), 92–93.

33. Sir Philip Sidney, *An Apology for Poetry; or, The Defence of Poesy*, ed. Geoffrey Shepherd, rev. R. W. Maslen (Manchester, U.K.: Manchester University Press, 2002), 81; my italics.

34. Ibid., 88. It is worth calling attention to the *Defence*'s split ends here. Which is the *actual* end of learning: the "final end" or the "ending end"? Logically, virtuous action (the ending end) is the means to the perfection of our degenerate souls (the final end). The sequence of Sidney's writing, however, seems to invert the causality insofar as the ending end actually ends the paragraph. In other words, the ending end subverts, insofar as it follows, the finality of the final end. The path of Sidney's rhetoric could perhaps be read in terms of Calvinism's reversal of the causality of virtue: where Catholic doctrine asserts that humans are chosen to receive salvation because they perform virtuous action, Calvinist doctrine asserts that humans perform virtuous action because they are chosen to receive salvation. In any case, the quote enacts the ways in which the "ends" of poetry are neither self-evident nor self-identical.

35. Sir Philip Sidney, *The Countess of Pembroke's Arcadia*, ed. Maurice Evans (1977; repr., New York: Penguin Classics, 1987), 93.

36. Ibid., 85, 103, 95.

37. D. A. Miller, *Jane Austen; or, The Secret of Style* (Princeton, N.J.: Princeton University Press, 2003), 64.

38. Berger, *Revisionary Play*, 222.

39. Douglas A. Northrop, "The Uncertainty of Courtesy in Book VI of *The Faerie Queene*," *Spenser Studies* 14 (2000): 216, 219.

40. Lodowick Bryskett, *A discourse of ciuill life containing the ethike part of morall philosophie* (London, 1606), sig. E1v–E2r.

41. See Gordon Teskey, "Positioning Spenser's 'Letter to Raleigh,'" in *Craft and Tradition: Essays in Honour of William Blissett*, ed. H. B. de Groot and Alexander Leggatt (Calgary: University of Calgary Press, 1990), 35–46, and Goldberg, *Seeds of Things*, 64–65.

42. This shift in tone is particularly acute in the case of the Legend of Courtesy. Richard Neuse acknowledges, in "Book VI as Conclusion to *The Faerie Queene*," *ELH* 35, no. 3 (1968), that "the dominant sense of Book VI is one of disillusionment, of the disparity between the poet's ideals and the reality he envisions" (331). Similarly, George E. Rowe writes, in "Privacy, Vision,

and Gender in Spenser's Legend of Courtesy," *Modern Language Quarterly* 50, no. 4 (1989), "that the sixth book of *The Faerie Queene* ends in bitterness and cynicism few readers would, I think, deny" (309).

43. For a thorough account of Spenser's tricky relationship with Burghley, see Bruce Danner, *Edmund Spenser's War on Lord Burghley* (New York: Palgrave Macmillan, 2011).

44. Goldberg, *Seeds of Things*, 65.

45. For more on the literary and philosophical resonance of the accident, see Michael Witmore, *Culture of Accidents: Unexpected Knowledges in Early Modern England* (Stanford, Calif.: Stanford University Press, 2002), and Ross Hamilton, *Accident: A Philosophical and Literary History* (Chicago: University of Chicago Press, 2007).

46. Goldberg, *Endlesse Worke*, 28–29.

47. Sir John Harington, "An Apology for Ariosto: Poetry, Epic, Morality (1591)," in *English Renaissance Literary Criticism*, ed. Brian Vickers (Oxford: Clarendon, 1999), 320.

48. For example, in a flashback, Timias pursues the Blatant Beast into a "woody glade" after being bitten by the monster, and there he is ambushed by Despetto, Decetto, and Defetto: "at length unto a woody glade / He came, whose covert stopt his further sight, / There his three foes shrowded in guilefull shade, / Out of their ambush broke, and gan him to inuade" (6.5.17). Indeed, the entire legend can be read as an attempt to dramatize the "guile" lurking behind apparently safe "shades." On the legend's, specifically Calidore's, tendency to disrupt shady secret spaces, see Richard Rambuss, *Spenser's Secret Career* (Cambridge: Cambridge University Press, 1993), 116.

49. Parker, *Inescapable Romance*, 105; my italics.

50. Maria R. Rohr Philmus, "*The Faerie Queene* and Renaissance Poetics: Another Look at Book VI as 'Conclusion' to the Poem," *English Studies* 76, no. 6 (1995): 512, 515; my italics.

51. Dolven, *Scenes of Instruction*, 233.

52. Here I disagree with Parker's foundational reading that this stanza "seems to gather up and remove the sting from images and phrases which earlier in the poem suggested more dangerous kinds of delay"—or, rather, I place more emphasis on the word "seems" than Parker herself seems to do. See Parker, *Inescapable Romance*, 102.

53. C. S. Lewis, *The Allegory of Love: A Study in Medieval Tradition* (1936; repr., New York: Galaxy, 1958), 350.

54. William V. Nestrick, "The Virtuous and Gentle Discipline of Gentlemen and Poets," *ELH* 29, no. 4 (1962): 363.

55. Nancy Armstrong and Leonard Tennenhouse, "The Literature of Conduct, the Conduct of Literature, and the Politics of Desire: An Introduc-

tion," in *The Ideology of Conduct: Essays on Literature and the History of Sexuality*, ed. Nancy Armstrong and Leonard Tennenhouse (New York: Methuen, 1987), 1.

56. Here I have in mind Daniel Juan Gil's perceptive comment in *Before Intimacy: Asocial Sexuality in Early Modern England* (Minneapolis: University of Minnesota Press, 2006), that "if *The Faerie Queene* is a conduct manual, then it is a very strange one for, as a genre, conduct manuals are marked by an overwhelming degree of explicitness. . . . Any reader of *The Faerie Queene*, by contrast, knows that if rules of conduct are being offered at all, they are almost impossible to understand" (49).

5. BEYOND SUBLIMATION

1. Richard Hurd, *Letters on Chivalry and Romance*, ed. Hoyt Trowbridge (Los Angeles: William Andrews Clark Memorial Library, University of California, 1963), 4.

2. John Milton, *Paradise Lost*, in *The Complete Poetry and Essential Prose of John Milton*, ed. William Kerrigan, John Rumrich, and Stephen M. Fallon (New York: Modern Library, 2007), 9.40–41. Unless otherwise noted, all quotations of Milton's work will be taken from this edition and cited in the text. Citations to Milton's prose works, such as *Areopagitica*, will refer to page numbers; citations to *Paradise Lost* and *Paradise Regained* will refer to book and line numbers; and citations to Milton's other poetry, such as *Comus*, will refer to line numbers only.

3. See Victoria Kahn's discussion, in *Wayward Contracts: The Crisis of Political Obligation in England, 1640–1674* (Princeton, N.J.: Princeton University Press, 2004), of Thomas Hobbes's attack on romance. For Hobbes, Kahn writes, "romance does not simply narrate the story of emulous desire but also excites the desire for imitation in the reader" (142).

4. John Milton, "*Eikonoklastes* (Selections)," in *Complete Poems and Major Prose*, ed. Merritt Y. Hughes (Indianapolis: Hackett, 2003), 793–94. The word "orts" denotes scraps of food; cf. Shakespeare's *Timon of Athens*: "Where should he have this gold? It is some poor fragment, some slender ort of his remainder. The mere want of gold and the falling-from of his friends drove him into this melancholy" (4.3.392–95).

5. On romance's royalist associations in the seventeenth century, see Kahn, *Wayward Contracts*, 139–40.

6. Milton, "*Eikonoklastes*," 793.

7. Steven Knapp, *Personification and the Sublime: Milton to Coleridge* (Cambridge, Mass.: Harvard University Press, 1985), 54.

8. William Blake, *The Marriage of Heaven and Hell*, in *The Norton Anthology of English Literature*, 7th ed., 2 vols., gen. ed. M. H. Abrams (New York: Norton, 2000), 2:75.

9. That tension was identified as early as the eighteenth century by Samuel Johnson, *Lives of the English Poets*, 2 vols. (London: Oxford University Press, 1906), who wrote of *Paradise Lost*: "Its perusal is a duty *rather than* a pleasure. We read Milton for instruction, retire harassed and overburdened, and look elsewhere for recreation; we desert our master, and seek for companions" (1:127; my italics).

10. Patricia Parker, *Inescapable Romance: Studies in the Poetics of a Mode* (Princeton, N.J.: Princeton University Press, 1979), 11.

11. For a summary of the tenets of contemporary Milton studies, see Peter C. Herman, *Destabilizing Milton: "Paradise Lost" and the Poetics of Incertitude* (New York: Palgrave Macmillan, 2005), 1–24. I will have more to say about Herman's study below.

12. David Scott Kastan, ed., *Paradise Lost* (New York: Hackett, 2005), xvi.

13. Stephen Guy-Bray, *Against Reproduction: Where Renaissance Texts Come From* (Toronto: University of Toronto Press, 2009), 154.

14. See Peter C. Herman and Elizabeth Sauer, eds., *The New Milton Criticism* (Cambridge: Cambridge University Press, 2012).

15. William Empson, *Milton's God* (London: Chatto and Windus, 1961), 13.

16. Herman, *Destabilizing Milton*, 7.

17. Stanley Fish, *How Milton Works* (Cambridge, Mass.: Belknap Press of Harvard University Press, 2001), 5.

18. Ibid., 14.

19. One could argue further that Herman also does to *Milton* what he accuses Fish of doing to Milton. Although Herman is intent on analyzing what he calls "a poetics of incertitude," he ultimately tethers that incertitude to a single political and historical cause: "It is out of the turmoil of not knowing what to affirm in the wake of the Revolution's failure that Milton creates some of his finest poetry" (*Destabilizing Milton*, 21). He argues later, for example, that "the Miltonic 'Or' in *Paradise Lost* reflects Milton's uncertainties after the Revolution collapses" (58). The metaphor of reflection, which is characteristic of a particularly unreflective version of historicist criticism, implies a stable mirroring between text and context. Precisely because it "reflects" Milton's political and historical incertitude, textual incertitude is thus sublimated as certain—and indeed redeemed in terms of aesthetic value, as Milton is thereby able to create "his finest poetry." For an incisive critique of Herman's study, see Stephen M. Fallon, *Milton's Peculiar Grace: Self-Representation and Authority* (Ithaca, N.Y.: Cornell University Press, 2007): "Herman's opposition to reading Milton as monolithic does not go far enough, for in the place of the real disjunctions in Milton's texts Herman provides a catalogue of the pervasive binaries and alternatives composing what has been called Milton's poetics of choice" (xiii).

20. As Fish writes immediately after attacking the Romantic strain of Milton criticism, "Then why, one might ask, is the poetry so full of what it finally asks us to affirm against? The answer is that the lesson [Milton] would teach us—that we must forsake the letter for the spirit—can be taught only in the discursive forms the letter provides. Those forms are at once the vehicles of our instruction and the habitation of temptation—that is, of the temptation to take them seriously for themselves rather than as instruments of a supreme pedagogical intention, Milton's intention and . . . the intention of his God" (*How Milton Works*, 14–15)

21. Herman, *Destabilizing Milton*, 179n26, quoting Fish, *How Milton Works*, 572.

22. Fish, *How Milton Works*, 572. In a recent critique of reviews of *How Milton Works*, Fish points out that most reviewers hone in on "only one half of the [book's] thesis, the half that presents a Milton who insists on an absolute fidelity to a single obligation." The half that conveniently gets ignored, Fish writes, "is the half that emphasizes the difficulty, both for fallen and unfallen creatures, first of discerning God's will in the midst of signs pointing in multiple directions, and the subsequent difficulty of determining what course of action among the many possible would be the appropriate vehicle of obeying that will." See Stanley Fish, *Versions of Antihumanism: Milton and Others* (Cambridge: Cambridge University Press, 2012), 123–24. For a more direct critique of the New Milton Criticism propounded by Herman and others, see 131–44.

23. Fish, *How Milton Works*, 572.

24. Ibid., 573.

25. Matthew Arnold, *Essays by Matthew Arnold* (London: Humphrey Milford, Oxford University Press, 1914), 291.

26. In explaining *la relève*, for example, Derrida situates Hegel's metaphysical system in relation to eschatological and theological concerns that are relevant for any understanding of Milton's ends: "*Aufheben* is *relever*, in the sense in which *relever* can combine to relieve, to displace, to elevate, to replace and to promote, in one and the same movement. . . . This equivocal relationship of *relief* doubtless marks the end of man, man past, but by the same token it also marks the achievement of man, the appropriation of his essence. . . . The *relève* or *relevance* of man is his *telos* or *eskhaton*. . . . Such a discourse, in Hegel as in the entirety of metaphysics, indissociably coordinates teleology with an eschatology, a theology, and an ontology." Jacques Derrida, *Margins of Philosophy*, trans. Alan Bass (Chicago: University of Chicago Press, 1982), 121.

27. Jacques Derrida, *Eyes of the University: Right to Philosophy 2*, trans. Jan Plug et al. (Stanford, Calif.: Stanford University Press, 2004), 133.

28. Ibid.

29. Quoted in ibid.

30. Ibid., 134. One cannot help but think here of the "bridge" that Sin and Death construct in *Paradise Lost* (10.301) through the abyss of Chaos in order to connect Hell to earth.

31. Ibid., 130.

32. Francis Bacon, *Essays and "New Atlantis"* (Roslyn, N.Y.: Walter J. Black, 1949), 4–5.

33. In this context, too, the word "vale" in the translated quotation from Lucretius likely operates as a pun on "veil." Parker writes, "The 'vale' of exile and the 'veil' of language were assimilated long before even Blake's combination of the mysterious and the lachrymose in the romance figure of Vala, and the figure of the veil and unveiling is one of the oldest of narrative—and semiotic—images, from the Book of Revelation to the series of romance enchantresses whose uncovering is related both to the discovery of meaning and to a sense of narrative ending" (*Inescapable Romance*, 221). Indeed, the title of one of the sections in Parker's chapter on Spenser is "The Vale of Vision."

34. Bacon, *Essays*, 5.

35. John M. Steadman, *The Hill and the Labyrinth: Discourse and Certitude in Milton and His Near-Contemporaries* (Berkeley: University of California Press, 1984).

36. One of the most recent statements of this view of Milton's sublimity can be found in Gordon Teskey, *The Poetry of John Milton* (Cambridge, Mass.: Harvard University Press, 2015), 409–35. "What is most striking about Milton's poetry, especially in *Paradise Lost*," Teskey remarks, "is not just that it is sublime, that it is elevated and 'high.' What is striking is that at every moment we feel its uplifting power in a moral sense, too, as a development subsequent to the experience of this height, without leaving the highness behind" (413).

37. All quotations are from *The Bible: Authorized King James Version* (Oxford: Oxford University Press, 1997); citations will appear in the text and refer to book as well as chapter and verse numbers; all italics are in the original.

38. On general parallels between Milton's tract and Michael's education of Adam, see Ann Baynes Coiro, "'To Repair the Ruins of Our First Parents': *Of Education* and Fallen Adam," *Studies in English Literature, 1500–1900* 28, no. 1 (1988): 133–47.

39. Fish, *How Milton Works*, 256.

40. See Paul de Man, *Aesthetic Ideology*, ed. Andrzej Warminski (Minneapolis: University of Minnesota Press, 1996), esp. 163–84.

41. Ibid., 177; my italics.

42. Lee Edelman, "Aesthetic Value and Literary Language: Elizabeth Bishop and Paul de Man," in *Never Again Would Birds' Songs Be the Same: Essays*

on Early Modern and Modern Poetry in Honor of John Hollander, ed. Jennifer Lewin (New Haven, Conn.: Beinecke Library, 2002), 231. On associations among sublimity, sublimation, and alchemy, see also Richard Halpern, *Shakespeare's Perfume: Sodomy and Sublimity in the Sonnets, Wilde, Freud, and Lacan* (Philadelphia: University of Pennsylvania Press, 2002), esp. chap. 1.

43. See John Milton, *Lycidas*, ed. H. B. Cotterill (London: Blackie and Son, 1902), 56–57.

44. In "Aesthetic Value," Edelman juxtaposes two texts published in 1978: Elizabeth Bishop's poem "Santarém" (which draws, for its context, on the discovery of gold in South America) and Paul de Man's essay "The Epistemology of Metaphor" (which analyzes John Locke's discussion of gold in *An Essay Concerning Human Understanding*). The juxtaposition of these two texts allows Edelman to speculate, so to speak, on questions of aesthetic value; his analysis centers, not incidentally for our discussion of Milton, on Bishop's use of the conjunction "or," "a word," Edelman points out, that is "always ready, in romance languages, to turn into gold itself. . . . Like a version of Rumpelstiltskin, the economy of aesthetic value turns even the refusal or undoing of the aesthetic into more aesthetic gold. . . . 'Santarém' thus enacts an allegory of literature as the gold standard of aesthetic value by tracing that value to the conjunction of linguistic possibilities *in* a conjunction" (225). On the complexities of the word "or" in Shakespeare's *Hamlet*, see also Edelman's essay "Against Survival: Queerness in a Time That's Out of Joint," *Shakespeare Quarterly* 62, no. 2 (2011): 148–69, esp. 165.

45. See Michael Lieb, *The Dialectics of Creation: Patterns of Birth and Regeneration in "Paradise Lost"* (Amherst: University of Massachusetts Press, 1970). (Part 1 is called "The Process of Creation," part 2 is called "The Process of Uncreation," and part 3 is called "The Process of Re-Creation.")

46. Ibid., 5.

47. Ibid., 6.

48. David L. Sedley, *Sublimity and Skepticism in Montaigne and Milton* (Ann Arbor: University of Michigan Press, 2005), 15.

49. Ibid., 124.

50. G. W. F. Hegel, *Phenomenology of Spirit*, trans. A. V. Miller (Oxford: Oxford University Press, 1977), 124–25.

51. Ibid., 124. In using the phrase "negative dialectics," I am drawing on Theodor Adorno's *Negative Dialectics*, trans. E. B. Ashton (New York: Continuum, 2007). At the outset of his opus, Adorno points out that his title "is a phrase that flouts tradition. As early as Plato, dialectics meant to achieve something positive by means of negation. . . . This book seeks to free dialectics from such affirmative traits without reducing its determinacy. The unfoldment of the paradoxical title is one of its aims" (xix). Later in the book, Adorno offers an extended reading of Hegel (300–60).

52. Hegel, *Phenomenology of Spirit*, 125. For help in understanding this point (from a poetic perspective, at least), recall Charles Lamb's horror at seeing *Lycidas* in manuscript form: where he had thought of the poem as a "full-grown beauty," as self-identical and whole, he had to confront it in the form of its unsublimated contingency: "mortal, alterable, displaceable . . . fluctuating, successive, indifferent." Quoted in Milton, *Lycidas*, 57.

53. Ibid. Let me note here that a colleague responded to this chapter by pointing out that this detour through Hegel seemed possibly unessential, rather than entirely necessary and relevant, to the unfolding argument. While I understand the basis of this response, I have retained this discussion of *Phenomenology of Spirit* because the blurred line between essentiality and nonessentiality, necessity and contingency, that my reliance on Hegel apparently enacts (beyond my intentions) is precisely what is at stake in both Hegel's discussion of skepticism and in *Paradise Lost*.

54. Jean Hyppolite, *Genesis and Structure of Hegel's "Phenomenology of Spirit,"* trans. Samuel Cherniak and John Heckman (Chicago: Northwestern University Press, 1974), 186–87. Hyppolite, it is worth pointing out here, was Derrida's thesis advisor; Derrida pays tribute to his teacher in the essay "Punctuations: The Time of a Thesis," which immediately precedes "The Principle of Reason," his Cornell lecture, in *Eyes of the University* (117).

55. Hyppolite, *Genesis and Structure*, 188–89.

56. Nancy Armstrong and Leonard Tennenhouse, *The Imaginary Puritan: Literature, Intellectual Labor, and the Origins of Personal Life* (Berkeley: University of California Press, 1992), 111.

57. Parker, *Inescapable Romance*, 138; my italics.

58. In *The End of Learning: Milton and Education* (New York: Routledge, 2006), for example, Thomas Festa sides with John Rumrich against Fish's didactic reading of the poem, but his rhetoric nonetheless reinscribes the value system undergirding the conventional reading of Milton. "What we gain by seeing Milton in [Rumrich's] way," he writes in his introduction, "is a new set of problems, a new *vantage* from which to challenge our own epistemological and ideological positions" (20; my italics). Festa's reading of books 11 and 12 culminates in the understanding that "Adam finally attains a serviceable understanding of Michael's teachings" (154). In addition to Festa, other critics who reproduce the assumptions of Fish's reading of books 11 and 12 include Marshall Grossman, *"Authors to Themselves": Milton and the Revelation of History* (New York: Cambridge University Press, 1987), who argues that "Milton represents the process whereby historical experience is integrated with a scripturally derived sense of providence" (183); and Catherine Gimelli Martin, *The Ruins of Allegory: "Paradise Lost" and the Metamorphosis of Epic Convention* (Durham, N.C.: Duke University Press, 1998), who sees Adam gaining "the rewards of self-deliverance through trial" (296).

59. Lee Edelman, *No Future: Queer Theory and the Death Drive* (Durham, N.C.: Duke University Press, 2004), 10.

60. Stanley Fish, "Transmuting the Lump: *Paradise Lost*, 1942–1979," in *Doing What Comes Naturally: Change, Rhetoric, and the Practice of Theory in Literary and Legal Studies* (Durham, N.C.: Duke University Press, 1989), 247–93.

61. Quoted in ibid., 252.

62. C. S. Lewis, *A Preface to "Paradise Lost"* (London: Oxford University Press, 1961), 129.

63. Quoted in Fish, "Transmuting the Lump," 247.

64. Parker, *Inescapable Romance*, 138.

65. "Education" and "seduction" share the same root: *educere*, to lead forth.

66. I'm thinking not only of the euphrasy and rue with which Michael cures the problems with Adam's vision, but also *A Maske*'s haemony, the root "more med'cinal . . . than that Moly/That Hermes once to wise Ulysses gave" and the "sov'reign use" of which works "'Gainst all enchantments" (636–40). "Moly," as Roger Ascham reminds us in *The Scholemaster*, is the herb that Hermes gives to Odysseus specifically to counteract the poisonous enchantments of Circe (see Chapter 3).

67. See, for e.g., Stephen M. Fallon, *Milton among the Philosophers: Poetry and Materialism in Seventeenth-Century England* (Ithaca, N.Y.: Cornell University Press, 1991), esp. 203–6, where he convincingly links Descartes's philosophy to Milton's devils.

68. René Descartes, *"Discourse on Method" and Related Writings*, trans. Desmond M. Clarke (New York: Penguin, 2003), 8–9. Derrida offers a reading of Descartes's relationship to romance in *Eyes of the University*, 20–42.

69. Descartes, *"Discourse on Method,"* 9.

70. For Guy-Bray, for example, this tension manifests itself as Milton's "discomfort with his own poetic audacity" (*Against Reproduction*, 162); Fallon similarly identifies it as "the question of overreaching" (*Milton's Peculiar Grace*, 207); Gordon Teskey, in *Delirious Milton: The Fate of the Poet in Modernity* (Cambridge, Mass.: Harvard University Press, 2009), reads it as a "delirium" that "arises from an inner conflict between the authority of God the Creator . . . and the poet's need to be a creator . . . in his own right" (5); and Noam Reisner, in *Milton and the Ineffable* (Oxford: Oxford University Press, 2009), recasts the terms of Teskey's claim as an opposition between "the Hermetic poet, self-propelling himself towards God in ever-more ambitious poetic flights, and the passive prophet, lying in his bed as the 'heavenly Muse' dictates accommodated divine truths to him in verse" (177).

71. Fallon, *Milton's Peculiar Grace*, 221, 232.

72. Fish comments on the ever-present, and always resonant, pun in *Paradise Lost* that makes it difficult to distinguish between what is "raised" and what is "razed" (*How Milton Works*, 479–84).

73. Reisner, *Milton and the Ineffable*, 184–85.

74. Ibid., 185.

75. Fallon, *Milton's Peculiar Grace*, 221.

76. Ibid., 223. See also Fish, *How Milton Works*, 289–90, and Guy-Bray, *Against Reproduction*, 162.

77. Sir Philip Sidney, *Apology for Poetry; or, The Defence of Poesy*, ed. Geoffrey Shepherd, rev. R. W. Maslen (Manchester, U.K.: Manchester University Press, 2002), 87.

78. I am grateful to Jean Feerick for calling this language to my attention.

79. See Ernest Sirluck, "Milton Revises *The Faerie Queene*," *Modern Philology* 48 (1950): 90–96; Harold Bloom, *A Map of Misreading* (New York: Oxford University Press, 1975), 127–28; John Guillory, *Poetic Authority: Spenser, Milton, and Literary History* (New York: Columbia University Press, 1983), 131–35; and Maureen Quilligan, *Milton's Spenser: The Politics of Reading* (Ithaca, N.Y.: Cornell University Press, 1983), 50–53.

80. George F. Butler, "Milton's 'sage and serious Poet *Spencer*': Error and Imitation in *The Faerie Queene* and *Areopagitica*," *Texas Studies in Literature and Language* 49, no. 2 (2007): 104.

81. Here we should recall Adorno's statement, in *Negative Dialectics*, that dialectics has traditionally meant "achiev[ing] something positive *by means of* negation" (xix; my italics).

82. Jacques Derrida, *Archive Fever: A Freudian Impression*, trans. Eric Prenowitz (Chicago: University of Chicago Press, 1995), 12–13. The passage to which Derrida is referring can be found in Sigmund Freud, *Civilization and Its Discontents*, trans. and ed. James Strachey (New York: Norton, 1989), 79–80.

83. Augustine, *Confessions*, ed. Henry Chadwick (Oxford: Oxford University Press, 1991), I.xiii.22.

84. Augustine, *The Confessions of the Incomparable Doctor S. Avgvstine, Translated into English* (London, 1620), sig. C2v.

85. John E. Hankins, "Chaos," in *The Spenser Encyclopedia*, gen. ed. A. C. Hamilton (Toronto: University of Toronto Press, 1990), 139.

86. Major contributions to the debate include the following studies: A. B. Chambers, "Chaos in *Paradise Lost*," *Journal of the History of Ideas* 24 (1963): 55–84; Regina Schwartz, *Remembering and Repeating: Biblical Creation in "Paradise Lost"* (Cambridge: Cambridge University Press, 1988), 8–39; John Rumrich, "Milton's God and the Matter of Chaos," *PMLA* 110, no. 5 (1995): 1035–46; Rumrich, "Of Chaos and Nightingales," in *Living Texts: Interpreting Milton*, ed. Kristin A. Pruitt and Charles W. Durham (Selinsgrove, Pa.: Susquehanna University Press, 2000), 218–29; John Leonard, "Milton, Lucretius, and 'the Void Profound,'" in Pruitt and Durham, *Living*

Texts, 198–217; John Rogers, *The Matter of Revolution: Science, Poetry, and Politics in the Age of Milton* (Ithaca, N.Y.: Cornell University Press, 1996), 103–43; Teskey, *Delirious Milton*, 65–85; Paul Cefalu, *English Renaissance Literature and Contemporary Theory: Sublime Objects of Theology* (New York: Palgrave Macmillan, 2007), 101–40; and Goldberg, *The Seeds of Things: Theorizing Sexuality and Materiality in Renaissance Representations* (New York: Fordham University Press, 2009), 204–9.

87. Schwartz, *Remembering and Repeating*, 31.

88. Rogers, *Matter of Revolution*, 134.

89. Ibid., 133.

90. See, for e.g., Michael C. Schoenfeldt, *Bodies and Selves in Early Modern England: Physiology and Inwardness in Spenser, Shakespeare, Herbert, and Milton* (Cambridge: Cambridge University Press, 1999), 131–68; Denise Gigante, "Milton's Aesthetics of Eating," *diacritics* 30, no. 2 (2000): 88–112; and Kent R. Lehnhof, "Scatology and the Sacred in Milton's *Paradise Lost*," *English Literary Renaissance* 37 (2007): 429–49.

91. Dominique Laporte, in his *History of Shit*, trans. Nadia Benabid and Rodolphe el-Khoury (Cambridge, Mass.: MIT Press, 2003), situates such dynamics in relation to the purification of language and the urban management of waste begun in the Renaissance: "*Where shit was, so gold shall be*. And with its entrance, gold proclaims its implicit and ambivalent relation to excrement. Beautified, ordered, aggrandized, and sublimated, the town opposes itself to the mud of the countryside. But in so doing, it also exposes itself . . . as a place of corruption. . . . If the shit that glows in the fields becomes the lasting gold of city streets, the stench of shit lingers where gold sleeps" (39).

92. Jacques Lacan, *The Ethics of Psychoanalysis, 1959–1960: The Seminar of Jacques Lacan, Seminar VII*, ed. Jacques-Alain Miller, trans. Dennis Porter (New York: Norton, 1997), 93.

93. Ibid., 92–93.

94. Teskey, *Delirious Milton*, 39.

95. Ibid., 39–40.

96. See Bataille, "Hegel, Death and Sacrifice," trans. Jonathan Strauss, *Yale French Studies* 78 (1990): 9–28; for a lucid reading of Bataille's reading of Hegel, see Jacques Derrida, "From Restricted to General Economy: A Hegelianism without Reserve," in *Writing and Difference*, trans. Alan Bass (Chicago: University of Chicago Press, 1978).

97. Georges Bataille, *Visions of Excess: Selected Writings, 1927–1939*, trans. Allan Stoekl (Minneapolis: University of Minnesota Press, 1985), 137–38, 140, 142.

98. The heterogeneous, Bataille writes in *Visions of Excess*, includes not only "the properly sacred things that constitute the common realm of religion

or magic," but also "the waste products of the human body and certain analogous matter (trash, vermin, etc.)" (142). This conjunction perversely reveals what he calls the "identical nature . . . of God and excrement" (102n1). Although it doesn't address Milton, Will Stockton's *Playing Dirty: Sexuality and Waste in Early Modern Comedy* (Minneapolis: University of Minnesota Press, 2011) is the best recent investigation of these sorts of dynamics in relation to early modern literature. His chapter on Chaucer (97–118)—which brings "The Pardoner's Tale" into conversation with Bataille, as well as Laporte and Lacan—has been absolutely fundamental, so to speak, to my attempt to read Milton's (e)sc(h)atalogical imagination in *Paradise Lost.*

99. Bataille, *Visions of Excess*, 96, 97.

100. J. Hillis Miller, "Zero," in *Glossalalia: An Alphabet of Critical Keywords*, ed. Julian Wolfreys (New York: Routledge, 2003), 374.

101. De Man, *Aesthetic Ideology*, 59.

102. Ibid., 61.

103. Paul de Man, "The Concept of Irony," in *Aesthetic Ideology*, 181.

104. Quoted in ibid.

105. Quoted in ibid., 183.

106. Ibid., 184.

107. Paul de Man, *Blindness and Insight: Essays in the Rhetoric of Contemporary Criticism*, 2nd ed. (Minneapolis: University of Minnesota Press, 1983), 222; my italics.

108. Edelman, *No Future*, 101.

109. Ibid., 92.

110. Ibid., 101.

111. Fallon, *Milton's Peculiar Grace*, 13.

112. Bataille, *Visions of Excess*, 8.

113. Jacques Derrida, *Acts of Religion*, ed. Gil Anidjar (New York: Routledge, 2002), 196, 197–98.

CODA: LESS MATTER, MORE ART

1. John Milton, *Paradise Lost*, in *The Complete Poetry and Essential Prose of John Milton*, ed. William Kerrigan, John Rumrich, and Stephen M. Fallon (New York: Modern Library, 2007), 4.458–59. Unless otherwise noted, all quotations of *Paradise Lost* will be taken from this edition and cited in the text by book and line number.

2. Lee Edelman, *Homographesis: Essays in Gay Literary and Cultural Theory* (New York: Routledge, 1994), 102.

3. Judith Roof, *Come As You Are: Sexuality and Narrative* (New York: Columbia University Press, 1996), 7, 8. See also D. A. Miller, *Narrative and Its Discontents: Problems of Closure in the Traditional Novel* (Princeton, N.J.: Princeton University Press, 1981): "Once the ending is enshrined as an all-

embracing cause in which the elements of a narrative find their ultimate justification, it is difficult for analysis to assert anything short of total coherence. One is barred even from suspecting possible discontinuities between closure and the narrative movement preceding it, not to mention possible contradictions and ambiguities within closure itself" (xiii).

4. Madhavi Menon, *Unhistorical Shakespeare: Queer Theory in Shakespearean Literature and Film* (New York: Palgrave, 2008), 32.

5. Barbara Johnson, "Poison or Remedy? Paul de Man as Pharmakon," in *The Barbara Johnson Reader: The Surprise of Otherness*, ed. Melissa Feuerstein et al. (Durham, N.C.: Duke University Press, 2014), 358.

6. Patricia Parker, *Inescapable Romance: Studies in the Poetics of a Mode* (Princeton, N.J.: Princeton University Press, 1979), 147.

7. At the end of book 4 of *Paradise Lost*, the incipient battle between Satan and Gabriel is left hanging in the balance by the very emblem of hanging and balance, the constellation Libra:

> Th'Eternal to prevent such horrid fray
> Hung forth in Heav'n his golden scales, yet seen
> Betwixt Astrea and the Scorpion sign,
> Wherein all things created first he weighed,
> The pendulous round Earth with balanced air
> In counterpoise, now ponders all events,
> Battles and realms: in these he put two weights
> The sequel each of parting and of fight;
> The latter quick up flew, and kicked the beam.
>
> (4.996–1004)

Parker provocatively reads this moment in relation to the rhetoric of suspension, pendancy, and crepuscularity that pervades *Paradise Lost*, a constellation of figures that she connects to the dilations and errancy of romance (*Inescapable Romance*, 117).

8. Leah S. Marcus, "Recent Studies in the English Renaissance," *SEL: Studies in English Literature, 1500–1900* 54, no. 1 (2014): 242.

9. Will Stockton, *Playing Dirty: Sexuality and Waste in Early Modern Comedy* (Minneapolis: University of Minnesota Press, 2011), xx–xxi.

10. G. W. F. Hegel, *Phenomenology of Spirit*, trans. A. V. Miller (Oxford: Oxford University Press, 1977), 17.

11. Judith Haber, *Desire and Dramatic Form in Early Modern England* (Cambridge: Cambridge University Press, 2009), 6.

12. As far as I can tell, this notion originates with Yvor Winters's critique of what he calls, in reference to the poetry of Marianne Moore, "the fallacy of expressive, or imitative, form," by which he means "the procedure in which

the form succumbs to the raw material of the poem." Yvor Winters, *In Defense of Reason* (Denver: Alan Swallow, 1947), 41.

13. Sean Keilen, *Vulgar Eloquence: On the Renaissance Invention of English Literature* (New Haven, Conn.: Yale University Press, 2006), 31.

14. As Joseph Litvak asserts in *The Un-Americans: Jews, the Blacklist, and Stoolpigeon Culture* (Durham, N.C.: Duke University Press, 2009), even the "affection and respect" with which postmodern cultural critics treat nonelite cultural texts "typically stop short of that point at which cultural studies begins to assume the features of its unreasonable, undignified object," the point, he adds, "where critical engagement with the object ceases to be merely conceptual or interpretative and takes on the character of stylistic mimesis: where the object's unseriousness crosses over into the commentary on it" (17).

15. See Paul de Man, *Allegories of Reading: Figural Language in Rousseau, Nietzsche, Rilke, and Proust* (New Haven, Conn.: Yale University Press, 1979): "Literature as well as criticism—the difference between them being delusive—is condemned (or privileged) to be forever the most rigorous and, consequently, the most unreliable language in terms of which man names and transforms himself" (19).

16. Geoffrey Hartman, *Criticism in the Wilderness: The Study of Literature Today* (1980; New Haven, Conn.: Yale University Press, 2007), 175.

17. See Michel Chaouli, "Criticism and Style," *New Literary History* 44, no. 3 (2013): 323–44; Andrew H. Miller, "Implicative Criticism; or, The Display of Thinking," *New Literary History* 44, no. 3 (2013): 345–60; and Eric Hayot, "Academic Writing, I Love You. Really, I Do," *Critical Inquiry* 41, no. 1 (2014): 53–77.

18. Andrew H. Miller, "Implicative Criticism," 347.

19. Ibid., 351.

20. D. A. Miller, *The Novel and the Police* (Berkeley: University of California Press, 1988), vii.

21. Hayot, "Academic Writing," 68.

22. Ibid., 61.

23. Ibid., 59.

24. Chaouli, "Criticism and Style," 343n8.

BIBLIOGRAPHY

Abrams, M. H., gen. ed. *The Norton Anthology of English Literature*. 7th ed. 2 vols. New York: Norton, 2000.

Adams, Robert. "Bold Bawdry and Open Manslaughter: The English New Humanist Attack on Medieval Romance." *Huntington Library Quarterly* 23, no. 1 (1959): 33–48.

Adorno, Theodor. *Negative Dialectics*. Translated by E. B. Ashton. New York: Continuum, 2007.

Ahmed, Sara. *The Promise of Happiness*. Durham, N.C.: Duke University Press, 2010.

Andersen, Jennifer. "Blame-in-Praise Irony in *Lenten Stuffe*." In *The Age of Thomas Nashe: Text, Bodies, and Trespasses of Authorship in Early Modern England*, edited by Stephen Guy-Bray, Joan Pong Linton, and Steve Mentz, 45–62. Burlington, Vt.: Ashgate, 2013.

Armstrong, Nancy, and Leonard Tennenhouse. *The Imaginary Puritan: Literature, Intellectual Labor, and the Origins of Personal Life*. Berkeley: University of California Press, 1992.

———. "The Literature of Conduct, the Conduct of Literature, and the Politics of Desire: An Introduction." In *The Ideology of Conduct: Essays on Literature and the History of Sexuality*, edited by Nancy Armstrong and Leonard Tennenhouse, 1–24. New York: Methuen, 1987.

Arnold, Matthew. *Essays by Matthew Arnold*. London: Humphrey Milford, Oxford University Press, 1914.

Ascham, Roger. *The Scholemaster*. Edited by Lawrence V. Ryan. Ithaca, N.Y.: Cornell University Press for Folger Shakespeare Library, 1967.

Augustine. *Confessions*. Edited by Henry Chadwick. Oxford: Oxford University Press, 1991.

———. *The Confessions of the Incomparable Doctor S. Avgvstine, Translated into English*. London, 1620.

Bacon, Francis. *Essays and "New Atlantis."* Roslyn, N.Y.: Walter J. Black, 1949.

Baker, David. *On Demand: Writing for the Market in Early Modern England*. Stanford, Calif.: Stanford University Press, 2010.

Barthes, Roland. *Le plaisir du texte.* Paris: Éditions du Seuil, 1973.
———. *The Pleasure of the Text.* Translated by Richard Miller. New York: Hill and Wang, 1975.
———. *Roland Barthes.* Translated by Richard Howard. New York: Farrar, Straus and Giroux, 1977.
Bataille, Georges. "Hegel, Death and Sacrifice." Translated by Jonathan Strauss. *Yale French Studies* 78 (1990): 9–28.
———. *Visions of Excess: Selected Writings, 1927–1939.* Translated by Allan Stoekl. Minneapolis: University of Minnesota Press, 1985.
Belsey, Catherine. *A Future for Criticism.* Malden, Mass.: Blackwell, 2011.
Benjamin, Walter. "The Storyteller: Reflections on the Works of Nikolai Leskov." In *Illuminations*, edited by Hannah Arendt, translated by Harry Zohn, 83–110. New York: Schocken, 1968.
Berger, Harry, Jr., *Revisionary Play: Studies in the Spenserian Dynamics.* Berkeley: University of California Press, 1988.
Berlant, Lauren. *Cruel Optimism.* Durham, N.C.: Duke University Press, 2011.
Berlant, Lauren, and Lee Edelman. *Sex, or the Unbearable.* Durham, N.C.: Duke University Press, 2014.
Bersani, Leo. *The Culture of Redemption.* Cambridge, Mass.: Harvard University Press, 1990.
Bersani, Leo, and Ulysse Dutoit. *Forms of Being: Cinema, Aesthetics, Subjectivity.* London: British Film Institute, 2004.
Bewes, Timothy. *Reification; or, The Anxiety of Late Capitalism.* London: Verso, 2002.
The Bible: Authorized King James Version. Oxford: Oxford University Press, 1997.
Blake, William. *The Marriage of Heaven and Hell.* In *The Norton Anthology of English Literature*, 7th ed., 2 vols., gen. ed. M. H. Abrams, 2:72–82. New York: Norton, 2000.
Bloom, Harold. *A Map of Misreading.* New York: Oxford University Press, 1975.
Bretzius, Stephen. *Shakespeare in Theory: The Postmodern Academy and the Early Modern Theater.* Ann Arbor: University of Michigan Press, 1997.
Brinkema, Eugenie. *The Forms of the Affects.* Durham, N.C.: Duke University Press, 2014.
Britton, Dennis Austin. *Becoming Christian: Race, Reformation, and Early Modern English Romance.* New York: Fordham University Press, 2014.
Bromley, James M. *Intimacy and Sexuality in the Age of Shakespeare.* Cambridge: Cambridge University Press, 2011.
Brooks, Cleanth. "The Heresy of Paraphrase." In *The Well-Wrought Urn: Studies in the Structure of Poetry*, 192–214. New York: Harvest, 1947.

Brown, Georgia. *Redefining Elizabethan Literature*. Cambridge: Cambridge University Press, 2004.

———. "Sex and the City: Nashe, Ovid, and the Problems of Urbanity." In *The Age of Thomas Nashe: Text, Bodies, and Trespasses of Authorship in Early Modern England*, edited by Stephen Guy-Bray, Joan Pong Linton, and Steve Mentz, 11–26. Burlington, Vt.: Ashgate, 2013.

Brown, Judith. "Pretty Richard (in Three Parts)." In *Shakesqueer: A Queer Companion to the Complete Works of Shakespeare*, edited by Madhavi Menon, 286–93. Durham, N.C.: Duke University Press, 2011.

Bruni, Frank. "College, Poetry and Purpose." *New York Times*. Feb. 18, 2015. http://www.nytimes.com/2015/02/18/opinion/frank-bruni-college-poetry-and-purpose.html.

———. "From 'Hamlet' to Hillary." *New York Times*. May 2, 2015. http://www.nytimes.com/2015/05/03/opinion/sunday/frank-bruni-from-hamlet-to-hillary.html.

Bryskett, Lodowick. *A discourse of ciuill life containing the ethike part of morall philosophie*. London, 1606.

Bushnell, Rebecca. *A Culture of Teaching: Early Modern Humanism in Theory and Practice*. Ithaca, N.Y.: Cornell University Press, 1996.

Butler, George F. "Milton's 'sage and serious Poet *Spencer*': Error and Imitation in *The Faerie Queene* and *Areopagitica*." *Texas Studies in Literature and Language* 49, no. 2 (2007): 101–24.

Butler, Judith. *Subjects of Desire: Hegelian Reflections in Twentieth-Century France*. New York: Columbia University Press, 1987.

Cahill, Edward. *Liberty of the Imagination: Aesthetic Theory, Literary Form, and Politics in the Early United States*. Philadelphia: University of Pennsylvania Press, 2012.

Campana, Joseph. *The Pain of Reformation: Spenser, Vulnerability, and the Ethics of Masculinity*. New York: Fordham University Press, 2012.

Campbell, Lily B., ed. *The Mirror for Magistrates*. New York: Barnes and Noble, 1873.

Castiglia, Christopher, and Christopher Reed. *If Memory Serves: Gay Men, AIDS, and the Promise of the Queer Past*. Minneapolis: University of Minnesota Press, 2012.

Cave, Terence. *The Cornucopian Text: Problems of Writing in the French Renaissance*. Oxford: Clarendon, 1979.

Cefalu, Paul. *English Renaissance Literature and Contemporary Theory: Sublime Objects of Theology*. New York: Palgrave Macmillan, 2007.

———. *Moral Identity in Early Modern English Literature*. Cambridge: Cambridge University Press, 2004.

Cesario, Robert L., et al. "The Antisocial Thesis in Queer Theory." *PMLA* 121, no. 3 (2006): 819–26.

Chambers, A. B. "Chaos in *Paradise Lost*." *Journal of the History of Ideas* 24 (1963): 55–84.

Chambers, Ross. *Loiterature*. Lincoln: University of Nebraska Press, 1999.

Chaouli, Michel. "Criticism and Style." *New Literary History* 44, no. 3 (2013): 323–44.

Chaucer, Geoffrey. *The Canterbury Tales: Complete*. Edited by Larry D. Benson. Boston: Houghton Mifflin, 2000.

Cohen, Stephen. "Between Form and Culture: New Historicism and the Promise of a Historical Formalism." In *Renaissance Literature and Its Formal Engagements*, edited by Mark David Rasmussen, 17–41. New York: Palgrave, 2002.

Coiro, Ann Baynes. "'To Repair the Ruins of Our First Parents': *Of Education* and Fallen Adam." *Studies in English Literature, 1500–1900* 28, no. 1 (1988): 133–47.

Corum, Richard. "Henry's Desires." In *Premodern Sexualities*, edited by Louise Fradenburg and Carla Freccero, 71–97. New York: Routledge, 1996.

Cotterill, Anne. *Digressive Voices in Early Modern English Literature*. Oxford: Oxford University Press, 2004.

Craik, Katherine. *Reading Sensations in Early Modern England*. New York: Palgrave Macmillan, 2007.

Craik, Katherine, and Tanya Pollard, eds. *Shakespearean Sensations: Experiencing Literature in Early Modern England*. Cambridge: Cambridge University Press, 2013.

Crewe, Jonathan. *Unredeemed Rhetoric: Thomas Nashe and the Scandal of Authorship*. Baltimore: Johns Hopkins University Press, 1982.

Crockett, Clayton. *Interstices of the Sublime: Theology and Psychoanalytic Theory*. New York: Fordham University Press, 2007.

Dalrymple, Roger. *Language and Piety in Middle English Romance*. Cambridge: D. S. Brewer, 2000.

Danner, Bruce. *Edmund Spenser's War on Lord Burghley*. New York: Palgrave Macmillan, 2011.

Davis, Alex. *Chivalry and Romance in the English Renaissance*. Cambridge: D. S Brewer, 2003.

Dean, Tim. "The Biopolitics of Pleasure." *South Atlantic Quarterly* 111, no. 3 (2012): 477–96.

de Man, Paul. *Aesthetic Ideology*. Edited by Andrzej Warminski. Minneapolis: University of Minnesota Press, 1996.

———. *Allegories of Reading: Figural Language in Rousseau, Nietzsche, Rilke, and Proust*. New Haven, Conn.: Yale University Press, 1979.

———. *Blindness and Insight: Essays in the Rhetoric of Contemporary Criticism*. 2nd ed. Minneapolis: University of Minnesota Press, 1983.

———. *Critical Writings, 1953–1978*. Edited by Lindsay Waters. Minneapolis: University of Minnesota Press, 1989.

———. *The Resistance to Theory*. Minneapolis: University of Minnesota Press, 1986.

Derrida, Jacques. *Acts of Religion*. Edited by Gil Anidjar. New York: Routledge, 2002.

———. *Archive Fever: A Freudian Impression*. Translated by Eric Prenowitz. Chicago: University of Chicago Press, 1995.

———. *Dissemination*. Translated by Barbara Johnson. Chicago: University of Chicago Press, 1981.

———. *Eyes of the University: Right to Philosophy 2*. Translated by Jan Plug et al. Stanford, Calif.: Stanford University Press, 2004.

———. "From Restricted to General Economy: A Hegelianism without Reserve." In *Writing and Difference*, translated by Alan Bass, 251–77. Chicago: University of Chicago Press, 1978.

———. *Margins of Philosophy*. Translated by Alan Bass. Chicago: University of Chicago Press, 1982.

———. "'This Strange Institution Called Literature': An Interview with Jacques Derrida." In *Acts of Literature*, edited by Derek Attridge, 33–75. New York: Routledge, 1992.

Descartes, René. *"Discourse on Method" and Related Writings*. Translated by Desmond M. Clarke. New York: Penguin, 2003.

DiGangi, Mario. *The Homoerotics of Early Modern Drama*. Cambridge: Cambridge University Press, 1997.

Dinshaw, Carolyn. *Getting Medieval: Sexualities and Communities, Pre- and Postmodern*. Durham, N.C.: Duke University Press, 1999.

DiPietro, Cary, and Hugh Grady, eds. *Shakespeare and the Urgency of Now: Criticism and Theory in the 21st Century*. London: Palgrave, 2013.

Dolven, Jeff. *Scenes of Instruction in Renaissance Romance*. Chicago: University of Chicago Press, 2007.

———. "When to Stop Reading *The Faerie Queene*." In *Never Again Would Birds' Songs Be the Same: Essays on Early Modern and Modern Poetry in Honor of John Hollander*, edited by Jennifer Lewin, 35–54. New Haven, Conn.: Beinecke Library, 2002.

Donno, Elizabeth Story, ed. *Andrew Marvell: The Complete Poems*. 1972. Reprint, London: Penguin, 2005.

Doran, Madeleine. *Endeavors of Art: Studies of Form in Elizabethan Drama*. Madison: University of Wisconsin Press, 1954.

Dubrow, Heather. "Guess Who's Coming to Dinner? Reinterpreting Formalism and the Country House Poem." In *Reading for Form*, edited by Susan J. Wolfson and Marshall Brown, 80–98. Seattle: University of Washington Press, 2006.

Duncan-Jones, Katherine. "Nashe and Sidney: The Tournament Scene in *The Unfortunate Traveller*." *Modern Language Review* 63 (1968): 3–7.

Edelman, Lee. "Aesthetic Value and Literary Language: Elizabeth Bishop and Paul de Man." In *Never Again Would Birds' Songs Be the Same: Essays on Early Modern and Modern Poetry in Honor of John Hollander*, edited by Jennifer Lewin, 222–31. New Haven, Conn.: Beinecke Library, 2002.

———. "Against Survival: Queerness in a Time That's Out of Joint." *Shakespeare Quarterly* 62, no. 2 (2011): 148–69.

———. "Ever After: History, Negativity, and the Social." *South Atlantic Quarterly* 106 (2007): 469–76.

———. *Homographesis: Essays in Gay Literary and Cultural Theory*. New York: Routledge, 1994.

———. *No Future: Queer Theory and the Death Drive*. Durham, N.C.: Duke University Press, 2004.

Ellinghausen, Laurie. *Labor and Writing in Early Modern England, 1567–1667*. Aldershot, U.K.: Ashgate, 2008.

Elmslie, Bruce, and Edinaldo Tebaldi. "Sexual Orientation and Labor Market Discrimination." *Journal of Labor Research* 28 (2007): 436–53.

Empson, William. *Milton's God*. London: Chatto and Windus, 1961.

Fallon, Stephen M. *Milton among the Philosophers: Poetry and Materialism in Seventeenth-Century England*. Ithaca, N.Y.: Cornell University Press, 1991.

———. *Milton's Peculiar Grace: Self-Representation and Authority*. Ithaca, N.Y.: Cornell University Press, 2007.

Feerick, Jean E. *Strangers in Blood: Relocating Race in the Renaissance*. Toronto: University of Toronto Press, 2010.

Felski, Rita. *Uses of Literature*. Oxford: Blackwell, 2008.

Ferguson, Arthur B. *The Indian Summer of English Chivalry: Studies in the Decline and Transformation of Chivalric Idealism*. Durham, N.C.: Duke University Press, 1960.

Ferguson, Frances. "Now It's Personal: D. A. Miller and Too-Close Reading." *Critical Inquiry* 41, no. 3 (2015): 521–40.

Fernie, Ewan. "Shakespeare and the Prospect of Presentism." *Shakespeare Survey* 58 (2005): 169–84.

Festa, Thomas. *The End of Learning: Milton and Education*. New York: Routledge, 2006.

Fineman, Joel. "The History of the Anecdote: Fiction and Fiction." In *The New Historicism*, edited by H. Aram Veeser, 49–76. New York: Routledge, 1989.

Fish, Stanley. *How Milton Works*. Cambridge, Mass.: Belknap Press of Harvard University Press, 2001.

———. *Surprised by Sin: The Reader in "Paradise Lost."* New York: St. Martin's Press, 1967.

———. "Transmuting the Lump: *Paradise Lost*, 1942–1979." In *Doing What Comes Naturally: Change, Rhetoric, and the Practice of Theory in Literary and Legal Studies*, 247–93. Durham, N.C.: Duke University Press, 1989.

———. *Versions of Antihumanism: Milton and Others*. Cambridge: Cambridge University Press, 2012.

Foucault, Michel. *The Use of Pleasure*. Vol. 2 of *The History of Sexuality*. Translated by Robert Hurley. New York: Vintage, 1990.

Freccero, Carla. *Queer/Early/Modern*. Durham, N.C.: Duke University Press, 2006.

Freeman, Elizabeth. *Time Binds: Queer Temporalities, Queer Histories*. Durham, N.C.: Duke University Press, 2010.

Freud, Sigmund. *Civilization and Its Discontents*. Translated and edited by James Strachey. New York: Norton, 1989.

———. *Three Essays on the Theory of Sexuality*. Translated by James Strachey. New York: Basic Books, 2002.

Frost, Laura. *The Problem with Pleasure: Modernism and Its Discontents*. New York: Columbia University Press, 2013.

Frye, Northrop. *Anatomy of Criticism: Four Essays*. Princeton, N.J.: Princeton University Press, 1957.

———. *The Secular Scripture: A Study of the Structure of Romance*. Cambridge, Mass.: Harvard University Press, 1976.

Fumerton, Patricia. "Introduction: A New New Historicism." In *Renaissance Culture and the Everyday*, edited by Patricia Fumerton and Simon Hunt, 1–17. Philadelphia: University of Pennsylvania Press, 1999.

Gajowski, Evelyn, ed. *Presentism, Gender, and Sexuality in Shakespeare*. New York: Palgrave, 2009.

Gallop, Jane. *Anecdotal Theory*. Durham, N.C.: Duke University Press, 2002.

———. "Beyond the *Jouissance* Principle." *Representations* 7 (1984): 110–15.

Garber, Marjorie. *A Manifesto for Literary Studies*. Seattle: University of Washington Press, 2003.

———. *Shakespeare After All*. New York: Pantheon, 2004.

———. *The Use and Abuse of Literature*. New York: Pantheon, 2011.

Gaudet, Paul. "The 'Parasitical' Counselors in Shakespeare's *Richard II*: A Problem in Dramatic Interpretation." *Shakespeare Quarterly* 33, no. 2 (1982): 142–54.

Gigante, Denise. "Milton's Aesthetics of Eating." *Diacritics* 30, no. 2 (2000): 88–112.

Gil, Daniel Juan. *Before Intimacy: Asocial Sexuality in Early Modern England*. Minneapolis: University of Minnesota Press, 2006.

Glimp, David. *Increase and Multiply: Governing Cultural Reproduction in Early Modern England*. Minneapolis: University of Minnesota Press, 2003.

Goldberg, Jonathan. *Endlesse Worke: Spenser and the Structures of Discourse.* Baltimore: Johns Hopkins University Press, 1981.

———. *The Seeds of Things: Theorizing Sexuality and Materiality in Renaissance Representations.* New York: Fordham University Press, 2009.

———. *Shakespeare's Hand.* Minneapolis: University of Minnesota Press, 2003.

———. *Sodometries: Renaissance Texts, Modern Sexualities.* 1992. Reprint, New York: Fordham University Press, 2010.

Goldberg, Jonathan, and Madhavi Menon. "Queering History." *PMLA* 120, no. 5 (2005): 1608–17.

Gosson, Stephen.*"The Schoole of Abuse" (1579) and "A Short Apologie of 'The School of Abuse'" (1579).* Edited by Edward Arber. London: A. Murray and Son, 1869.

Grady, Hugh, and Terence Hawkes, eds. *Presentist Shakespeares.* Abingdon, U.K.: Routledge, 2007.

Greenblatt, Stephen. *Learning to Curse: Essays in Early Modern Culture.* 1990. Reprint, New York: Routledge Classics, 2007.

———. *Marvelous Possessions: The Wonder of the New World.* Chicago: University of Chicago Press, 1991.

———. *Renaissance Self-Fashioning: From More to Shakespeare.* 1980. Reprint, Chicago: University of Chicago Press, 2005.

Greene, Thomas M. *The Light in Troy: Imitation and Discovery in Renaissance Poetry.* New Haven, Conn.: Yale University Press, 1982.

Grogan, Jane. *Exemplary Spenser: Visual and Poetic Pedagogy in "The Faerie Queene."* Burlington, Vt.: Ashgate, 2009.

Grossman, Marshall. *"Authors to Themselves": Milton and the Revelation of History.* New York: Cambridge University Press, 1987.

Guillory, John. *Poetic Authority: Spenser, Milton, and Literary History.* New York: Columbia University Press, 1983.

Guy-Bray, Stephen. *Against Reproduction: Where Renaissance Texts Come From.* Toronto: University of Toronto Press, 2009.

———. "Middleton's Language Machine." In *The Oxford Handbook of Thomas Middleton*, edited by Gary Taylor and Trish Thomas Henley, 346–59. Oxford: Oxford University Press, 2012.

———. "No Present." In *Sex, Gender, and Time in Fiction and Culture*, edited by Ben Davies and Jana Funke, 38–52. New York: Palgrave Macmillan, 2011.

Guy-Bray, Stephen, Joan Pong Linton, and Steve Mentz, eds. *The Age of Thomas Nashe: Text, Bodies, and Trespasses of Authorship in Early Modern England.* Burlington, Vt.: Ashgate, 2013.

Haber, Judith. *Desire and Dramatic Form in Early Modern England.* Cambridge: Cambridge University Press, 2009.

Halperin, David. *How to Be Gay.* Cambridge: Belknap Press of Harvard University Press, 2012.

Halpern, Richard. *Shakespeare's Perfume: Sodomy and Sublimity in the Sonnets, Wilde, Freud, and Lacan.* Philadelphia: University of Pennsylvania Press, 2002.

Hamilton, Ross. *Accident: A Philosophical and Literary History*. Chicago: University of Chicago Press, 2007.

Hammill, Graham L. *Sexuality and Form: Caravaggio, Marlowe, and Bacon.* Chicago: University of Chicago Press, 2000.

Hankins, John E. "Chaos." In *The Spenser Encyclopedia*, edited by A. C. Hamilton, 139. Toronto: University of Toronto Press, 1990.

Hanson, Victor Davis, John Heath, and Bruce S. Thornton. *Bonfire of the Humanities: Rescuing the Classics in an Impoverished Age*. Wilmington, Del.: ISI Books, 2001.

Harington, Sir John. "An Apology for Ariosto: Poetry, Epic, Morality (1591)." In *English Renaissance Literary Criticism*, edited by Brian Vickers, 302–24. Oxford: Clarendon, 1999.

Harlow, C. G. "Shakespeare, Nashe, and the Ostrich Crux in *I Henry IV*." *Shakespeare Quarterly* 17, no. 2 (1966): 171–74.

Harris, Jonathan Gil. *Untimely Matter in the Time of Shakespeare.* Philadelphia: University of Pennsylvania Press, 2009.

Hartman, Geoffrey. *Criticism in the Wilderness: The Study of Literature Today.* 1980. Reprint, New Haven, Conn.: Yale University Press, 2007.

———. *Scars of the Spirit: The Struggle against Inauthenticity.* New York: Palgrave Macmillan, 2002.

Hawkes, Terence. *Shakespeare in the Present.* London: Routledge, 2002.

Hayot, Eric. "Academic Writing, I Love You. Really, I Do." *Critical Inquiry* 41, no. 1 (2014): 53–77.

Hegel, G. W. F. *Phenomenology of Spirit.* Translated by A. V. Miller. Oxford: Oxford University Press, 1977.

Helgerson, Richard. *The Elizabethan Prodigals.* Berkeley: University of California Press, 1976.

———. *Forms of Nationhood: The Elizabethan Writing of England.* Chicago: University of Chicago Press, 1992.

———. *Self-Crowned Laureates: Spenser, Jonson, Milton, and the Literary System.* Berkeley: University of California Press, 1983.

Herbert, George. *The Complete English Poems.* Edited by John Tobin. New York: Penguin, 2004.

Herman, Peter C. *Destabilizing Milton: "Paradise Lost" and the Poetics of Incertitude.* New York: Palgrave Macmillan, 2005.

Herman, Peter C., and Elizabeth Sauer, eds. *The New Milton Criticism.* Cambridge: Cambridge University Press, 2012.

Hilliard, Stephen S. *The Singularity of Thomas Nashe.* Lincoln: University of Nebraska Press, 1986.

Horace. "The Art of Poetry." *Ancient Literary Criticism: The Principal Texts in New Translations*, edited by D. A. Russell and M. Winterbottom, 279–91. Oxford: Oxford University Press, 2003.

Howard, Jean E., and Phyllis Rackin. *Engendering a Nation: A Feminist Account of Shakespeare's English Histories*. London: Routledge, 1997.

Howie, Cary. "Stay." In *Shakesqueer: A Queer Companion to the Complete Works of Shakespeare*, edited by Madhavi Menon, 146–51. Durham, N.C.: Duke University Press, 2011.

Hurd, Richard. *Letters on Chivalry and Romance*. Edited by Hoyt Trowbridge. Los Angeles: William Andrews Clark Memorial Library, University of California, 1963.

Hutson, Lorna. *Thomas Nashe in Context*. Oxford: Clarendon, 1989.

Hyman, Wendy. "Authorial Self-Consciousness in Nashe's *The Vnfortunate Traveller*." *SEL: Studies in English Literature, 1500–1900* 45, no. 1 (2005): 23–41.

Hyppolite, Jean. *Genesis and Structure of Hegel's "Phenomenology of Spirit."* Translated by Samuel Cherniak and John Heckman. Chicago: Northwestern University Press, 1974.

Innes, Stephen. *Creating the Commonwealth: The Economic Culture of Puritan New England*. New York: Norton, 1995.

Jameson, Fredric. "Pleasure: A Political Issue." 1983. In *The Ideologies of Theory: Essays 1971–1986*. Vol. 2 of *Syntax of History*, 61–74. Minneapolis: University of Minnesota Press, 1988.

———. *Postmodernism; or, The Cultural Logic of Late Capitalism*. Durham, N.C.: Duke University Press, 1991.

Javitch, Daniel. *Proclaiming a Classic: The Canonization of "Orlando Furioso."* Princeton, N.J.: Princeton University Press, 1991.

Johnson, Barbara. "Art for Something's Sake." *Journal of Aesthetic Education* 36, no. 3 (2002): 28–30.

———. *Mother Tongues: Sexuality, Trials, Motherhood, Translation*. Cambridge, Mass.: Harvard University Press, 2003.

———. *Persons and Things*. Cambridge, Mass.: Harvard University Press, 2007.

———. "Poison or Remedy? Paul de Man as Pharmakon." In *The Barbara Johnson Reader: The Surprise of Otherness*, edited by Melissa Feuerstein et al., 357–70. Durham, N.C.: Duke University Press, 2014.

———. *The Wake of Deconstruction*. Cambridge, Mass.: Blackwell, 1994.

———. *A World of Difference*. Baltimore: Johns Hopkins University Press, 1987.

Johnson, Samuel. *Lives of the English Poets*. 2 vols. London: Oxford University Press, 1906.

Jones, Ann Rosalind. "Inside the Outsider: Nashe's *Unfortunate Traveller* and Bakhtin's Polyphonic Novel." *ELH* 50, no. 1 (1983): 61–81.

Jusdanis, Gregory. *Fiction Agonistes: In Defense of Literature*. Stanford, Calif.: Stanford University Press, 2010.

Kahn, Coppélia. *Man's Estate: Masculine Identity in Shakespeare*. Berkeley: University of California Press, 1981.

Kahn, Victoria. "The Passions and the Interests in Early Modern Europe: The Case of Guarini's *Il Pastor fido*." In *Reading the Early Modern Passions: Essays in the Cultural History of Emotion*, edited by Gail Kern Paster, Katherine Rowe, and Mary Floyd-Wilson, 217–39. Philadelphia: University of Pennsylvania Press, 2004.

———. *Wayward Contracts: The Crisis of Political Obligation in England, 1640–1674*. Princeton, N.J.: Princeton University Press, 2004.

Kaske, Carol. "How Spenser Really Used Stephen Hawes in the Legend of Holiness." In *Unfolded Tales: Essays on Renaissance Romance*, edited by George M. Logan and Gordon Teskey, 119–21. Ithaca, N.Y.: Cornell University Press, 1989.

Kastan, David Scott, ed. *Paradise Lost*. New York: Hackett, 2005.

———. *Shakespeare after Theory*. New York: Routledge, 1999.

Keilen, Sean. *Vulgar Eloquence: On the Renaissance Invention of English Literature*. New Haven, Conn.: Yale University Press, 2006.

Kermode, Frank. *The Sense of an Ending: Studies in the Theory of Fiction*. London: Oxford University Press, 1966.

———. *Shakespeare, Spenser, Donne: Renaissance Essays*. 1971. Reprint, Abingdon, U.K.: Routledge, 2005.

Kimball, Roger. *Tenured Radicals: How Politics Has Corrupted Our Higher Education*. Rev. ed. Chicago: Elephant Paperbacks, 1998.

Kinney, Clare Regan. *Strategies of Poetic Narrative: Chaucer, Spenser, Milton, Eliot*. Cambridge: Cambridge University Press, 1992.

Knapp, Steven. *Personification and the Sublime: Milton to Coleridge*. Cambridge, Mass.: Harvard University Press, 1985.

Kojève, Alexandre. *Introduction to the Reading of Hegel*. Edited by Allan Bloom. Translated by James H. Nichols Jr. Ithaca, N.Y.: Cornell University Press, 1980.

Krause, Virginia. *Idle Pursuits: Literature and Oisiveté in the French Renaissance*. Newark: University of Delaware Press, 2003.

Lacan, Jacques. *The Ethics of Psychoanalysis, 1959–1960: The Seminar of Jacques Lacan, Seminar VII*. Edited by Jacques-Alain Miller. Translated by Dennis Porter. New York: Norton, 1997.

———. "The Instance of the Letter in the Unconscious or Reason since Freud." In *Écrits: The First Complete Edition in English*, translated by Bruce Fink, 412–41. New York: Norton, 2006.

Landreth, David. "Wit without Money in Nashe." In *The Age of Thomas Nashe: Text, Bodies, and Trespasses of Authorship in Early Modern England*, edited by Stephen Guy-Bray, Joan Pong Linton, and Steve Mentz, 135–52. Burlington, Vt.: Ashgate, 2013.

Laporte, Dominique. *History of Shit*. Translated by Nadia Benabid and Rodolphe el-Khoury. Cambridge, Mass.: MIT Press, 2003.

Leggatt, Alexander. "Artistic Coherence in *The Unfortunate Traveller*." *Studies in English Literature, 1500–1900* 14, no. 1 (1974): 31–46.

Lehnhof, Kent R. "Scatology and the Sacred in Milton's *Paradise Lost*." *English Literary Renaissance* 37 (2007): 429–49.

Lentricchia, Frank. *Criticism and Social Change*. Chicago: University of Chicago Press, 1983.

Leonard, John. "Milton, Lucretius, and 'the Void Profound.'" In *Living Texts: Interpreting Milton*, edited by Kristin A. Pruitt and Charles W. Durham, 198–217. Selinsgrove, Pa.: Susquehanna University Press, 2000.

Levine, Caroline. *Provoking Democracy: Why We Need the Arts*. Malden, Mass.: Blackwell, 2007.

Lewis, C. S. *The Allegory of Love: A Study in Medieval Tradition*. 1936. Reprint, New York: Galaxy, 1958.

———. *English Literature in the Sixteenth Century*. Oxford: Clarendon, 1954.

———. *A Preface to "Paradise Lost."* 1942. Reprint, London: Oxford University Press, 1961.

Lieb, Michael. *The Dialectics of Creation: Patterns of Birth and Regeneration in "Paradise Lost."* Amherst: University of Massachusetts Press, 1970.

Little, Arthur L., Jr. *Shakespeare Jungle Fever: National-Imperial Re-Visions of Race, Rape, and Sacrifice*. Stanford, Calif.: Stanford University Press, 2000.

Litvak, Joseph. *Strange Gourmets: Sophistication, Theory, and the Novel*. Durham, N.C.: Duke University Press, 1997.

———. *The Un-Americans: Jews, the Blacklist, and Stoolpigeon Culture*. Durham, N.C.: Duke University Press, 2009.

Lockey, Brian C. *Law and Empire in English Renaissance Literature*. Cambridge: Cambridge University Press, 2006.

Loesberg, Jonathan. *Aestheticism and Deconstruction: Pater, Derrida, and de Man*. Princeton, N.J.: Princeton University Press, 1991.

Love, Heather. *Feeling Backward: Loss and the Politics of Queer History*. Cambridge, Mass.: Harvard University Press, 2007.

Marcus, Leah S. "Recent Studies in the English Renaissance." *SEL: Studies in English Literature, 1500–1900* 54, no. 1 (2014): 193–242.

Marshall, Cynthia. *The Shattering of the Self: Violence, Subjectivity, and Early Modern Texts*. Baltimore: Johns Hopkins University Press, 2002.

Martin, Catherine Gimelli. *The Ruins of Allegory: "Paradise Lost" and the Metamorphosis of Epic Convention*. Durham, N.C.: Duke University Press, 1998.

Martines, Lauro. *Fire in the City: Savonarola and the Struggle for Renaissance Florence*. New York: Oxford University Press, 2006.

Marx, Karl. *Grundrisse: Foundations of the Critique of Political Economy*. Translated by Martin Nicolaus. London: Penguin, 1993.

Marx, Karl, and Frederick Engels. *The German Ideology (Selections)*. Edited by C. J. Arthur. New York: International Publishers, 2001.

Maslen, R. W. *Elizabethan Fictions: Espionage, Counter-Espionage, and the Duplicity of Fiction in Early Elizabethan Prose Narratives*. Oxford: Clarendon, 1997.

Masten, Jeffrey. *Textual Intercourse: Collaboration, Authorship, and Sexualities in Renaissance Drama*. Cambridge: Cambridge University Press, 1997.

Matz, Robert. *Defending Literature in Early Modern England: Renaissance Literary Theory in Social Context*. Cambridge: Cambridge University Press, 2000.

Maxwell, J. C. "The Truancy of Calidore." *ELH* 19, no. 2 (1952): 143–49.

McKerrow, Ronald, ed. *The Works of Thomas Nashe*. 6 vols. London: A. H. Bullen, 1904–10. Reprint, Oxford: Basil Blackwell, 1958.

McLuhan, Marshall. *The Classical Trivium: The Place of Thomas Nashe in the Learning of His Time*. Corte Madera, Calif.: Ginko, 2005.

Menon, Madhavi. "Introduction: Queer Shakes." In *Shakesqueer: A Queer Companion to the Complete Works of Shakespeare*, edited by Madhavi Menon, 1–27. Durham, N.C.: Duke University Press, 2011.

———. "*Richard II* and the Taint of Metonymy." *ELH* 70, no. 3 (2003): 653–75.

———. *Unhistorical Shakespeare: Queer Theory in Shakespearean Literature and Film*. New York: Palgrave, 2008.

Mentz, Steve. *Romance for Sale in Early Modern England: The Rise of Prose Fiction*. Aldershot, U.K.: Ashgate, 2006.

Miller, Andrew H. "Implicative Criticism; or, The Display of Thinking." *New Literary History* 44, no. 3 (2013): 345–60.

Miller, D. A. *8 1/2*. BFI Film Classics. Houndmills, U.K.: Palgrave Macmillan, 2008.

———. "Foutre! Bougre! Ecriture!" *Yale Journal of Criticism* 14, no. 2 (2001): 503–11.

———. "Hitchcock's Hidden Pictures." *Critical Inquiry* 37, no. 1 (2010): 106–30.

———. "Hitchcock's Understyle: A Too-Close View of *Rope*." *Representations* 121 (2013): 1–30.

———. *Jane Austen; or, The Secret of Style*. Princeton, N.J.: Princeton University Press, 2003.

———. *Narrative and Its Discontents: Problems of Closure in the Traditional Novel*. Princeton, N.J.: Princeton University Press, 1981.

———. *The Novel and the Police*. Berkeley: University of California Press, 1988.

Miller, J. Hillis. "Presidential Address 1986. The Triumph of Theory, the Resistance to Reading, and the Question of the Material Base." *PMLA* 102, no. 2 (1987): 281–91.

———. "Zero." In *Glossalalia: An Alphabet of Critical Keywords*, edited by Julian Wolfreys, 369–90. New York: Routledge, 2003.

Miller, Shannon. *Invested with Meaning: The Raleigh Circle in the New World.* Philadelphia: University of Pennsylvania Press, 1998.

Milton, John. *The Complete Poetry and Essential Prose of John Milton.* Edited by William Kerrigan, John Rumrich, and Stephen M. Fallon. New York: Modern Library, 2007.

———. "*Eikonoklastes* (Selections)." In *Complete Poems and Major Prose.* Edited by Merritt Y. Hughes, 781–816. Indianapolis: Hackett, 2003.

———. *Lycidas.* Edited by H. B. Cotterill. London: Blackie and Son, 1902.

Morton, Donald. "Changing the Terms: (Virtual) Desire and (Actual) Reality." In *The Material Queer: A Lesbigay Cultural Studies Reader*, edited by Donald Morton, 1–33. Boulder, Colo.: Westview, 1996.

Moss, Daniel D. *The Ovidian Vogue: Literary Fashion and Imitative Practice in Late Elizabethan England.* Toronto: University of Toronto Press, 2014.

Muñoz, José Esteban. *Cruising Utopia: The Then and There of Queer Futurity.* New York: New York University Press, 2009.

Nancy, Jean-Luc. *Hegel: The Restlessness of the Negative.* Translated by Jason Smith and Steven Miller. Minneapolis: University of Minnesota Press, 2002.

Nardizzi, Vin. "Grafted to Falstaff and Compounded with Catherine: Mingling Hal in the Second Tetralogy." In *Queer Renaissance Historiography: Backward Gaze*, edited by Vin Nardizzi, Stephen Guy-Bray, and Will Stockton, 149–69. Farnham, U.K.: Ashgate, 2009.

Nestrick, William V. "The Virtuous and Gentle Discipline of Gentlemen and Poets." *ELH* 29, no. 4 (1962): 357–71.

Netzley, Ryan. *Reading, Desire, and the Eucharist in Early Modern Religious Poetry.* Toronto: University of Toronto Press, 2011.

Neuse, Richard. "Book VI as Conclusion to *The Faerie Queene.*" *ELH* 35, no. 3 (1968): 329–53.

Ngai, Sianne. *Ugly Feelings.* Cambridge, Mass.: Harvard University Press, 2005.

Nicholl, Charles. *A Cup of News: The Life of Thomas Nashe.* London: Routledge and Kegan Paul, 1984.

Nietzsche, Friedrich. *Daybreak: Thoughts on the Prejudices of Morality.* Edited by Maudemarie Clark and Brian Leiter. Translated by R. J. Hollingdale. Cambridge: Cambridge University Press, 1997.

Nims, John Frederick, ed. *Ovid's Metamorphoses: The Arthur Golding Translation, 1567.* Philadelphia: Paul Dry, 2000.

Northrop, Douglas A. "The Uncertainty of Courtesy in Book VI of *The Faerie Queene.*" *Spenser Studies* 14 (2000): 215–32.

Nussbaum, Martha C. *Not for Profit: Why Democracy Needs the Humanities.* Princeton, N.J.: Princeton University Press, 2010.

Ord, Melanie. *Travel and Experience in Early Modern English Literature.* New York: Palgrave Macmillan, 2008.

Orvis, David L. "'Thy glorious household-stuffe': Doctrinal (Re)Inscription in George Herbert's Church Furnishing Poems." In *The Sacred and Profane in English Renaissance Literature*, edited by Mary A. Papazian, 285–320. Newark: University of Delaware Press, 2008.

Ossa-Richardson, Anthony. "Ovid and the 'Free Play with Signs' in Thomas Nashe's *The Unfortunate Traveller.*" *Modern Language Review* 101, no. 4 (2006): 945–56.

Ovid. *Ovid's Metamorphoses: The Arthur Golding Translation, 1567.* Edited by John Frederick Nims. Philadelphia: Paul Dry, 2000.

———. *The Poems of Exile.* Translated by Peter Green. New York: Penguin, 1994.

Panofsky, Erwin. *Hercules am Scheideweg.* Leipzig: B. G. Teubner, 1930.

Parker, Patricia. *Inescapable Romance: Studies in the Poetics of a Mode.* Princeton, N.J.: Princeton University Press, 1979.

Paster, Gail Kern, Katherine Rowe, and Mary Floyd-Wilson, eds. *Reading the Early Modern Passions: Essays in the Culture History of Emotion.* Philadelphia: University of Pennsylvania Press, 2004.

Philips, Katherine. *Poems.* London, 1664.

Phillips, Joshua. "Chronicles of Wasted Time: Anthony Munday, Tudor Romance, and Literary Labor." *ELH* 73 (2006): 781–803.

———. *English Fictions of Communal Identity, 1485–1603.* Farnham, U.K.: Ashgate, 2010.

Philmus, Maria R. Rohr. "*The Faerie Queene* and Renaissance Poetics: Another Look at Book VI as 'Conclusion' to the Poem." *English Studies* 76, no. 6 (1995): 497–519.

Pollard, Tanya. *Drugs and Theater in Early Modern England.* Oxford: Oxford University Press, 2005.

Prendergast, Maria Teresa Micaela. *Renaissance Fantasies: The Gendering of Aesthetics in Early Modern Fiction.* Kent, Ohio: Kent State University Press, 1999.

Puttenham, George. *The Art of English Poesy: A Critical Edition.* Edited by Frank Whigham and Wayne A. Rebhorn. Ithaca, N.Y.: Cornell University Press, 2007.

Quilligan, Maureen. *Milton's Spenser: The Politics of Reading.* Ithaca, N.Y.: Cornell University Press, 1983.

Quint, David. *Epic and Empire: Politics and Generic Form from Virgil to Milton.* Princeton, N.J.: Princeton University Press, 1993.

Rambuss, Richard. *Closet Devotions*. Durham, N.C.: Duke University Press, 1998.

———. *Spenser's Secret Career*. Cambridge: Cambridge University Press, 1993.

Reisner, Noam. *Milton and the Ineffable*. Oxford: Oxford University Press, 2009.

Robinson, Benedict S. *Islam and Early Modern English Literature: The Politics of Romance from Spenser to Milton*. New York: Palgrave Macmillan, 2007.

Roche, Mark William. *Why Literature Matters in the 21st Century*. New Haven, Conn.: Yale University Press, 2004.

Rogers, John. *The Matter of Revolution: Science, Poetry, and Politics in the Age of Milton*. Ithaca, N.Y.: Cornell University Press, 1996.

Ronell, Avital. *Crack Wars: Literature, Addiction, Mania*. 1992. Reprint, Urbana: University of Illinois Press, 2004.

Roof, Judith. *Come As You Are: Sexuality and Narrative*. New York: Columbia University Press, 1996.

Rooney, Ellen. "Form and Contentment." In *Reading for Form*, edited by Susan J. Wolfson and Marshall Brown, 25–48. Seattle: University of Washington Press, 2006.

———. *Seductive Reasoning: Pluralism as the Problematic of Contemporary Theory*. Ithaca, N.Y.: Cornell University Press, 1989.

Rowe, George E. "Privacy, Vision, and Gender in Spenser's Legend of Courtesy." *Modern Language Quarterly* 50, no. 4 (1989): 309–36.

Rumrich, John. "Milton's God and the Matter of Chaos." *PMLA* 110, no. 5 (1995): 1035–46.

———. "Of Chaos and Nightingales." In *Living Texts: Interpreting Milton*, edited by Kristin A. Pruitt and Charles W. Durham, 218–29. Selinsgrove, Pa.: Susquehanna University Press, 2000.

Ryan, Lawrence V. *Roger Ascham*. Stanford, Calif.: Stanford University Press, 1963.

Sawday, Jonathan. *Engines of the Imagination: Renaissance Culture and the Rise of the Machine*. New York: Routledge, 2007.

Schaff, Philip. *History of the Christian Church*. Vol. 5. Part 2. New York: Charles Scribner's Sons, 1910.

Schoenfeldt, Michael C. *Bodies and Selves in Early Modern England: Physiology and Inwardness in Spenser, Shakespeare, Herbert, and Milton*. Cambridge: Cambridge University Press, 1999.

Schwartz, Regina. *Remembering and Repeating: Biblical Creation in "Paradise Lost."* Cambridge: Cambridge University Press, 1988.

Schwarz, Daniel. *In Defense of Reading: Teaching Literature in the Twenty-First Century*. Malden, Mass.: Wiley-Blackwell, 2008.

Schwarz, Kathryn. "Queer Futility; or, *The Life and Death of King John.*" In *Shakesqueer: A Queer Companion to the Complete Works of Shakespeare*, edited by Madhavi Menon, 163–170. Durham, N.C.: Duke University Press, 2011.

———. *Tough Love: Amazon Encounters in the English Renaissance*. Durham, N.C.: Duke University Press, 2000.

Sedgwick, Eve Kosofsky. *Epistemology of the Closet*. 1990. Reprint, Berkeley: University of California Press, 2008.

———. "Paranoid Reading and Reparative Reading; or, You're So Paranoid You Probably Think This Essay Is about You." In *Touching Feeling: Affect, Pedagogy, Performativity*, 125–51. Durham, N.C.: Duke University Press, 2003.

Sedley, David L. *Sublimity and Skepticism in Montaigne and Milton*. Ann Arbor: University of Michigan Press, 2005.

Seward, Desmond. *The Burning of the Vanities: Savonarola and the Borgia Pope*. Stroud, U.K.: Sutton, 2006.

Shakespeare, William. *The Norton Shakespeare, Based on the Oxford Edition*. Gen. ed. Stephen Greenblatt. New York: Norton, 1997.

———. *Richard II*. Arden Shakespeare. 3rd ser. Edited by Charles R. Forker. London: Arden Shakespeare, 2002.

Sherman, Donovan. "'What more remains?': Messianic Performance in *Richard II*." *Shakespeare Quarterly* 65, no. 1 (2014): 22–48.

Sidney, Sir Philip. *An Apology for Poetry; or, The Defence of Poesy*. Edited by Geoffrey Shepherd. Rev. ed. R. W. Maslen. Manchester, U.K.: Manchester University Press, 2002.

———. *The Countess of Pembroke's Arcadia*. Edited by Maurice Evans. New York: Penguin Classics, 1987.

Sirluck, Ernest. "Milton Revises *The Faerie Queene*." *Modern Philology* 48 (1950): 90–96.

Snediker, Michael. *Queer Optimism: Lyric Personhood and Other Felicitous Persuasions*. Minneapolis: University of Minnesota Press, 2009.

Sontag, Susan. *"Against Interpretation" and Other Essays*. 1966. Reprint, New York: Picador, 2001.

Spenser, Edmund. *The Faerie Queene*. 2nd ed. Edited by A. C. Hamilton. Harlow, U.K.: Pearson Longman, 2007.

———. *The Shorter Poems*. Edited by Richard A. McCabe. New York: Penguin, 1999.

Spiller, Elizabeth. *Reading and the History of Race in the Renaissance*. Cambridge: Cambridge University Press, 2011.

Stark, Ryan J. "Protestant Theology and Apocalyptic Rhetoric in Roger Ascham's *The Scholemaster*." *Journal of the History of Ideas* 69, no. 4 (2008): 517–32.

Steadman, John M. *The Hill and the Labyrinth: Discourse and Certitude in Milton and His Near-Contemporaries.* Berkeley: University of California Press, 1984.

Stephanson, Raymond. "The Epistemological Challenge of Nashe's *The Unfortunate Traveller.*" *SEL: Studies in English Literature, 1500–1900* 23, no. 1 (1983): 21–36.

Stewart, Alan. *Close Readers: Humanism and Sodomy in Early Modern England.* Princeton, N.J.: Princeton University Press, 1997.

Stillman, Robert E. "Spenserian Autonomy and the Trial of New Historicism: Book Six of *The Faerie Queene.*" *English Literary Renaissance* 22, no. 3 (1992): 299–314.

Stockton, Will. *Playing Dirty: Sexuality and Waste in Early Modern Comedy.* Minneapolis: University of Minnesota Press, 2011.

Strier, Richard. *The Unrepentant Renaissance: From Petrarch to Shakespeare to Milton.* Chicago: University of Chicago Press, 2011.

Tasso, Torquato. *Discourses on the Heroic Poem.* Translated by Mariella Cavalchini and Irene Samuel. Oxford: Clarendon, 1973.

Tennenhouse, Leonard. *Power on Display: The Politics of Shakespeare's Genres.* New York: Methuen, 1986.

Teskey, Gordon. *Delirious Milton: The Fate of the Poet in Modernity.* Cambridge, Mass.: Harvard University Press, 2009.

———. *The Poetry of John Milton.* Cambridge, Mass.: Harvard University Press, 2015.

———. "Positioning Spenser's 'Letter to Raleigh.'" In *Craft and Tradition: Essays in Honour of William Blissett*, edited by H. B. de Groot and Alexander Leggatt, 35–46. Calgary: University of Calgary Press, 1990.

Tonkin, Humphrey. *Spenser's Courteous Pastoral: Book Six of "The Faerie Queene."* Oxford: Clarendon, 1972.

Traub, Valerie. "The New Unhistoricism in Queer Studies." *PMLA* 128, no. 1 (2013): 21–39.

Turner, Victor. *From Ritual to Theatre: The Human Seriousness of Play.* New York: PAJ Publications, 1982.

Vives, Juan Luis. *The Education of a Christian Woman: A Sixteenth-Century Manual.* Edited and translated by Charles Fantazzi. Chicago: University of Chicago Press, 2000.

Weber, Max. *"The Protestant Ethic and the 'Spirit' of Capitalism" and Other Writings.* Edited and translated by Peter Baehr and Gordon C. Wells. New York: Penguin, 2002.

Werth, Tiffany J. *The Fabulous Dark Cloister: Romance in England after the Reformation.* Baltimore: Johns Hopkins University Press, 2011.

Wilde, Oscar. *The Picture of Dorian Gray.* Edited by Robert Mighall. London: Penguin, 2000.

Williams, Arnold. *Flower on a Lowly Stalk: The Sixth Book of "The Faerie Queene."* East Lansing: Michigan State University Press, 1967.

Winters, Yvor. *In Defense of Reason*. Denver: Alan Swallow, 1947.

Witmore, Michael. *Culture of Accidents: Unexpected Knowledges in Early Modern England*. Stanford, Calif.: Stanford University Press, 2002.

Wolfe, Jessica. *Humanism, Machinery, and Renaissance Literature*. Cambridge: Cambridge University Press, 2004.

Xenophon. *Memorabilia*. Translated by Amy L. Bonnette. Ithaca, N.Y.: Cornell University Press, 1994.

Yates, Julian. *Error, Misuse, Failure: Object Lessons from the English Renaissance*. Minneapolis: University of Minnesota Press, 2003.

Yeats, William Butler. *The Cutting of an Agate*. New York: Macmillan, 1912.

Zurcher Sandy, Amelia. *Seventeenth-Century English Romance: Allegory, Ethics, and Politics*. New York: Palgrave, 2007.

INDEX